LAW AND THE PUBLIC SPHERE IN AFRICA

WORLD PHILOSOPHIES

Bret W. Davis, D. A. Masolo, and Alejandro Vallega, *editors*

LAW AND THE PUBLIC SPHERE IN AFRICA

La Palabre *and Other Writings*

Jean Godefroy Bidima

Translated and edited by Laura Hengehold
Foreword by Souleymane Bachir Diagne

Indiana University Press

Bloomington and Indianapolis

This book is a publication of

Indiana University Press
Office of Scholarly Publishing
Herman B Wells Library 350
1320 East 10th Street
Bloomington, Indiana 47405 USA

iupress.indiana.edu

| Telephone orders | 800–842–6796 |
| Fax orders | 812 855 7931 |

Manufactured in the United States of America

Bidima, Jean Godefroy, [date]
  [Palabre. English]
  Law and the public sphere in Africa : La palabre and other writings / Jean Godefroy Bidima ; translated by Laura Hengehold ; foreword by Souleymane Bachir Diagne.
    pages cm. — (World philosophies)
  Includes bibliographical references and index.
  ISBN 978-0-253-01124-4 (cloth : alk. paper)
  ISBN 978-0-253-01128-2 (ebook)
  1. Political anthropology—Africa. 2. Public meetings—Africa. 3. Dispute resolution (Law)—Africa. 4. Africa—Politics and government. 5. Africa—Social conditions. I. Title.
  GN645.B5213 2013
  306.2—dc23
                                                            2013034754

1 2 3 4 5 19 18 17 16 15 14

When I was very young, my mother hung a world map next to the couch so that I would always learn the location and name of places in the news. This translation is dedicated to her, for without my mother's encouragement to learn French and explore other cultures, it would never have come about. She is the one who gave me the courage to learn.

Contents

Acknowledgments

Jean Godefroy Bidima

THE READER WILL have ample opportunity to decide whether this book is a symphony or a cacophony. However they may choose, readers are no fools and know that the signed personal adventure of any book or article responds like an echo to many individuals who have discreetly and patiently set this symphony or cacophony to music. The responsibility for errors and rough statements in this text should be laid at my own feet as the author; I turn over all the gratitude to those before me, who made this book possible at so many levels.

I have to start with the most heartfelt thanks to Antoine Garapon, magistrat and secrétaire général of the Institut des Hautes Études of Justice in Paris, who not only strongly encouraged this publication by welcoming it into the *le Bien Commun* series with Éditions Michalon, but also drew my attention to the relationship between Paul Ricoeur's work and problems associated with justice. I also give the friendliest recognition to Professor Laura Hengehold, who committed herself to translating and making this book available to the American public, and whose questions pushed me to reconsider the relations between mystification and politics in the African public space. Many thanks as well to Publications de la Sorbonne, Éditions Michalon, Les Éditions de l'UNESCO, the journal *Diogenes*, and other publishers who gave permission for the reproduction of these texts.

A particular note of acknowledgement goes to Francis Abiola Irele, who tirelessly convinced me of the importance of orality despite the bad favor into which it has fallen due to the chorus of those opposing ethnophilosophy. A warm thanks to philosophical friends and critics who enabled me to enrich this meditation and whose integrity and works, at once diverse and rich, have been a source of inspiration to me: Souleymane Bachir Diagne, Nick Nesbitt, Seloua Luste Boulbina, Mylène Botbol-Baum, and Emmanuel Hirsch.

I will be forever indebted to the philosophical styles and the erudition of my professors at the Sorbonne: Olivier Bloch, Olivier Revault d'Allonnes, and Hélène Védrine. I am more than cognizant of the devotion and the enthusiasm shown by my teachers at the primary school St. Pie X in the village of Mfoumassi in Cameroon: Madame Kavolo, Messieurs Grégoire Sala Mendzana, Jean (Le Grand) Bidoung, Maurice Ateba Akono, Florent Bekolo, Aloys Mendogo, and Jean Bidoung (alias Petit Jean).

My residency at University of Bayreuth in Germany as *Gastdozent* (visiting associate professor) enhanced my exposure to debates about the dialogical public sphere animating the German philosophical scene at that time. My gratitude goes to Professor

Dr. János Riesz, who gave me an enormously enriching welcome and above all to the meticulous mind and intellectual vivacity of Dr. Katharina Städtler.

My time as program director at the Collège International de Philosophie in Paris enabled me to appreciate and to be inspired by the work of certain colleagues: on the question of genealogy, François Noudelmann, former president of the collegial assembly; Robert Harvey on the theme of testimony; and Eric Hamraoui on the imaginaries associated with that corporeal organ, the heart. My short stay as associate with the Centre d'études africaines (CEAF) at EHESS in Paris gave me the chance to appreciate the competence and the unfailing friendship of research librarian Patricia Bleton. I remain in permanent debt to the intellectual perspicacity of Luca Scarantino, who introduced me to the extremely subtle thought of Giulio Preti, one of the most important philosophers emerging from Italy in the twentieth century.

Nor should I miss the chance to express my special appreciation to the administrative personnel and colleagues I met at the Institut d'études avancées at Nantes during the course of our stay as 2011–12 EURIAS (European Institutes for Advanced Studies) lauréats. I was hugely impressed by their competence, whether their subjects were near or far from my own interests. In particular, let me thank Alain Supiot—an erudite mind, respectful of nonwestern cultures, former director of the IEA of Nantes and currently professor at the Collège de France—for his welcome and for his research findings on the importance of the dogmatic basis for cultures. I owe a great deal to the analyses of the philosopher Dany-Robert Dufour when it comes to the criticism of various kinds of economies that structure our contemporary lived experience, and would like to express that gratitude here. Nor could I fail to mention and thank Kwame Anthony Appiah, a philosopher sensitive to the universal, who, during the drama of Hurricane Katrina's assault on New Orleans, welcomed me and initiated a mutually beneficial residency at Princeton University. I also keep in mind Dismas Masolo, a Kenyan philosopher with remarkable pedagogical talents whose writings have fed my knowledge of African philosophical traditions in the English language.

I would like to make a special reference to my African friends, who over many long years have honored me with their friendship, their experiences, and their knowledge: Abel Kouvouama, José Kagabo, Boniface Mongo-Mboussa, Wilfrid Miampika, Victorien Lavou Zoungbo, Eloi Messi Metogo, and Auguste Owono-Kouma. Daniel Maximin, a restless thinker with admirable oral eloquence who provided my education in Caribbean problematics, deserves my gratitude here. My current interest in material culture also comes from assiduously reading the archeological works of Lucie-Blanche Miamouini-Nkouka, for which my sincere thanks. Finally, my long stay in France has given me the opportunity to appreciate the friendship of Frédérique Jardin-Donovan and Kevin Donovan, as well as that of Michel and Claudine Trougnou, Pierre and Marie Thérèse Lefort, and Maryline Gesret.

Thanks to my past and current colleagues at Tulane University, around whom I have learned so much about the vocabulary, the rhetoric, and the syntax of the United

States—I am particularly thinking of Richard Watts, Erec Koch, Beth Poe, Linda Carroll, and Michael Syrimis.

To conclude, I thank my parents—Godefroy Bidima Bela and Crescence Akoumou Evina—who taught me the art of *palabre*, and in connection with them, I hope I may also mention those who carry on their memory in bearing the name of Bidima: Afana Evina Bidima, Monique Evelyne Mbolle Afana Bidima, Hermine Akoumou Nsizoa Bidima, Godefroy Bidima Evina, Bilounga Andomzoa Bidima, Fomo Nsizoa Bidima, Joyce and her sister, Henri-Godefroy Mbolle Engbwang Bidima, Paul Mebe Ndjengue Bidima, Mosobalaje Bidima, Nsizoa Evina Bidima, and Olounou Nsizoa Bidima.

My thoughts at this last moment go especially to my sister, Lucie Marthe Nsizoa Bidima, who is facing some trying times just now, along with her children Pascal Ndzengue Nsizoa Bidima and Mimbang Nsizoa Bidima.

New Orleans, June 2013

Foreword

Souleymane Bachir Diagne

Wʜᴇɴ *Tʜᴇ Eᴄᴏɴᴏᴍɪsᴛ*, on the cover of its 13 May 2000 issue, labeled Africa "The Hopeless Continent," the magazine was certainly not betting on the seeds of change that had been appearing since the early 1990s on that continent, in spite of the wars and their attendant woes. When, a decade later, on the cover of its 3 December issue, the same magazine saluted a "Rising Africa," those seeds had started to produce palpable results. Among the reasons that led the continent from "hopeless" to "rising" were peace and democratization, which brought about political stability and rule of law. Of course, there is still a long way to go and the case of Mali is evidence that setbacks are still threatening countries struck by poverty. But in a continent where many economies are now consistently growing at high rates and where political changes are taking place through fair elections, thus setting the norm and showing the path for the future, the promises of democracy are real. Today, there is indeed a new context in which philosophers, African or Africanists, are invited to revisit the notion of "African democracy." This phrase, "African democracy," had been used by autocrats claiming that their regimes were versions of an authentic African tradition of leadership. Now the time has come to examine the phrase in the context of an African *appropriation* of the universal concept of democracy, defined everywhere by pluralism, a multiparty system, equality between men and women, and respect for human rights and the rights of minorities.

Jean Godefroy Bidima's *La Palabre* is certainly a pioneer work in that direction. It must be underlined that it was published in 1997, precisely when the democratic transitions were taking place in many African countries. Thus, eight years after the National Conference of Benin (which inaugurated those transitions in a majority of francophone countries) was the right time to point out, as Bidima does here, that democratization must not be solely for the elites, "intellectual, industrial, legal, or religious" (those were the main actors of the national conferences). It must also speak to the populations at large, to their sense of what constitutes a productive discussion that leads to a good settlement, and to their feeling that justice has been well served. This is precisely an appropriate definition for *palaver*. Beyond the context of state politics, Bidima claims, the process of democratization must engage a renewed meaning of the tradition of *palaver* as a way of structuring the public space, of providing a detour by which violence is bypassed and peace and active tolerance achieved.

The way in which Bidima construes *palaver* as a philosophical concept is quite enlightening: he explains that *palaver* is essentially dialogue and argumentation; he then shrewdly uses the fact that in French, the word *entretien* (which could be one of the many synonyms of *palabre*) means both "discussion" and "maintenance." This allows him to analyze *palaver* as a process of argumentation inextricably tied to the overarching goal of *maintaining* peace, harmony, and social consensus; he can then examine the "staging, ordering, and putting in words" of the strategy of resolving conflicts to maintain the social bond. As Bidima elegantly puts it, quoting Michel Foucault: the culture of *palabre* is about "discuss and redeem" and not "discipline and punish."

The question could be raised of the colonial construction of African societies as "cold" societies that wish to "freeze" themselves in time and avoid the turbulences of history, therefore "calling" unwittingly for colonization as a way to join into the mainstream of human development. This question is well posed and discussed by Bidima, as are other questions concerning the relationship between the culture of *palaver* and the many phases through which Africa has gone: colonialism, neocolonial regimes ruled by a one-party system, pseudodemocracies (christened "democratures"), African socialisms, democratic transitions, and so forth. There is no doubt that Bidima's meditation on *palaver* is essential to the reflection on the past, the present, and the future of democratization in a "rising Africa."

Preface to the English Edition

Justice, Deliberation, and the Democratic Public Sphere: Palabre *and its Variations*

Jean Godefroy Bidima

Rhythms and Terminologies

Rhythms

We never enter a house without crossing a *space* called the "threshold" and without "bearing tales" about ourselves or others that reveal how we are connected to them and to the world around us. If we may indulge in an association and a comparison, every book has an *immediate threshold*—such as the preface, the foreword, the introduction, or the note to readers; and also a *distant threshold,* which is the universe of tales, ambitions, actions, and failures that precondition it.

A book is a *space*—almost a trap. The book does not simply *reflect* the meaning that it weaves, shows, and conceals—either within the mind's eye of the author or at the level of the historical events that it recounts—indeed, it claims to exist as a *consequence* of that meaning. However, sometimes the book is more like a *symptom.* Not just in the sense of whatever evades easy explication, but in the sense of those complications linking the speaking, acting, suffering subject to the symbols that he or she manipulates and to institutions that either provoke hopelessness or offer him or her excuses for living. As a condensation of *time,* the book may outstrip the spirit of its age or lag behind events that are still unfolding. Most frequently, the book acts as a counterpoint to what we somewhat naively call current events. A book is always "untimely," which means one cannot expect its exposition of notions and concepts to be terribly uniform, or even to provide a lucid description and analysis of everything that happens.

The book—let's add this one last consideration—is always written in a serious spirit, because authors worry when they imagine being judged by their readership.[1] Tormented by private anxieties, the author nevertheless occasionally gives him- or herself away by building up the threshold with multiple warnings to the reader such as a "preface," an "introduction" or a "foreword," a "note to the reader," or a "reader's guide." Laboring over the "thresholds" of this book's thesis is actually a "work of mourning" worthy of several preliminary observations.[2] First, the author and the reader must get over the desire for *univocal comprehension.* By univocal comprehension, we mean the practice of reducing the extent of a book's meaning to the urgency of current events, often by means of the cruel question: "What good is this book right now?" Second, both would have to work at maintaining *a reasonable distance* from what the German philosopher Peter Sloterdijk describes as a *new theology*, one proclaimed today "by drawing on the trinity. . . .What is added to the Father is 'money,' to the Son 'success,' and to the Holy Spirit 'prominence.'"[3]

Only after laying these regrets to rest can we note that this book is the result of many texts written at different moments and rhythms. The work on *palabre* was published in the collection *Le Bien Commun* [The Common Good] with the Paris editor Michalon. It had to fit the required form of a French pocket edition, which means walking a fine, delicate line between academic writing and a broadly popular style. The chapters dealing with media and legal judgment were published in various specialist journals, each with their own distinct politics of expression. The chapter on "strategies for constructing belief" came from a doctoral dissertation on the Frankfurt School.[4] The text on books in Africa was published with the educational mission of UNESCO in the background. Therefore, the reader ought to know that this book tries to play impersonal academic writing, with its tics and manias, against a style that frequently becomes political.[5] We often prefer to say that academic writing is objective, dispassionate, or professional—though the seriousness of the subject is mocked by the unforeseeable and ironic nature of reality. But politics is unavoidable, given that the question of the African public sphere has stakes transcending purely philosophical and juridical discourses.

Palabre, a "Flexible Law": Cui Bono?

It must be said that these texts dealing with law and justice were written against the cultural backdrop of the Napoleonic civil code, whose tradition is still alive—with modifications and local adaptations—in latter-day francophone Africa and in Louisiana.[6] However, the problems that appear in these texts surrounding the act of judging, the status of consensus, and reconciliation, as well as the persistence of ritual in the staging of the law, are universal problems.

Terminologies

On the terminological plane, the notion of law [*droit*] poses a problem. This book's title contains the word "law," which can be translated either by *loi* or by *droit* in French. But things rarely coincide with words. Even if most African languages have the term *loi*, many do not have *droit*. But this does not mean that, lacking a form of law guaranteed by the state, such societies lack a domain in which norms are formulated and discussed, and prohibitions or statutes [*loi*] are enacted. In this respect, *palabre* permits African society to diversify the sources of its law.

To give just a few examples: the positivist and unitarist tradition finds the sources of law in the state's organization and the will's autonomy. But today there is only a slight difference between what is considered law and what is not. Phenomena like *palabre* were frequently considered simple problems of behavior, manners, and customs, barely connected to a code underwritten by the state; in other words, to law [*droit*]. *Palabre* would not be an antilaw, therefore, but rather a nonlegal phenomenon. But nonlegal or infralegal phenomena make up an integral part of law, and the difference between these phenomena and positive law is one of degree, not one of kind. This is affirmed by French law professor Jean Carbonnier: "All the same, the difference between law and nonlaw . . . can be brought down to a difference of degree."[7] Moreover, the epistemological effect of integrating these phenomena into questions related to law is juridical pluralism. As we are told by the Spanish jurist Manuel Atienza: "When the notion of law is separated from that of the state, it loses its kernel of clear signification and is then situated in the penumbral zone: law in primitive societies, canon law . . . rules referring to social relations . . . similar efforts enlarge the object of juridical reflection, but at the cost of giving up a unitary understanding of law."[8]

Attention to *palabre* might motivate jurists in Africa and the postcolonies to think about rescuing law from the state's monopoly and making it into a "common good." This good is necessary to build a public sphere in which the notion of justice would transcend the state's narrow purview and reenter the dimension of ethics. *Palabre* will thus reactivate a certain form of memory (a), one that also privileges the passions of the public sphere (b). Examining "regimes of historicity" (c) is one way to reopen the question of how collaboration [*concertation*] can generate power (d) and to revive conversation on the principles of law (e) and reconciliation (f). *Palabre* shows that law can no longer be conceived as anything but a network (g) and that it can be useful for "restorative justice" (h). All of this leads, on the one hand, to an evaluation of the notion of "constructing belief" (i) in the African public sphere and, on the other hand, to the extension of liberties (j) in the African public sphere.

Palabre as Renewal: A "Noble Form of Memory" (Merleau-Ponty) or the "Objectively Cynical" Melancholy of the Post- and Neocolonized (Žižek)?

Is it not a sign of archaism to try and put *palabre* back on the contemporary agenda? And is it not especially archaic at a moment when migrations, ecological risks, new definitions of identity, the development of nanotechnologies, transformations of international law with questions linked to "just" and "preventive" wars, the nomadism of financial capital, the irruption of new forms of precarity, new definitions of space and time emerging with electronic media, transformations of the family, and redefinitions of the state and its crises give humanity at the start of the twenty-first century the opportunity to reinterrogate itself and to redefine its relation to time, to action, to space, and to hope? What can *palabre* do besides put new clothes on an old-fashioned practice born in societies that had smaller populations and a specific relationship to illness, time, space, norms, and the law?

We could easily believe that *palabre* picks up on a kind of melancholy—according to Slavoj Žižek, one proper to postcolonial elites. In reworking and criticizing Freud, Žižek comments on the distinction between mourning and melancholy. It is in describing this distinction that he speaks of an objective cynicism among postcolonial elites that betrays an unacknowledged attachment to the lost ethnic object. For Žižek,

> With regard to mourning and melancholy, the predominant doxa is as follows: Freud opposed "normal" mourning (the successful acceptance of loss) to "pathological" melancholy (where the subject persists in his or her narcissistic identification with the lost object). Against Freud, one should assert the conceptual *and* ethical primacy of melancholy. . . . Mourning is a kind of betrayal, the "second killing" of the (lost) object, while the melancholic subject remains faithful to the lost object, refusing to renounce his or her attachment to it.[9]

In Žižek's view, this attachment to the lost object would be a ruse, not just a refusal to acknowledge the fact that the ethnic object is lost, but a strategy that also facilitates adaptation to the imperatives of the market economy's globalized society.

> For this very reason, however, it is all the more necessary to denounce the "objective cynicism" that such a rehabilitation of melancholy enacts: the melancholic link to the lost ethnic Object allows us to claim that we remain faithful to our ethnic roots, while fully participating in the global capitalist game. . . . Melancholy is thus an exquisitely *postmodern* stance, the stance that allows us to survive in a global society by maintaining the appearance of fidelity to our lost "roots."[10]

According to Žižek, this postmodern posture is found as often among queer movements as in the postcolonial ethnic version: "(when ethnic groups enter capitalist modernization and are under threat that their specific legacy will be swallowed up by the new global culture, they should not renounce their tradition through mourning, but retain their melancholic attachment to their lost roots)."[11]

In recalling the existence of *palabre* and its potential ability to consolidate a public sphere of deliberation and discussion in Africa; in making *palabre* one of the models (imperfect, to be sure) for the resolution of conflicts in Africa, we do not think we are signing on to this cynical melancholy with respect to the postcolonial world and its attachment to what is "lost," as Žižek puts it. Rather we count on taking the notion of tradition seriously as a "reworking" [*reprise*]. It must be said that what Žižek describes as the "lost (ethnic) object"—he employs the term "loss" in his qualification of mourning and of melancholia—was never truly lost. Social changes in the cultures dominated by the colonial adventure never led to the pure and simple loss or disappearance of customs. Despite the colonizer's efforts to eradicate them (above all the French colonial policy of assimilation), what happened was more like a *bracketing* of certain elements in that culture and a *marginalization* (rather than disappearance) of its practices. In supposing that the adventure of the global economy has brought about "loss of the ethnic object," as Žižek believes, one thereby assumes that the holders of that "ethnic object" were passive and did not resist its disappearance; or, put otherwise, that the postcolonized lacked real *agency*. Moreover, this "loss of the ethnic object" is inscribed within a vision of progressive temporality with gains and losses.

Contrary to Žižek's thesis on the "total loss of the *ethnic object*," we might affirm its persistence in various ways alongside "visible objects and official practices," as well as its claim to be a *counterpoint* either existing alongside authorized practices (as a parallel object) or rowing against their current (as a paradoxical object). In resuming talk about *palabre*, we would like to emphasize its dual status as an auxiliary and parallel form of justice that sometimes works in Africa; it is also a "paradoxical justice" that seems, unlike forms of justice tied to the state, to pursue peace rather than truth. It is therefore another way of carrying out justice, opposing not just the inflation of the realm of criminal justice in our post-postmodernity, where punishment is the only response to transgression, but also the extreme litigiousness that haunts our social life.

Rwanda provides an example. The practice of arbitration and judgment called *gacaca*—with its flaws and political face-saving—survived German and Belgian colonization. When it was a matter of judging certain agents of the genocide and their accomplices, we might say that *gacaca* came to the rescue of the international criminal court for Rwanda located in Tanzania. The criminal court for Rwanda had great difficulty judging the *génocidaires* and their accomplices in the limited time it was allotted, and since it was necessary to judge everyone if reconciliation were to be possible, judgment could no longer be rendered in terms of the civil code or the common law but only in terms known to the users of the criminal justice system. *Gacaca*, the traditional *palabre* of the Rwandan people, with its defects and its false steps, was there to say that where justice is concerned, the important thing once condemnation or pardon have been given is what *comes next* [*l'après*]. There is nothing nostalgic about reviving *palabre* today and placing it at the center of African action, because it is a matter of shedding light on another conception of justice, one that uses truth to bring about peace.

In Africa, *palabre* has sometimes served—and been situated alongside—the state's system of justice, with its colonial heritage. But it reminds the state that punishment and truth cannot be made the chief issues at stake in mangled societies unless reconciliation and peace are also respected. As a result, with its various moments of staging, articulating, submitting to deliberation, and enacting judgment, *palabre* reminds humanity that, constituted as we are by speech, no space of deliberation and negotiation is possible without staging, theatricality, and ritual. All commerce in signs is drawn on the depth of the symbolic dimension. Thus we are put in an awkward position by any "negotiations" established by the managerial system in which, under the rule of *efficiency*, this depth is replaced by "officialese" and "paperwork."

For us, the "renewal" of *palabre* as an element of tradition is a way to reconnect with a noble form of African memory. Commenting on Husserl, Merleau-Ponty explains that "*tradition . . . is . . . the power to forget origins*, the duty to start over again and to give to the past, not survival, which is the hypocritical form of forgetfulness, but the efficacy of renewal or 'repetition,' which is the noble form of memory."[12]

Renewing the "noble form of memory" is one reason to invoke *palabre* as a building block in the ever-renovating construction of an African public sphere. However, most of the postcolonized countries are glazed over with Roman-canonical juridical culture; members of the chorus of human rights, they draw simultaneously on Athens, Rome, and Jerusalem, and on the French, English, and American revolutions. For them, the only kind of law and justice that count are the kind fed and framed by state texts or emerging from commercial contracts. From the period of colonization into our globalized postmodernity, the traditional practices of *palabre* were first recuperated by the colonizers and then despised by the postcolonial elite—who wore the robes and wigs of Louis XIV in court so proudly despite their regular criticisms of colonialism. African intellectuals often make passing references to *palabre* without seeing its capacity to nourish contradictions and resolve certain problems posed in the contemporary public sphere.

Here we are pulled by Gershom Scholem's question regarding the German Jewish elite's relationship to its own heritage: "What is a heritage worth if the elite among its heirs worked so hard to disavow it?"[13] In response, our task was to renew this practice so any unfinished deeds it might yet accomplish could bear their fruit. Every cultural practice stored in the drawer of tradition conceals some pending accomplishment that has yet to be identified—the famous *nondum:* the *not-yet* of which Ernst Bloch speaks to us.[14]

Palabre and the Oppositional Public Sphere: *Beyond* Habermas *through* Habermas

Jürgen Habermas was right to criticize the straitjacket imposed by the philosophies of consciousness, especially their subject-object paradigm, and to replace this with a philosophy focusing on the intersubjectivity of one subject who speaks to another subject. This speaking subject, who tries to validate his or her arguments when addressing an other so as to produce a public sphere free from tyranny and manipulations, is not a self-referential subject. He or she is only constituted by his or her interaction with the other in a public space.

Where the notion of the public sphere is concerned, Habermas has been criticized for taking an interest only in the bourgeois public sphere while neglecting an oppositional and proletarian public sphere. This is the view of Oskar Negt, whom Laura Hengehold, however, has critiqued for not explaining more clearly how a counterpublic with its dialects and practices comes into existence.[15] A further critique comes from Axel Honneth, who reproaches him for downplaying the notion of contempt in the construction of a notion of public space.[16] From the side of postcolonial critique, Nick Nesbitt points out that Habermas, who speaks about the French bourgeois public sphere, did not have the chance to deal with the plebeian one. However, the premises and consequences of the Haitian Revolution show precisely this kind of space rising up against French colonial arrogance.[17] Other critics of Habermas have stressed his failure to consider the "people on the bottom," but our critique bears on the exclusion of anger from the constitution of the public sphere. The emphasis on argumentation, the exclusion of passion and affects, present another angle from which we can interrogate the notion of the public sphere in Habermas's work.

The public sphere cannot be constituted without special attention to *anger*, because after all, discussion about what concerns the common good and our common world and the need for a space of discussion and deliberation cannot happen without people having outbursts, becoming aggravated, or withdrawing due to misunderstandings and bad faith. It is somewhat striking that Habermas, whose concept of the public sphere focused on the period of the Enlightenment, in which the French Revolution was a major event, did not reserve a role for *anger* in the notion of "publicity," to say nothing of Kant's oversight in *Project for a Perpetual Peace*. The French Revolution was nothing if not the "people in anger," as well as the expression of the "people's anger," and one cannot study publicity if one is limited to discussion of the "better argument."

In ancient Greece, privileged site of gods and heroes, as Sloterdijk tells us, rage was more or less mastered and in Rome it was considered a demon harmful not only to the soul's peace but also to cohesiveness between the city's members. Seneca's work is quite significant in this respect when he opposes reason—"which wants to decide what is just"—and anger—"which wants what has been decided to be found just."[18] From this ironic angle, Sloterdijk distinguishes the rage of the gods—a "metaphysical revenge bank"—from the rage of the proletarian people—a "communist world bank of rage."[19] Today, the historical uses of rage are deteriorating into a scattered sense of fury: small claims of anger that leave peoples at best dreamers and at worst cynics. "If one wanted to express the strong character of the contemporary psychopolitical international situation in one sentence, it would have to be: We have entered an era without rage collection points of global perspective."[20]

It is urgent that we give anger back what it is due and integrate it into the public sphere, on condition that it should be anger associated with intelligence. Rage needs intelligence, just as intelligence is nothing without anger toward the vicissitudes of our societies. *Ira quaerens intellectum* (rage needs intelligence) and *intellectus quaerens iram* (intelligence needs rage): these two formulas of Sloterdijk show us that there are problems with the purely argumentative public sphere; moreover, we must take the doublet *rage-intelligence* into consideration in our ways of conceiving and applying theories of justice.[21] In this context, *palabre* builds a public space of discussion allowing people to express their anger, and thereby suggests that the public space of discussion and deliberation must pay attention to fits of rage as well as arguments. All procedures must be considered in the constitution of the public sphere, as they are in the adventure of knowledge described by Cioran: "reasoning, intuition, disgust, enthusiasm, complaint. A vision of the world supported by concepts is no more legitimate than another born of tears: arguments, or sighs."[22] During *palabre*, the progression of actors' narratives matters, as well as their capacity to break that progression through laughter, sighs, mimicry, or gesture. There is hardly a public sphere if we ignore the body, passion, and *pathic* dimension of the subject.

Palabre between Religions and Markets: Examining "Regimes of Historicity" in the Arab Spring

In the context of building and consolidating oppositional public spheres in Africa, conflict resolution and the evaluation of media present us with a challenge. For why restore the dignity of a practice that seems in every way to be merely a relic, unrelated to the present and probably also the future? We have seen that *palabre* puts a certain form of memory back into play, but what about its relation to history? "History is only born for an epoch when it is completely dead. The domain of history is therefore the past. The present comes down to politics, and the future belongs to God."[23] Beyond the narrow character of his conception of past and future, this remark of the nineteenth-century French thinker Champagne Thiénot asks us to consider whether the privilege accorded to *palabre* is well-founded, and whether it has a future. How could *palabre* relate to a conception of the present as nothing but a political illusion?

By opening society's wounds in public and then striving to close them provisionally through speech, gesture, and ritual, *palabre*—a practice from the past—weaves a relation to the future. It does this by permitting the present to explore what historians call "regimes of historicity." Every relationship to history explores the past, the present, and the future using methods that equally privilege traces, evidence, and stories. But meanwhile, beyond this exploration of history's meaning or of one's own place in it, over which schools of thought contend, what interests us is that the relations between subjects, communities, and practices of history can be evaluated in light of the historicity they embody. By this term we mean to bring the notions of *happening*, of *transformation*, of *crisis*, and of *tension* into a conception of time that is not linear. Historicity is *happening*. This is an understanding we draw from Herbert Marcuse's comment on Hegel: "Historicity signifies the meaning we intend when we say of something that it is 'historical.' Historicity signifies the meaning of this 'is,' namely the meaning of the being of the historical. . . . History will be our problem as a process of happening and as a form of motility."[24]

Interrogating African historicity with respect to *palabre* implies that we see it as a factor of mobility and of social transformation. The "national conferences," major African *palabres* that threatened authoritarian regimes during the 1990s, would be a historical example. Despite their weaknesses, the positive point of these conferences was that in order to secure political mobility, they put public speech back into circulation in Africa. Historicity is also the *transformation of self by self*, as we are told by sociologist Alain Touraine: "Societies are not defined by their functioning, but by their capacity to transform themselves . . . [we] call historicity this work on the work, this action of society's self-transformation. . . . We are led . . . to think society as a hierarchy of systems. Historicity, in other words the transformation of the self by the self, is the highest system."[25] *Palabre* aims at the transformation of the self by the self. To commit oneself to *palabre* implies relativizing one's own convictions in order to be open to others and to new events. This opening is a self-transformation in the adventure of speech and of action.

Historicity is also the *crisis* within a temporal continuum arising when "the articulations of past, present, and future" lose their "self-evident character."[26] But as the historian Reinhart Koselleck tells us, each historical period actually articulates a "space of experience" and a "horizon of expectation." Historicity would be therefore the *gap* between the two and the diverse combinations that we could make from them. What does the field of experience offer us, and what are our expectations regarding this experience? In fact, it is "the tension between experience and expectation which, in ever-changing patterns, brings about new resolutions and through this generates historical time."[27] *Palabre* is precisely this moment of tension between a society's achievements and its potentials; it is also the crisis between what is owed and what can be realized. During *palabre*, a society also tells the story of its own odysseys, its sociodicies, and its theodicies, because discussion is not simply limited to the litigation at hand. Society takes advantage of the situation to evoke the events of preceding generations and the utopias yet to be realized. Reconsidering *palabre* is a way of asking about the succession between regimes of historicity.

Whatever motivations and obscure forces may influence their trajectories and changes from the sidelines, the political upheavals in the Maghreb resulting from the famous Arab springs are *indicative of a change in the regime of historicity*, insofar as these societies are expressing the tension between the field of their experience (constituted by corrupt political regimes) and the indeterminate horizon of their expectations. Between experience coming to a close and expectations of what is to come, we find political regimes that may be either populist or fundamentalist, depending on what makes stock markets and commercial contracts happiest. This situation calls for a *palabre* on the notion of crisis in postcolonial and emerging countries. What is the relationship between peoples' histories and their subjugation?

Palabre and Power: From the Power to *Dominate* to the Power to *Collaborate*

Several fundamental problems linked to power have been periodically demonstrated in colonial and postcolonial African history: (a) networks of legitimation in the precolonial and neocolonial periods; (b) the disqualification of traditional forms of power by colonization, followed by the introduction of Islam and Christianity; (c) the agents of these powers, represented first and foremost by colonial and postcolonial elites; (d) questions linked to the inequality of commercial exchanges; (e) relations between human rights and the security of peoples; (f) relations between nation-building and diverse cosmopolitanisms; (g) the role of religion in the elaboration of political strategies; (h) the role played by the translation of legal and political languages into terms that match up with the reality of African traditions. A conception of power as domination over persons, groups, or peoples was the common denominator in all these investigations.

To account for the changing nature of domination, scholars employed the analyses of Max Weber, of Karl Marx, of Michel Foucault and of Antonio Gramsci. Power was thought from below, or rather on the basis of counter-powers that, since the colonial period, have always posed alternatives to the powers imposed from above. Sometimes this took the form of messianism—as in Angola (Kimpa Vita), the Congos (Simon Kimbangu, André Grenard Matsoua), or Cameroon (Thong Likeng)—at other points during the colonial and neocolonial periods, it took the form of independence movements. But whether it is a matter of conceiving power from the grassroots or other similar notions, the *habitus* of political and juridical philosophy for most francophone African thinkers has always been to conceive *power as a form of domination-over*. . . . As a society's expanded conversation about itself, its institutions and what is other than itself, *palabre* allows us to have a different notion of power—namely, one involving collective action. From power as "*domination over . . .*" to power as "*collaboration with . . .*"

The spirit of *palabre* is closer to the conceptions of Hannah Arendt and Paul Ricoeur. Indeed, the former gives a primary place in her thought to the *space of appearance*. No longer disdained as the kingdom of tyrannical common sense or, as Plato would say, of opinion (*doxa*), this space becomes an experimental laboratory where we find the human Logos deployed in its multiple expressions. Further, Arendt shows us that power cannot be conceived solely in terms of command and obedience, but is primarily this capacity to do something in common. "It is only after one has ceased to reduce public affairs to the business of domination that the original data of the realm of human affairs will appear, or, rather, reappear in their authentic diversity."[28]

Certainly, we must recognize that domination remains present within political power, but once domination has been fought, subjects have to somehow act together. Power is thus the art of collaborating and not only the art of domination. "Power corresponds to the human ability not just to act but to act in concert. Power is never the property of an individual."[29] To be sure, we must not forget that humans have the ability to do evil and particularly to exercise power over each other, but doing something in common is more difficult, because the notions of debate, deliberation, and consensus enter into consideration.

Although Ricoeur spent no time in African societies, he too seems to give collective life [*vivre-ensemble*] the objective of power-in-common, as would be the case in *palabre*: "We have also called power-in-common the capacity of the members of a historical community to exercise in an indivisible manner their desire to live together, and we have been careful to distinguish this power-in-common from the relation of domination in which political violence resides, the violence of those who govern as well as that of the governed."[30] *Palabre* is not uniquely bound to the affair under discussion during hearings; its goal is to stage "Reference," that *in whose name*, as Pierre Legendre puts it, a society confronts the temptation of the absurd and the abyss.[31] This staging of "Reference" requires power-in-common.

A genuine action is one that can be enacted in concert. What are the modalities that favor collective action among citizens in contemporary Africa? And in what ways do the processes circulating financial capital and scientific knowledge encourage reciprocity? What aspects of reciprocity do African traditions promote or obstruct? The being-with (*Mitsein*) referred to by Heidegger can only be achieved in "acting-with;" starting here, what are the current economic and anthropological parameters that might redefine the notion of action (*Handeln*) in Africa today? Are the state, churches, families, or workplace environments liable to promote cooperation? Beyond the structural obstacles, what are the new possibilities of reciprocity at the level of the African Union that could assist with African integration?

Palabres within Law: Beyond Deliberation and Argumentation, the Conversation over Principles

Palabre prioritizes conversation, an element of law that is constitutive—though one might argue only peripherally so. Norms, rules, principles, and applications are a way of ordering society and the individual and there is no reason these cannot be *discussed*. When it comes to the *staging* of law, we tend to deliberate and to interpret either with respect to *doctrines*, with respect to *past cases* (jurisprudence), or with respect to current *experience*. Doctrines, history, and experience are some of the foundations on which law is "staged," "put into language," and "put into images."

In the *staging* and the practice of law, hermeneutic questions often lead to controversies (what hermeneutic canons to adopt and on what bases?) and to abstractions (the jurist or judge often adopts theories about theories), but all of this distracts from the fact that ordinary conversation is also an integral component of law. The role of conversation is more and more frequently recognized by jurists when it comes to the essential role of citizens and judges in the matter of constitutional interpretation. Commenting on the book by American Supreme Court justice Stephen Breyer, the French judge Antoine Garapon notes quite rightly that "the Constitution articulates principles, in whose light all laws—meaning all positive laws—must be evaluated. These two vectors of law—principles and statutes—do not have the same discursive etiquette: if the laws impose silence, principles by contrast demand speech. The law is not to be discussed; principles are."[32]

As the principles are only elaborated and only survive in confrontation with a real situation that is also deceptive and mobile, subjects must adopt the dialogical path of conversation. One follows the laws, even if they are in some ways unjust, but the conditions of possibility for law, the principles, must be the object of conversations and consultations; in short, of irenic *palabres*. These are the kinds of *palabres*/conversations about constitutions that Breyer recommends when, referencing Benjamin Constant's "liberty of the ancients," he describes "an active liberty . . . [that] consisted in the sharing of a nation's sovereign authority among that nation's citizens. From the citizen's perspective it meant 'an active and constant participation in collective power;' it included the citizen's right to 'deliberate in the public place,' to 'vote for war or peace,' to 'make treaties,' to 'enact laws,' to examine the actions and accounts of those who administer government."[33]

The strength of citizens' awareness tends to be shaped by conversation over principles guiding law and the idea of justice. Can we still converse? This is not so certain! Max Horkheimer, following Walter Benjamin, lamented the passing of the kind of speech we find in conversation: "We complain that no one can talk any longer. People are mute even when they talk continually. Meanwhile we forget . . . that language dies from the fact that the individual, addressing another as an individual, let's say as a thinking subject, has no more to say—in the sense that we say, 'there is nothing more to say about that;' namely, he is powerless, he can realize nothing, his speech changes nothing at all."[34] This apparently hollow and impotent speech is precisely where politics takes place. Its seeming impotence already plays against the cynicism of straight talk, of authorized and channeled speech. This is where the Sisyphean task of always resuming conversation must find its foothold.

But from the standpoint of the practice of *palabre*, conversation is a cornerstone. During *palabre*, before delivering a judgment or a resolution, one talks through several smaller consultations that are *palabres* within *palabres*, deliberations nested within deliberation and minor conversations inside of the large conversation that provoked the hearings. As the place of politics, the model of *palabre* would give post-postmodern subjects—accustomed to depoliticization by the logic of the market on the one hand and by the discouragement born of resentment and the sentiment of powerlessness on the other—the possibility of avoiding a reified and standardized language evoking the logic of command and obedience. In the apparent disorder and inefficiency of interminable conversation, meaning emerges.

A conversation, or rather a *palabre*, could be held today on many challenges facing Africa. The question of international peace, the demands made by the extension and development of this reality called the constitutional state [*état de droit*], the complications and complementarities between written laws and those that are informal or traditional, the influences and conflicts between religious laws and rights (such as Islam) and those that are secular, and the problem of the suppression of minority rights by those of dominant groups all show us how urgent it is to reflect, converse, and to hold *palabre*.

Where postcolonial states are concerned, this must happen on two axes: (a) the encounter between laws/rights; and (b) the simultaneous presence of many kinds of law and right within postcolonial cultures. In relying on these two ideas (*the* encounter between legal systems and the copresence of systems), our *palabre* could build each axis on the other while questioning not just the encounter between types of law but also, and especially, the current status of traditional African legal rights. For this, we could consider the case of Cameroon (a country that, just like Louisiana, once had both the civil code and the common law) and the Islamic republic of Mauritania, which has adopted the model of a republic—the *res publica* is first (and not only!) *pro-fanum* or "outside the temple"—but with an Islamic connotation. We could then turn our conversation toward the problems linked to the encounter between traditional laws and rights and those of the state, which largely date from the colonial period.

How has this law been transformed at the level of the production of norms? What has happened when the application of norms comes up against questions related to procedure? How are the steps of codification in these laws articulated (what is the place of myths, religions, semantics, and behaviors in these processes of codification?) How is the notion of juridical competence justified in traditional law? And were the problems that we—today's interpreters—have with these rights the most important ones for those who established traditional law? To what extent are power, the sacred, and language linked? What does it mean to become acculturated to law? And how can we translate new juridical concepts into present-day African languages?

All these questions we can pose with respect to traditional legal systems could have a single goal: that of understanding transformations between types of law and their current importance for democratic states.[35] In this conversation, it will be a matter of making stories work and confronting them with one another, because if law's job is to produce narratives that *put the collectivity in order*, we might well ask what challenges the legal stories emerging from oral traditions—which some hesitate to give the name of "law" because they have hitherto regarded them only as customs—pose to the notion of a judicial narrative today. How can we give a *transversal interpretation* of rights today when we face situations where state-based law is tested by traditional systems of law and also where traditional law is controlled by the law of the state, or finally when religious laws (Islam) want to regulate both of them?

The current political situation of Mali poses a juridical problem of this kind. Today Mali is occupied by politico-military groups who for the most part want to create a republic whose law follows Shari'a. How can we reconcile religious claims, political necessities, the question of territory, and the form of the Malian state, which claims to be secular? The conversation could focus on this question: Starting with the presence of the Islamic religion in most African states south of the Sahara, how is Islam situated with respect to traditional African law and to the laws of the state emerging from colonization? We could finish with this general question, whose significance is not limited to African states: Is it really possible to have a secular state from which all religious characteristics have been purged?[36] In any case, *palabre* shows us that the secularization of law is only a figment of the imagination because law is materialized by personnel and through rituals during any trial.

We could also pose a last series of questions: What is the place of the market, the arms economy and geostrategy in the question of the collapse of contemporary African states that we find debated so frequently? How do law and military buildup, law and obedience, and law and economic interests intersect in the African public sphere?

Palabre: Revenge and Reconciliation

Michel Foucault's studies of imprisonment emphasized two particular aspects of our modernity: surveillance and punishment. But his study did not sufficiently emphasize the notions of revenge and hate, which seem to constitute additional pillars of our post-postmodernity. In his 1978–79 course at the Collège de France, *The Birth of Biopolitics,* Foucault stated that *"homo penalis,* the man who can legally be punished, the man exposed to the law and who can be punished by the law is strictly speaking a *homo economicus."*[37] Beginning in the nineteenth century, Foucault contends, *homo economicus* evolved into *homo criminalis* and all this, he continues, led to what he calls law "enforcement;" i.e., "the set of instruments employed to give social and political reality to the act of prohibition in which the formulation of the law consists. . . . [This] will be the quantity of punishment provided for each crime. It will be the size, activity, zeal, and competence of the apparatus responsible for detecting crimes. It will be the size and quality of the apparatus responsible for convicting criminals and providing effective proof that they have committed a crime."[38] What Foucault does not foresee at this level is that the same apparatus can degenerate into a pure and simple instrument of revenge and hate.

Palabre is an antidote to revenge and recidivism. In certain traditions, the end of *palabre* is not definitive. *Palabre* is an adjournment of discussion, a gap between the violence of words and that of actions. *Palabre* never says *"causa finita,"* but rather, "let's stop there and resume another time, on another occasion; meanwhile, let's try to do something together." Philosophically speaking, *palabre* goes beyond the model of revenge that also seems to haunt the unconscious of criminal law. As Gérard Courtois says so well, "vengeance also constitutes a repressive notion for the construction of a 'history of criminal law.' The model is simple: since revenge is supposed to be the most archaic 'stage' . . . the meaning and evolution of punishment would be reduced to a gradual increase in the repression of vengeance, which culminates in the state's monopoly over punishment."[39] Our post-postmodernity tries as hard as possible to persuade itself that the reign of vengeance is mediated by law: "One could therefore have the feeling that the theme of revenge is out of date, that it is only practiced by disaffiliated brutes who respond to crimes with crime—which is against the law. Meanwhile in the same historical period . . . one observes . . . a growing visibility of extreme acts of violence."[40]

Vengeance remains in our globalized societies. It takes the form of an extreme judicialization of human relations and a propensity to "make wrongdoers pay for what they have done," no longer with the sword but with the law itself, which is reduced to its punitive dimension. It is not surprising that it should be two North American jurists, one from the United States and the other from Canada, who deplore this camouflaged form of revenge that is enveloping their societies; "Juridicization . . . may signal that a greater number of aspects of life become formally subjected to a juridical rule . . . judicialization is thus a function of certain elements in the juridical culture, notably the propensity to initiate legal proceedings, to act on claims or more generally to assert one's rights . . . judicialization is the sign of a juridicization realized by means of recurrent recourse to the courts."[41] Thus *palabre* shows how to escape the cycle of revenge by regulating conflict in a way that does not privilege the aspect of obligatory payment or punishment. Certain *palabres* demand nothing but apologies on the part of the one who did wrong (*bidjuga* in the Beti *palabres* of Cameroon). Democracy is only possible if there exists an atmosphere of pacification that employs a nonpunitive logic.

Palabre between "Jupiter, Hercules, and Hermes"?

Whether we consider *palabre* a substitute or auxiliary form of justice matters little; what is important, however, is that it is a practice of the "in-between" [*l'entre deux*], combining rules that come from the weight of tradition with practices that the users of *palabre* invent and reinvent in light of new experiential data. If, for example, the oath and the preliminary *palabres* contained within the large *palabre* are kept, if reference to the ancestors is still invoked in several cases, and if the role of speech is always foundational, then practices like the ordeal, on the other hand, always tend to disappear. To better understand the role of the "in-between" and the socializing function of *palabre*, we draw on notions of the network and the polyphony (as opposed to a cacophony) of law developed by the philosopher and jurist François Ost. For Ost, the diverse transformations of the figure of law can be summed up in three moments.

1. The Code (the pyramid) with its norms and rules. This model is symbolized by the figure of Jupiter. Here judgment is rendered on the basis of a transcendent source, as at Sinai or, in another register, Rousseau's general will. The law "expresses itself in the imperative and tends to take on the nature of the prohibition it finds inscribed in a sacred depository, tables of laws or modern codes and constitutions."[42] This conception of law, which we continue to find in thinkers like Hans Kelsen, is very widespread in francophone Africa—and often characterized as juridical monism.

2. In the second moment, which Ost assimilates to the image of Hercules, law can no longer rely so heavily on codes but depends on the decision of the judge, who is there less to assure that a norm is applied than to evaluate the consequences of certain acts. The judge in this case "decides and awards . . . but he also carries out other kinds of work. For those about to enter litigation, he orients, advises, warns; for those emerging from it, he follows the evolution of the case, adapts his decisions willingly to circumstances and needs, controls the application of penalties. The Jupiterian judge was a man of the law; whereas Hercules is also a social engineer."[43] This image of the judge

is very compatible with a realist conception of law that relies on juridical atomization, as it fractures the law into a multitude of decisions. The preoccupations of this figure center on the notion of interest.

3. The third figure compares the judge to Hermes. This means that law is not simply implicated in a multiplicity of meanings and interpretations but is also presented as a game: "before being a rule and an institution, law is Logos, discourse, suspended signification. It is articulated between things: between the rule (which is never entirely normative) and the deed (which is never entirely factual), between order and disorder, between the letter and the spirit, between force and justice."[44]

Given its method of conflict resolution, *palabre* would probably be situated alongside this last model. *Palabre* reminds us that the events woven around and by law are primarily a *celebration of speech* and that this speech is *expressed by rituals* in which the *application* of what has been instituted and the *invention* of new rules are combined. *Palabre*, as a jurisdiction of speech, attempts to play this continuous game interior to every institution—simultaneously applying conventions and organizing transgressions. Our post-postmodernity has so extensively developed rituals of *empty speech* (arbitrating only between strategies of interest), of *vain speech* (which deteriorates into a strategy of mastery), and of *neutral speech* (which hides its brutal character behind "objectivity" or "technicality") that there is great benefit in a court or *jurisdiction of speech* like *palabre* (a speech that conveys meaning and evokes the absurdity of an ethic not based on egoistic gain). The model of justice offered by *palabre* privileges neither procedure, nor retribution, nor distribution—but a logic of inclusion and deliberation.

International Criminal Law: *Palabre* and "Reparative/Restorative" Forms of Justice

Since the end of the First World War, where the figure of the victim was central to the Treaty of Versailles, the topic of international justice has gained increasing currency. One recalls that the demand for the extradition of Kaiser Wilhelm II, then a refugee in Holland, posed questions regarding the *impunity* and the *responsibility* of German leaders. One also recalls that, among other problems of strategy and geopolitics, the Teheran and Moscow Conferences in 1943, like those of Potsdam and Yalta in 1945, dealt with planning for the postwar situation. During these conferences, it was a matter of knowing what to do with the conquered and with those responsible for atrocities. The question of damages was posed, but never the question of what would happen to the social bond.

The tribunals created after the two world wars lacked clauses that could have mended the social bond. Once those guilty are punished, what should the society that suffered from this torn connection do? These courts lacked a conception of restorative and reparative justice. Where reparative justice is concerned, there is one open question: What should happen to the honor of the conquered and the guilty? Punishing or rendering those who have committed heinous crimes responsible is a worthy goal of our post-postmodern societies, in conformity with equity, but the ethical question remains as to whether the condemned, the criminal who must give the victims their due, has any right to consideration. Can we still save anything honorable about him?

Starting with Nuremberg, and developing via Yugoslavia, Arusha in Tanzania, and The Hague, these tribunals had two principal goals: to *escape the logic of revenge* and to promote a justice that would avoid impunity by pursuing *the truth*. But when we observe closely, not only have these tribunals never judged the citizens of the great military powers, but they also contain some curious elements.[45] If, for example, the tribunal at Nuremberg was right to punish Nazi officers and officials who admitted to unpardonable crimes like the Jewish Holocaust, it also had one rather strange feature. Article 19 of its statutes stipulates: "the tribunal shall not be bound by technical rules of evidence. It shall adopt and apply to the greatest extent possible expeditious and nontechnical procedure, and shall admit any evidence which it deems to have probative value."[46] Is a tribunal that does without evidence still democratic? Can we imagine American, Russian, French, British, or Chinese generals guilty of war crimes being judged by an international criminal tribunal? One could also mention the difficulties of the International Criminal Tribunal for Rwanda, whose procedural requirements made rape victims reiterate the acts that recalled their worst memories.

These two problems—the fact that the International Criminal Tribunals lack a truly democratic and international character, and their poor adaptation to the way local cultures verbalize conflicts—oblige us to turn toward other modes of *restorative justice*. In this respect, one finds that *palabre* can be very useful. The *spirit* of *palabre* is one that reminds participants that problems of justice must transcend the law's narrow context to the point where they reconnect with morality; moreover, its *objective* is less to punish than to reconcile and make good. Finally, we may note that its *strategy* is to never insist on unanimity but to reiterate that every society has a foundational *dissensus*, which makes the task of multiplying occasions for consultation, altercation, deliberation, and opposition all the more urgent.

Perhaps two observations are in order with respect to the international criminal tribunals: (a) there is no will to rehabilitate the individuals freed from punishment. In any case, the international criminal courts are not set up in a way that gives them functional authority to influence the *future social bond that the offender, the criminal or the génocidaire will have with his or her community*. The goal is to make them pay for what they have done, rather than to rehabilitate them. (b) *Palabre* offers Africans a way to *resist these new ways of defining anthropological bonds* (i.e., transformations of the family, sexual difference, connections with one's habitat and the environment), and their relation to *truth*, to *equity*, and above all to *time*. By managing violence through debate and deliberation, *palabre* allows us to assess the fundamental values defining what is forbidden within African societies, in a world where the logic of economic production and the pressure of new information technologies tends to produce frightened persons and societies, willing and able to integrate buying and selling into most forms of human exchange.

Today, the goals of *palabre* are fostered by the—non-Africanist—partisans of "restorative justice" in the United States and around the world. In his preface to the French translation of *Restorative Justice*, Robert Cario links the main points of restorative justice as defended by Howard Zehr to our conception of *palabre*.[47] The important thing to take away is that criminal justice does not allow responsibility to develop either toward the victims or toward the community. According to the logic of criminal justice: "Crime is a violation of the law and the state. . . . Justice requires the state to determine blame (guilt) and impose pain (punishment). . . . *Central focus: offenders getting what they deserve.*"[48] Restorative justice borrows from the spirit of *palabre* when it considers that "crime is a violation of people and relationships . . . justice involves victims, offenders, and community members in an effort to put things right."[49]

The task of *palabre* and other restorative forms of justice is to move beyond the *deontological necessity* of duty and of laws to respect for *practical wisdom*. This wisdom is unsatisfied with the alternative of true and false, or just and unjust, but attends to the fragility of expressions, actions, and destinies. This practical wisdom is just the kind required for an injured person or a society that wants to rebuild itself. This practical wisdom is indeed, as Ricoeur puts it, a call to a "transformation of the idea of justice . . . [having] to do with the difficult decisions that have to be made in circumstances marked by incertitude and conflict under the sign of the tragic dimension of action."[50]

Constructed Belief [*faire-croire*] and the Media

The Book

In its multiple variants, the African public sphere has been structured by the strategies of constructed belief. One fetish that has burst into the African universe is the book. Writing is associated with the way that the fantasy of mystery functions in Africa. There has never been a society without prostheses for its imaginaries. Apart from the questions of power it posed in the African universe, the book was one of these prostheses. Four moments are important if we are to understand the book's adventure in Africa: its presence, its virtualization, its disappearance, and its ties with the economy.

When it burst onto the African scene, the book found other types of extant writing, those of the brute matter of sculptures in stone, wood, and skins, and that of the body with its tattoos and scarifications. Writing expressed a mysterious voice and when religion was involved, it became sacred. Koranic verses and biblical passages were so many holy objects having a therapeutic and cathartic function in societies that adopted revealed religions without abandoning the ancestral basis of their beliefs. The book and its writing also participated in this mythology that consisted of pretending that the Reference—in other words: that in *whose name* society manages its relations to action and to its self-justification—is materialized in the book that, thereby, becomes a totem. In certain courts one swears on a book, perhaps the Bible or the Koran; the assumption of political power, at the level of inaugural rituals, also involves an oath that one takes on a book—for example, the Constitution. This gives the book a mysterious aspect in the eyes of Africans.

An instrument of power when it helps to disqualify the regime of orality in Africa and above all when it is the object of competition between colonizers in the colonies (for example, the competition between German and French publications in Cameroon after the First World War), the book oppresses and emancipates subjects and communities. For certain African populations, it symbolizes access to capabilities and to power.[51] Today, however, we have been told that virtualization means the end of book, or at least of its *paper-form*. The electronic book, despite its advantages for distribution, therefore poses a challenge for Africa. What will become of the mysterious dimensions of paper and ink, which in some cases were mysterious symbols in the appropriation of the book's power? Reading is not just an intellectual act. It is also a tactile and olfactory one, an act of grappling between the body and the printed and bound thing. What will this virtualization do to the *jouissance* of touching paper and its smell?

To be sure, the digital revolution solves the problem of distribution posed by earlier formats of the book, but the loss of an olfactory and tactile relation to the book still makes us question our readiness to accept a sterile universe, of which the digital is only one modality. How is our sensibility reorganized when the *logic of stockpiles* (since printed books accumulate in piles) is progressively replaced by that of *streams* (digital books give us immaterial streams)? How is the public sphere of discussion reorganized when we move from the materiality of pedagogical sources to the predominance of immaterial ones? In Africa, the book invites a political examination of the system of the culture industry alongside the one made by Adorno and Horkheimer; the question that the book poses for Africa today involves its alliance with consumer technologies. As Michel de Certeau suggests in another context, "Books say nothing about their fabrication, or as much as nothing. They hide their relation to the hierarchized and socioeconomic machinery."[52]

The politics of book distribution in Africa and the official literacy campaigns carried out by states and by UNESCO these days do not consider the *noopolitics* of which digitization and the book are vectors. By *noopolitics*, the French philosopher Bernard Stiegler means "a politics of minds [*esprits*] aimed at developing and managing a national spirit [*esprit*] serving a national economy and a national industry."[53] Let us add that in Africa, the economy and the industry served by this noopolitics are at the beck and call of international financial speculators. Since the wave of made-to-order "democratization" during the 1990s, books in Africa are no longer seized en masse by censorship, but they are increasingly shaped by consumerism. The population is no longer controlled "as a producing machine, but rather as a *consuming machine*; and the danger is no longer biopower but psychopower as both control *and* production—production of motivations."[54]

Internet

Users of the Internet are also affected by this psychopower, which elicits, shapes, and controls motivations. This marks a major anthropological revolution in the development of humanity. Like electricity and the telephone, the Internet has allows homo sapiens to gain some perspective on changes in the grand anthropological reference points of space, time, being-with, memory, and the private-public division. With the revelations of Wikileaks, something similar has happened to the notions of secrecy and *raison d'état*. All of this has provoked both discomfort and encouragement among Africans, who were not stakeholders when the technology making the Internet possible emerged.

The Internet's advantage is that the logic of networks allows for the constitution of a global public sphere in which censorship becomes more and more difficult. True, its pretension to a supposedly panoptical memory may be criticized, and cybercrime and especially the privatization of digital access pose threats, but the Internet's challenge to Africa goes beyond this.[55] What will happen to our imaginary of space and time when the notion of time is reduced to the *instantaneity* of transmission and the reception of a message, but also to the *long memory* that preserves the very same message even after it has been erased? What will we make of the notion of space when borders no longer seem to exist?

With the use of the Internet and the multiplication of cybercafés in African cities, Africans subtly undermine the logic of solitude that subtends immersion in the network of this virtual and sanitized community. Often the virtual community constituted by the Internet is little more than an insubstantial universe of people who present themselves to the screen as simulacra. Spending time with simulacra on a screen is nothing but a denial of solitude, because the speed of the Internet is opposed to the slowness of a real encounter, and the difficulty one feels in writing manually contrasts with the tactile facility of typing on a keyboard. This difficulty and this slowness constitute the parameters of the real encounter. A two-dimensional world is constituted in African cybercafés: the subject who rattles across the keyboard and the universe of the machine in front of him or her. And to ease this two-dimensionality, the public often visits the cybercafés—not to deal with virtual networks but to talk with other people, to comment on the outcome of soccer games, to complain about politicians, and to marvel over the local news. Everything happens as if the space containing the computers, which tends to enclose the subject in the virtual, reintegrated the real and carnal dimension of human relations and thereby constituted a public sphere of discussion.

Thus the dialogical public sphere is duplicated: over the captivating virtual space is superimposed that of the real, which absorbs. The real characters who are at the cybercafé overshadow the characters on the net and remind them that the real dimension of existence cannot be supplanted by simulacra from the virtual dimension. This presence of the talkative public indicates that we may have to examine more closely this ideology of the "network" that masks the "techno-utopia" of intersections that can be used for manipulative ends. This is what is meant by "retiology"—in short, "the contemporary ideology of the network . . . the dilapidation of the symbolic dimension, the ensemble producing an inflation of intersecting images and discourses . . . an ideology with utopian pretensions, a technological utopia, in other words one whose referent is reduced to the fetishism of technical networks."[56] This fetishism of "networks" reinforces the spirit of instrumental rationality in Africa.[57]

There is one important problem remaining with these forms of media more generally—a problem that was not raised by the article in this collection. This is the bond that exists between the justice of the courts and that of the media. The timeframe of the courts is often long, while that of the media tends toward the instantaneous and to impatience or urgency. Even if it may help to prevent political or economic powers from covering up cases of injustice, the intrusion of the media into the rituals of justice can also be pernicious insofar as an extremely important ritual aspect—namely, procedure—is also implicit in the notion of justice. "The media abolish the three essential forms of distance which ground justice: the delimitation of a protected space, the deferred time of the trial, and the official quality of actors in this social drama."[58]

Constructing Belief

Palabre is all about returning to discussion and asking for clarification of the mechanisms by which belief is *constructed* in the public sphere. When a society opens its wounds during a conflict, when it reminds us that we have a collective memory that can determine the present, through various oaths and promises, society commits itself to a future relationship with the founding Reference. This is particularly exemplified by the relationship that societies hold with time and with mystery. Now, the kind of time to which we are accustomed in post-postmodernity is often flat and linear, ruled by the economy. This world spreads "constructed belief" when it sells certain products. First, it proposes a world *without mystery* to us in which everything can be dismantled, accounted for, and managed under the dictatorship of markets. In fact: "American-style industrial faith breaks with the question of humanity's destiny . . . it sells the origin without mystery . . . the creator God is technocratized. He presides over the immense machinery of networks announcing worldwide feudalism . . . techno-science-economy has rationalized myth. The human has become the modular individual, the psychosomatic marionette in the hands of life's managers."[59] In showing the ambiguities of human discourse by way of the peaceful management of misunderstandings, and in weaving between *transparency* (public debate in the course of *palabre*) and the *cult of the secret* (the preliminary hearings, or small consultations in the course of *palabre*), palabre tries to show us quite simply that the public sphere is at once opaque and transparent.

Next, the world we are promised announces *the end of convictions* for the benefit of multiple religions that take the market as a paradigm. In this "competition between good news," for which the example would be America's supermarket of religions, the relationship of faith between citizens is severed.[60] Citizens gather in a public space, but what or who do they expect to look like? The question of resemblance leads us to raise the place of mirrors in our societies. Thus the analysis of "constructed belief" provokes us to examine the nature of reflection, of duplication, and of the simulacrum at the interior of our public spheres. In contemporary African societies, how is the production of simulacra lived and how does the diminution of symbolic content in a life reduced to the struggle for survival produce a new kind of citizen whose words are hollow? How do people live out the disorganization of psychic, sexual, and political economies that comes with the intrusion of this new theology of the market and its cohort of subdeacons and sycophants?[61]

Palabre and the Extension of Citizens' Freedoms

Privilege of the Logos and Democratic Freedoms

Palabre is a jurisdiction of speech and by that very fact serves to promote the consolidation of democracy in the city. Historians remind us that, in the context of ancient Greece, what was essential about the *polis* was not initially constituted by the walls, nor by arms, but by speech; "The system of the *polis* implied, first of all, the extraordinary preeminence of speech over all other instruments of power.... Speech was no longer the ritual word, the precise formula, but open debate, discussion...."[62] However, since public speech can kill as well as liberate, *palabre* allows African citizens to set aside the quest for unanimity and to conceive of their societies in the very terms of their own dissension.[63]

The expression of dissent is not just a condition for freedom but also provides renewed opportunities for the reconstitution of the social bond. One significant weakness of democracy in the West is its lack of confidence in Logos and the dissolution of Logos into technocratic machinery: "If democracy is sick, this is because it has lost its relationship to the Logos and to the dynamical order of discourse. Words no longer take the side of creative genius, but rather the side of trauma, of shame and of blackmail; they weigh on individuals instead of helping to build them up."[64]

Freedom, Palabre, *and Fragility*

The speech of *palabre* and its creation of meaning through ritual are always as fragile as the social bond that ostensibly supports them. Taking the *floor*, the taking of *turns*, and the *distribution* of speech are the three modalities in which freedom is expressed. Taking the floor in *palabre* means taking the initiative to affirm something at a given moment (Ricoeur). This procedure, which consists in saying "I," is really important in our democracies, where self-affirmation must resist being reduced to a kind of self-withdrawal in which the notion of alterity is denied. Speaking up is a fragile act, because it can be evasive and sometimes deteriorates into "chatter." Taking the floor presupposes that one has considered the need for a common language and especially the possibility that speech may produce both consensus and dissensus. Speech is thus the place of reversibility and above all the prelude to action. By way of speech, we must try to examine the role of fragility in our civilizations, otherwise so sure of themselves.

The *taking of turns* that develops in the course of *palabre,* on the other hand, consists in letting the other person on stage play his or her part, and in recognizing the finitude of our communication. This is a perfect example for political regimes that become entrenched and seem unaware that competence is a matter of effacing oneself before the other and allowing alternation and alternatives. In *palabre,* no one monopolizes speech. The distribution of speech during *palabre,* finally, indicates that a people, a state, and better yet a community, only maintain themselves in making meaning circulate. Monopoly is the opposite of *palabre* and departs from democracy. It would be necessary to make a small addition or multiplication of the *types of power* or of the *states* that scheme to conserve monopolies (on thought, on interpretation, on the power to confer value on money and on nuclear power).

Freedom with Fictions

One cannot try to make people believe in freedoms without paying attention to *fictions*. Often, we forget that access to the symbolic cannot be achieved without fictions. What is the place of fiction in processes of liberation? *Palabre* articulates the meaning of this mystery through the practice of ordeals. At the level of responsibility, one creates fictions allowing individual responsibility to be discharged onto an abstract entity so as not to oppress the one who has committed a wrong *ad vitam aeternam*; one will say, for example, that it was the work of an evil spirit who carried away the culprit. We have often forgotten, in demanding freedom according to the rule of law, that law itself only functions thanks to fictions. In a way, this is a critique of our post-postmodernity that multiplies so many fictions only to hide them behind others, and that especially promises a utilitarian world containing one-dimensional beings.

Palabre *as Analytic Paradigm*

The reception of this book in the European world has fostered the rediscovery of *palabre*'s significance. On the side of specialists, teachers, and practitioners of law: Étienne Leroy, professor of law at the Sorbonne, salutes our approach to *palabre* as being useful in the construction of "maisons de justice" [houses of justice], places of mediation set up by the French state to avoid excessive judicialisation.[65] Chantal Delsol, professor at the Institut Universitaire de France, recognizes the importance of *palabre* in the establishment of majoritarian voting in French democracy, while the judge Denis Salas—following Michel Foucault—sees *palabre* as a critique of the privilege that society confers upon punishment and particularly the mania for the death penalty in the United States.[66] In his discussion of the notion of consensus in democracies, Pierre Rosanvallon, professor at the Collège de France, refers to our exposition of this notion with respect to *palabre* and, by the same token, interrogates the notion of unanimity in Western democracies.[67]

Certain researchers in medical ethics also recognize *palabre*'s importance for the elaboration of a "narrative ethics;" this is the sense in which Mylène Botbol-Baum, professor of medical ethics at the Catholic University of Louvain, speaks of *palabre* as an alternative model for generating an ethics out of the narratives of sick persons and their caregivers rather than from abstract principles.[68] Moral theology, further, has stressed the significance of *palabre* for a style of evangelization that focuses more on the aspirations of fleshly beings than on dogmas and abstractions.[69] Finally, psychiatry has also seen its value. In the *Lettre de la Psychiatrie Française*, Dr. Madeleine Rivière notes an important aspect of *palabre*—namely, its refusal to insist on the wrongdoer's guilt *ad vitam aeternum*.[70] By overcoming conflict with an eye toward restoring the social bond, *palabre* demonstrates that individuals and communities can manage to overcome certain defects and to bandage their wounds. Finally, Emmanuelle Danblon, specialist of rhetoric and of argumentation, has seen *palabre* as a style of rhetoric that creates relationships between speech, bodily posture, and gesture.[71]

The African development programs elaborated in Germany by the Klute team include plans for conflict resolution through discussion that are inspired by our conception of *palabre*.[72] From the side of sociology, the problematic of the gift that comes from Marcel Mauss and that has found a new formulation in France with Alain Caillé and in Canada with Jacques T. Godbout, professor at the University of Québec, coincides with a certain spirit of *palabre*. Godbout thinks that the spirit of *palabre* that I stressed in my book—the willingness to spend time in an open-ended way, to pardon without excessive conditions, to suspend conflict in order to preserve social relations, and to give while accepting that something will be lost—is the way to constitute a true critique of the circular and utilitarian notion of the gift/counter-gift. The understanding of the gift as gain must be replaced by a utopia in which the gift becomes a pure loss. To accept losing, as Godbout well understands, follows straight from the spirit of *palabre* in which one must accept partial loss of oneself in the conflictual relationship with another person.[73] Uses for the logic of *palabre* we described are today explored by research in criminology and in the law of international mediation.[74]

Séverine Kodjo-Grandvaux, a French philosopher, has done a doctoral dissertation in contemporary philosophy at the University of Rouen on our work, including *La Palabre*, as well as on the philosophers Kwasi Wiredu (Ghana), Souleymane Bachir Diagne (Senegal), and Odera Oruka (Kenya).[75] And finally, Francis Irele of Nigeria, who was visiting professor at Harvard, wrote an article in *Africana: The Encyclopedia of the African and African American Experience*, stating that:

> *La Palabre* . . . is arguably Bidima's most accomplished work. His scholarship is at its most precise and trenchant in this book, in which he cites ethnographic evidence from a wide range of relevant studies in order to demonstrate the existence of rules of procedure in the judicial systems of African traditional societies. . . . It is significant to note that Bidima's position runs counter to that advocated by Western anthropologists such as Jack Goody and Walter Ong, who deny the potential of oral discourse to formulate abstract ideas.[76]

These observations and commentaries show how many disciplines are affected by *palabre*.

This summary of positive responses to *palabre* and its importance in the domains of knowledge has another pedagogical goal, that of correcting a certain type of ethnocentrism. In French dictionaries, this ethnocentrism still defines *palabre* as a lazy, interminable, and disordered discussion produced by non-Western peoples.[77] This view implicitly bears the imprint of a certain degrading conception of the other. Individuals, communities, and peoples enter into contact through multiple means of expression, whose words freeze, kill, dissociate, and bind all in one stroke. For better and for worse, *palabre* contributes to the assurance of this *fragile linkage* between words and between humans and words. On the other side, among postcolonial African political scientists and philosophers, the questions bearing on future African societies, the vagaries of colonial history, the displacement of populations, wars and genocides, governmentality (as Foucault would put it), ethnophilosophy, endogenous forms of knowledge, religions, development, cosmopolitanism, modernity, the state, globalization, and gender have all become the object of brilliant studies.

But what is missing and what *palabre* brings back into view is that the construction of African history with its imperatives and requirements could begin from a less superficial relationship to time. An *intensive relation to temporality* frees itself from the petty tyranny of programs for the satisfaction of short-term needs, in order to interrogate and encourage a reading of African history from the point of view of the "longue durée" (Fernand Braudel). In the "longue durée," as in *palabre*, which opens a society's former wounds on the occasion of a conflict, the important thing is indeed what happened but particularly its emergence and becoming. *Palabre*, the practice of *singular* societies in Africa, also expresses the *universality of the human condition* with its fears, its forms of revenge, its hopes, its bonds and delinkages, its tentative words that evaporate, its strong words that encourage or break, and, finally, the *fragility* of *peace* as well as that of *conflict*.

Translated from the French by Laura Hengehold.

Translator's Acknowledgments

I<small>T IS A</small> good thing to have too many friends to thank properly. For continually encouraging my study of African culture and politics, I wish to thank Seloua Luste Boulbina, Cheryl Toman, and Gilbert Doho. Souleymane Bachir Diagne, Michael Naas, and Dee Mortensen deserve my gratitude for helping to navigate the publishing world. David Stute's interest in Habermas gave me an alibi for this project, which grew far beyond what we imagined at the start. Jean Coléno, Laurent Payot, Anthony Castellaneta, Arnaud Gerspacher, and Richard Rozewski have provided invaluable recommendations and assistance over the years. For inspiration and provocation, I thank Thérèse Kuoh-Moukoury, Andrew Cutrofello, Brent Adkins, and Olúfémi Táíwò, as well as Jean Godefroy Bidima himself, who has been a wonderful philosophical interlocutor, generous with his time and vast knowledge of legal and political thought, and for whom no question was ever silly.

LAW AND THE PUBLIC SPHERE IN AFRICA

Introduction

Speech, Belief, Power

Laura Hengehold

> To live in a political realm with neither authority nor the concomitant awareness that the source of authority transcends power and those who are in power, means to be confronted anew, without the religious trust in a sacred beginning and without the protection of traditional and therefore self-evident standards of behavior, by the elementary problem of human living-together.
>
> Hannah Arendt, *Between Past and Future: Eight Exercises in Political Thought*

WHAT IS THIS elementary but problematic social bond, "living-together"? How can it give authority to the law so that people find courts and legislatures trustworthy—even when their personal interests may be threatened—if not, as Burke warned, through tradition? When living-together becomes an elementary *problem*, we have to ask how we could ever have expected tradition to maintain our social world in the first place. We also ask how *criticism* of beliefs, including the belief in tradition, could turn out to be a way of preserving or renewing collective life [*vivre-ensemble*].

The hermeneutic tradition in French and German philosophy has always appealed to the social bond as a backdrop for interpretation and for the critique of distorted beliefs. On the French side, Durkheim, Beauvoir, Lévinas, Nancy, and Ricoeur have all explored the means by which such bonds are formed, maintained, or broken. In the German tradition, the Habermasian category of the *lifeworld* has its roots in Hegel's *Sittlichkeit* and Marx's notion of species being. But these categories are objects of faith among European thinkers that may or may not describe the social complexity they call us together to debate. As Paul Ricoeur has argued, some form of belief is necessary even for the emergence of a public *critical of* authority.

In *La Palabre,* neither the meaning of *tradition* nor the meaning of *community* and *modernity* are taken for granted by Jean Godefroy Bidima. These three concepts dominated Africa's philosophical conversation in the years since independence because they facilitated reflection on the apparent conflict between tradition and modernization, using tools from both hermeneutic and dialectical philosophy. The implicit goal of a hermeneutic project like Tsenay Serequeberhan's, to take one eminent example, is to discover the unity of present philosophical inquiry *with* an African tradition of thought that is grasped as a unity even amid its breadth and diversity.[1]

Fewer African philosophers have looked at the critical or self-critical potential of African traditions on the basis of their historical multiplicity and conflict, rather than beginning from the struggle to establish independence from colonial societies and systems of thought.[2] Usually, critiques of the power relations that construct and reinforce belief in the social bond have tried to demystify violently imposed European ideologies, not ideologies from within Africa itself. Consequently, the conflicts within and between the traditions shaping African political thought and practice have not been emphasized, nor the multiplicity of *modernities* emerging from those conflicts. When critique has been identified with "science," as in the work of the Althusserian Marcien Towa, this has been done in such a way that modernity is reduced to a version of science that even European philosophies find problematic.[3]

While he acknowledges that critique always refers to a context, Bidima is not in search of any uniquely non-Western metaphysics or epistemology, and still less, of a single positive cultural presence for Africans. Rather, he hopes to identify an opening or lacuna in modernity's discourse—an incomplete link in the causal chain of international history—that could be the site of an African response or contribution to what is also unfinished in the West.[4] This opening is neither a defect nor evidence of failure—terms that are used too often in discourses on African politics—but an opportunity. It corresponds to a belief (since there must be one) that democratic institutions in which public criticism is possible cannot be oriented by a nostalgic or utopian faith in communicative transparency—whether past (as in Hans-Georg Gadamer) or yet to come (as in Jürgen Habermas). It corresponds to a sober critical will to leave something about history and humanity undetermined; in short, to gamble.[5]

What form does this gamble take in *La Palabre*? Bidima wagers that local traditions and universalism need not be absolutely distinct ways of conceiving the social bond, as in the choice that Fanon famously accused Sartre of imposing on Africa in *Black Orpheus*.[6] Can legal and political systems, by remaining faithful to African meanings and tactics of living-together, create collective grounds for individual freedom? "It is against the mystery of collective life," Bidima writes, "that all questions of state, of institutions, of intermediate institutions, of action and of the subject run aground."[7]

The notion of living-together found in both Arendt and Ricoeur derives from Heidegger's *Mitsein*. In *On Revolution,* Arendt describes *functional* living-together as the result of mutual promising, not merely consent or freedom from coercion.[8] In other texts, Arendt's social bond rests on a principle of publicity and a community of shared aesthetic judgments.[9] Insofar as this idea has Kantian roots, the public space is grounded in a shared and constructive use of the imagination.[10]

There is a tension between the importance of imagination in Kant's philosophy and the principle that "all maxims which *require* publicity if they are not to fail in their purpose can be reconciled both with right and with politics," because imagination testifies to our plural embodiment and our inability to perceive or communicate without mediation and invention.[11] Aesthetic critics, for example, may justifiably believe that everyone *ought* to share their judgments about the common world but cannot be assured that unanimity will actually result. Media, including the voice and body, convey content but also constrain it and introduce ambiguity. Thus, despite its importance as a moral guide to conduct in politics that would forbid conspiracy or corruption, Kant's principle of publicity is unlikely to result in empirical consensus over actions, justifications, or the proper context in which these arise. As a result, one meaning of "transparency" (unanimity or elimination of ambiguity) raises problems for the other meaning (good faith in action). In fact, where people believe that transparency prevails in the sense of unanimity, they may well suffer from superstition or willed blindness. Neither of these make for a genuine public space, for Arendt thinks living together as a creative, revelatory *agôn* in which judgment makes manifest *who* spectators are as distinct individuals, along with what they are experiencing.

Like Habermas, Ricoeur criticizes Gadamer for assuming the European tradition did and should generate consensus, and Bidima elaborates on their critiques from within the even-more-profoundly mixed horizon of postcolonial African culture. Bidima suggests that the very *wish* to purge the collective life of embodiment or imagination would undermine the sense of reality that makes belief work, since reality is the result of effort, endlessly tested in confusion and conflict. Nor should one (like Habermas) idealize the *unity* of the communicative space, for truth and justice require ongoing dissensus. In other words, the regulative ideal of the public space can be no more disembodied or unified than the discussants who use it—this ideal must be an "imperfect mediation." If traditions are going to play a role in this public sphere and maintain faith in the social bond, they cannot hold up a (false) memory of common understanding or an (impossible) promise of future understanding, but can only give citizens the tools to structure their dissent as a *process*.

But doesn't every secular revolution need to endow law and government with authority over citizens in a way that is at least implicitly consensual? Arendt believed American revolutionaries drew upon colonial habits of self-government to invest their new constitution with authority. Societies that lack a functional experience of participatory power are at a disadvantage (Arendt's example is *ancien régime* France).[12] But many African societies do not suffer from this defect. *Palabre*, the traditional mechanism for conflict resolution and public decision making in many African societies (especially the decentralized societies referred to as "acephalous") is Bidima's historical example of African participatory power, whose *experiential* legitimacy could be tapped in the same way that early colonial Americans drew on the town-hall meeting. Furthermore, *palabre* is more than an empirical phenomenon; it is also a *standpoint* from which a society can "take a distance on its present reality"—the critical function attributed to *utopias* by Ricoeur.[13]

Thus *La Palabre* is not an apology for precolonial or rural systems of justice. Indeed, Bidima is very critical of contemporary states that exploit concepts such as *palabre* or traditional religion in order to claim legitimacy and to separate people from what is useful in their own culture. He is scathing toward African philosophers who fail to expose these deceptions, or who ignore the problem of tyranny by majorities that may come with the valorization of reconciliatory justice.[14] *Palabre* cannot replace technical governmental institutions or replace economic solutions to the problems of poverty and mistrust that make corruption and coercion so endemic. What *palabre* might be able to do, however, is provide a model for critique and public dialogue that *keeps people together* even while they disagree, and that teaches people to balance their interest in specific outcomes with their interest in having an open-ended future. In short, *palabre* is one example of how tradition can usefully contribute to the multiple modernities of contemporary Africa.

> With respect to the notion of conflict, a democratic state is that state which does not propose to eliminate conflicts but to invent procedures allowing them to be expressed and to remain open to negotiation. A State of law, in this sense, is a state of organized free discussion.[15]

Bidima's other writings in political philosophy, including *Théorie critique et modernité négro-africaine* and articles on the state of religion, journalism, and the Internet in Africa, show how democracy in postcolonial states often suffers from lack of a viable *public sphere*, though such an element was present in "tribal" African societies.[16] Like many thinkers in Africa and the West, including Habermas, Bidima is deeply concerned about the competitive or instrumental social bond that civil and common law legal systems tend to impose on every sphere of life. Recovery from colonization and brutal civil wars, moreover, *demands* a sophisticated notion of reconciliatory justice—one that can accommodate the persistence of conflict during peacetime.[17]

Palabre is both a method of everyday adjudication and a principle of publicity or collective legislation. It differs from Habermas's historical and transcendental models of law and the public sphere, in being a potentially agonistic as well as a fundamentally embodied practice[18] For example, *palabre* encompasses a greater variety of speech forms than Habermas's model—including rhetorical speech, as well as informational speech that allows various arguments to be compared. Furthermore, *palabre* is not *unified* or implicitly universal in the same way as Habermas's various communicative models. Indeed, there is no *need* for *palabre*, which renews the social bond, without the existence of conflict to which *palabre* simultaneously testifies and promises reconciliation. Nor, finally, is *palabre possible* unless speakers, litigants, and nations are willing to relinquish part of their sovereignty and their certainty: willing, in other words, to see the meanings of their terms and interests altered by discussion. The revelatory or productive capacity of *palabre* is not diminished when clarifying the existence of fundamental *différends*. Lyotard's warnings that modern legal "language games" have a totalitarian potential are heeded from the start.[19] *Différends* open onto an unfinished history, which, as Bidima contends in *Théorie critique*, is the only history with an actual future.

With respect to criminal law, *palabre* does involve set procedures and standards of evidence, which are capable of improvement and change. It offers a prototype for legal confrontation and legislation, which can be improved by implementing modern standards of evidence. Religious, ethnic, and age or gender prejudice must also be removed from the structures of legal authority found in both traditional *and modern* African justice, for these often reproduce the injustices of European and American models. However, Bidima does believe that without holding out a false promise of neutrality, the goals of justice cannot be simply adversarial or leave social antagonisms unexamined.

Because it acknowledges that age, sexuality, religion, and ethnicity exist and are relevant to law and politics, *palabre* also allows for critical discussion of the role these factors *ought* to play in African practices of legislation and adjudication. In the historical European public spheres studied by Habermas, these are factors that often disqualified speech as unreasonable and therefore incapable of genuine deliberation.[20] And yet the meaning of these factors is no less malleable or subject to rational reconsideration in African societies than in European or American ones. Every society, as Bidima draws from Montesquieu, is suffused with political *passions* and understands itself through bodily metaphors. Bodily integrity is intimately felt to be at stake in the exercise of political power.[21] Political philosophers often acknowledge these factors in analyses of *propaganda*, but are less likely to consider embodiment and libido as elements of the *critical stance*, as wellsprings of the will to modernity and democracy; rather, they are often relegated to being merely elements of deception and nostalgia.

Feminists will applaud Bidima's argument that the pre- and postcolonial legal and political structures in most African countries are suffused with a problematic masculinism.[22] This masculinism is often invisible, he explains, because functionalist and rationalist approaches to contemporary political and legal studies have incorporated Western philosophical and religious phobias toward corporeality. In *Théorie critique* and *La Palabre*, Bidima also expresses concern that postcolonial appropriations of Western religious and legal ideas have reinforced those trends in African cultures that are most anxious and oppressive regarding sexuality, leaving fewer cultural resources to defend citizens against religious opposition to biomedical phenomena procedures like abortion and genetic therapy.[23]

However, *palabre* also enables the law to bring litigants and their society back to a more robust notion of *responsibility* than simple *imputability* or culpability. Conflict resolution through *palabre* does not just assign a deed to an actor, but tries to renegotiate the action's meaning for the perpetrator, victim, and community in a way that preserves and enhances their capacity for *responsiveness*, regardless of the specific penalty arrived at.[24] Florence Bernault has argued that precolonial societies rarely considered prison an adequate means of punishment. However, colonial powers imposed punishments alien to local cultures—including prisons—and postcolonial governments generally continued the practice.[25] As a result, like the bourgeois reorganization of postrevolutionary law in France described by Foucault, the criminal justice system created new injustices and illegalities in Africa.[26]

In many countries today, political conflict is pursued by private rather than public means, which include both corruption and war.[27] Legal punishment is viewed by cynical citizens as an additional weapon in this conflict rather than as a tool for reestablishing a body politic torn by crime, even when it is deployed honestly. Religions are also used this way—dividing the "saved" from the "sorcerers," or fostering superstitious fear of politicians—rather than playing a more positive role, such as preserving openness to the unseen *possibilities* implicit in embodied individuality. Furthermore, because colonial police were difficult to distinguish from the military, ordinary citizens rightly doubt that the police has any protective role to play; in a constant state of anxiety, they trust "patrons" more than they trust the law, or the effectiveness of their own law-abiding behavior.

Conceiving collective life as obedience to commandments, imagining human lives as moral "bank accounts," and envisioning wrongs as "errors" to be confessed (and, ideally, interiorized with guilt) derives from Judeo-Christian and, sometimes, Islamic theology. "The relation to the other, which is never more on display than in the law, becomes a relationship of interest and of fear, because a demand placed on the justice system can have no outcome other than compensation or a penalty."[28] Such religious assumptions and economic metaphors ought to be challenged, not incorporated blindly into the state's workings. Here, Bidima's arguments join with those of North American and European critics of imprisonment and advocates of community mediation like Angela Davis, Hermann Bianchi, and Ruth Morris, for whom the political and moral goals of justice remain reconciliation and sanctuary, even if conflict cannot always be resolved or pain assuaged in a given time period.[29]

Meanwhile, at the level of constitutional law, state administration and economic policy are too often grounded in false claims that reconciliation is unnecessary because the polity contains no serious *différends*. Whether in the form of African socialism or anti-communist traditionalism, communitarianism was justified during the first years of independence in terms of a social bond that Bidima, for one, insists was *never* as unanimous as African ideologues would have liked to pretend. Nor was any positive attention given to the individualist values that were present in precolonial cultures. More recent governments have unburdened themselves of communitarian rhetoric. They do not pretend to rule in the name of community, but merely to manage national administration given severe economic pressures. But this means that neither the legislature nor the executive expresses much accountability—in other words, *responsibility* in the sense of being willing to tolerate responses from their citizenry and respond in turn.

When the world of administration is divorced from that of living-together, politics easily creates warring ethnic or linguistic communities around emotionally powerful but historically dubious identities. "Sociocryonics" is Olúfémi Táíwò's term for the colonial tactic of preserving authenticity by "forbidding" traditional institutions to adapt self-reflexively to internal critique and to develop common interests with neighboring ethnicities.[30] In Bidima's home country of Cameroon, the ruling party tried to repackage demands for democracy on the part of a new opposition movement headed by Anglophone citizens as ethnic conflict between Francophones and economically aggressive Anglophones. Fortunately, the government was unsuccessful in this venture, although eventual legalization of multiple parties scarcely changed the political structure. Without risking violence in the name of "absolute" transparency, one can certainly find enough lies and subterfuges to critique.[31]

One example of deceptive *palabre* or superficial dialogue to which Bidima repeatedly returns is the program of "inculturation" in African churches.[32] All Christian missionaries faced the challenge of inculturation—the discovery of Christian truths in the idioms and select practices of indigenous peoples. Indeed, one important source of contemporary African philosophy has been the work of African missionaries who tried to identify philosophical commonalities between African and Christian worldviews. But inculturation is also a signal example of the way in which "belief" is mobilized to support certain strategies of publicity, concealment, and power. Religion is certainly one of the ubiquitous frameworks for any structured public sphere in contemporary Africa.

After the Second Vatican Council, inculturation was the topic of an institutionalized debate within the Catholic Church, which is predominant in Francophone Africa. This debate was provoked, among other things, by the proliferation of independent and Pentecostal churches throughout the global south as resistance against the racist hierarchy of cultures that often accompanied evangelization. Inculturation demonstrates how economic power can influence the choice of religious symbols and rituals for that truth. However, the terms of this dialogue leave sexuality and gender out of the truths thereby formulated, and can easily mask a fear of social dissent. Moreover, it simply tries to replace African traditions rather than confronting and analyzing their superstitious exploitation.

Is any religious dialogue possible when one culture considers its truth to originate altogether beyond culture or language? Although he is critical of traditional religions and Islam when they covertly inform (and freeze) definitions of national life, Bidima's critique of inculturation also challenges the asexual versions of modernism and secularism imposed through the post-Christian West. Neither religion nor rationalism seems to leave room for addressing the role of sexuality in the African economy, or the ways in which Western understandings of sexuality are imported to fight against the influence of religion.[33] For Bidima, these are not problems of religion per se, but examples of the general problem of constructing belief or "making believe" (*faire croire*)—giving the social bond the emotional and institutional weight of inner as well as interpersonal and intergroup conflict.[34]

Palabre lets Bidima bring questions concerning the public sphere back to the original sources and goals of German critical theory prior to Habermas—breaking open totality and revealing the real existence and epistemological potential of nonidentity. As he argued in *Théorie critique*, *palabre* releases *possibilities* into the consciousness of actors, possibilities that have been concealed or inhibited in language as well as in material circumstances.[35] These are also possibilities for philosophy as a discipline, since Bidima fears that toward the end of the twentieth century, German critical theory became its own brand of universal, totalizing theory: indeed, a small culture industry in metropolitan countries.[36] Even the founding generation of the Frankfurt School for Social Research, in his view, failed to incorporate sufficient analysis of political economy in its analysis of culture.[37] But *palabre* is also Bidima's *philosophical* standpoint and practice on the complex relationship between social ontology and speech, and especially on the constitutive role of *conflict* in social bonds.[38] "Through conflict, society redefines its normative regimes, structures new expectations, produces and revises its procedures of interaction, probes heteronomy in the midst of its institutional order, and finally, puts some of its foundations back into perspective."[39]

Thus *palabre* is a critical project enabling the practice of philosophy in Africa and around the world to constructively reintroduce Africa into global modernity. *Palabre* was misrepresented and used by ideologues to justify false communitarianism and to aid the powerful in claiming consensus where none existed. But professional philosophers have also tended to fill the public sphere with discourse that does not reflect the real needs of people striving for freedom and possibility under hostile political circumstances.[40] Intentionally or unintentionally, philosophers have used the authority of education to silence those from less privileged classes, to *take up time* in public media so that other perspectives are not allowed to challenge their authority, and sometimes to become official employees of state cultural organs. How can these media be structured so that dissent allows new ideas to emerge, rather than blindly reproducing old forms of authority, or newer forms that wear its masks?

Language has been one of the most heated topics in African philosophy because so little professional philosophy is done in African languages.[41] At times, philosophical questions are posed regarding the meaning and metaphysical or moral implications of certain terms in African languages, but this ordinary language approach is usually carried out in a European language such as English. Now, *palabre* is first and foremost a matter of language. According to Bidima, simply writing in a non-European language will be insufficient to "decolonize" the mind. Because there are serious political conflicts within and between African linguistic communities, writing in an African language associated with power fails to address the interests of the powerless, who may well speak a minority language. Which African language is best at making social possibilities evident to the greatest number and at criticizing power relations? Which is best at exposing the myths exerted by the state and the *linguistic* forms of officialdom, such as academic citation or legalese?[42]

In addition, there is insufficient analysis of the pragmatics and political potential of ironic and rhetorical forms peculiar to African cultures, including *silence*, which can often make a point better than speech of any kind.[43] If philosophy is to do more than fill the airwaves, a language that criticizes oppressive states in a superficial way, or in a way that allows the state to recuperate its image, is of no use. Indeed, Bidima is critical of the technological triumphalism that celebrates the Internet's appearance in Africa without attending to the ways in which this new medium fails to provide for the important roles of forgetfulness, indirection, and temporal pacing or delay in everyday conversations that allow public matters to be revealed and acted upon. "Speech opens onto the unknown," therefore facilitating *action*, "whereas we communicate only what is known" and become mired in *doing*.[44]

Above all, *palabre* among philosophers must contribute to a better life. Here Bidima invokes the "promesse de bonheur" of the early Frankfurt School. Part of this *promesse* would include citizenship—not simply the ability to participate in nonauthoritarian government, but the ability to be released from the false "African individuality" imposed by colonial legal systems that never had any intention of protecting Africans' rights.[45] "Democracy," Bidima writes, "requires two tools: procedure and right opinion." But "these two essential dimensions of *palabre* . . . assume there are citizens" and that citizens see themselves as such.[46] Another part of that *promesse* would be acknowledging and overcoming the massive historical suffering of colonization and postindependence civil wars without whitewashing the past.[47]

The achievement of this promise is plausible because *palabre* is, above all, a nonviolent method for structuring conflicts, whether or not it can resolve them. One might think that the South African Truth and Reconciliation Commission was an exemplary case of *palabre*. But many people maintain that the material need for an amnesty and for compromise with former apartheid officials rushed the TRC to a consensus involving forgiveness that could not possibly be genuine.[48] By contrast, the *gacaca* courts put in place by the postgenocide government of Rwanda appealed more to traditional practices than to specific ideas like *ubuntu*.[49] But since tradition is never unified and must often be critically sifted for relevance to contemporary standards of justice, there is no guarantee of its success. For example, Bidima notes in *La Palabre* that traditional criminal justice often prevented rape from being publicized; this can protect the victim but also shelter the criminal. The human rights innovations resulting from the Rwanda case, such as the prosecution of rape as a war crime, were carried out by the parallel legal activities of the UN International Criminal Tribunal for Rwanda.

How, in closing, should we understand belief? For Arendt, the power of political communities emerges from their capacity to engage in mutual promising. Likewise, for Ricoeur:

Only a being capable of gathering his or her life into the form of a story, and therefore of recognizing himself or herself in a narrative identity, can accede to this other, superior identity—which is the identity of the kept promise. In *Oneself as Another*, I considered narrativity as a sort of transitional structure which, on the basis of the dispersion of everyday actions and practices, where each of us assumes simultaneously many roles . . . leads to the capacity to make a story of one's own life, traversing and dominating the multiplicity of roles.[50]

Promising does not mean the cessation of conflict, for it includes negativity and the perpetual temptation to suspicion. It is a "belief" that survives and draws upon these phenomena for its own social reality. Narration is a method for structuring conflicts, and is always, therefore, an ethical work even when it contributes to politics. Narration is also a way of being responsive to oneself and of safeguarding one's future capacity for responsibility. Self-otherness and the alterity of public conflict do not *disappear* in the act of narration.

Bidima would probably hesitate to equate narration with self-mastery, for true *palabre* requires the setting aside of sovereignty, the willingness to become another of one's possible selves. In the conflicts of South Africa and Rwanda mentioned above, the impossibility of a "pure" *palabre* might offer a way through the aporia of political forgiveness identified by Derrida.[51] Thus one might read *La Palabre* as a prolegomena to any critical theory of nonviolent or reconciliatory justice, which could complement and perhaps ground the prosecution of war criminals and the administrative restoration of democracy in a way that would not model peace on "war" between those who are free and those who are imprisoned.

Ultimately, the task of critical reason is to overcome people's *disempowering* depoliticization, including the opportunistic use of religion and spiritual confusion to keep populations submissive. Too many philosophers, Bidima believes, blame the state for the woes of ordinary people and too many ordinary people, in Africa just as elsewhere in the world, voice their criticisms of government in private. How can they become politicized in a *public* way, using means other than violence and deception? How can they band together for reasons other than *ressentiment*?[52] Bidima's goal is to hang onto the idea of a social bond that is logically, not historically, *prior* to the categories of tradition and modernity. His hope is that even *agôn* between the rich and poor, elite and popular, must become subjects of what is *not-yet* in African history, rather than being resolved in a superficial consensus.

Africans have always been part of the "philosophical discourse of modernity," if only because for so long Europeans took them as their example of nonmodernity; moreover, the material culture of European modernity was built on their material resources and labor. Hountondji, Mudimbe, and the first generation of Francophone African philosophers attempted to detach African modernity from Europe's nineteenth-century effort to imagine (and produce) its own alterity. By contrast, *La Palabre* and the other essays included in this volume are concerned with Africa's modernity as part of a global public sphere, in which the meaning of "constructed belief" changes and becomes more difficult to contest with new technologies and the end of the Cold War. These essays should be read for the insights they offer to all countries where law and libido join hands uneasily to suppress conflict rather than turn it, at propitious moments, into dialogue.

LA PALABRE
THE LEGAL AUTHORITY OF SPEECH

Introduction

Paradoxically, while African political and intellectual elites tend to scorn *palabre* and prefer a superficial legalism directly borrowed from the West, Western countries and Japanese businesses resort to *palabre* whenever a conflict requires settlement or a law requires interpretation.[1] The very people who overemphasized law are returning to practices of informal mediation, while those who spontaneously practiced the latter in their own tradition want to codify everything according to a rigid legal model. Strange how things turn out.

Palabre is original in its capacity to combine the code and the network, usually with success. Employing the one without ceasing to be the other, *palabre* is defined as an elusive medium. Derived from the Spanish *palabra* (word), *palabre* is a politics of the word because the word is political. How, indeed, does the word enter into the process by which a subject or a social group signifies its own history? How should we understand the word as "other," or the words spoken by others? How can we resist being carried away by words in a political space and tripping on our own tongues, exchanging only depraved words—that is, clichés or slogans?

Palabre is speech "given" or "addressed" to someone. This donation requires a speaker to envision the party he or she is addressing, to anticipate a form that would make a directed address meaningful. *Palabre* is therefore the place par excellence of politics. By means of *palabre*, society interrogates its reference points, looks at itself from a distance, and can enter into uninterrupted dialogue with itself and its other. In Africa, one encounters *palabre* at every level of civil society since words give rise to meaning on every occasion.

Consequently, there exist several types of *palabre*. These can be grouped into two categories: "irenic" *palabres* that occur in the absence of conflict (on the occasion of a marriage, a sale, etc.) and "agonistic" *palabres*[2] that result from a *différend*.[3] Here we will only treat the second [agonistic] form, defined as "conflict reduction through language; violence grasped humanely in discussion."[4] In the process, *palabre* is suspended between the rigidity of rules and rebellion against them, between polemic and collective meditation, between flattering hypocrisy and satirical aggressivity. It is an *entretien* in the political and juridical sense of the word.[5] But if there is no law apart from the process of maintaining, what makes *palabre* hold?

The history of *la palabre* is tumultuous because it is *too* essential to Africa's maintenance. Perhaps this explains why the African staging of deliberation (chapter 1), which is a genuine political paradigm (chapter 2), has been minimized again and again by authoritarian traditional powers (chapter 3) or denied in African political thought (chapter 4).

1 The Public Space of *Palabre*

W̲HAT IS P̲A̲L̲A̲B̲R̲E̲? Not just an exchange of words, but also a social drama, a procedure, and a series of human interactions. *Palabre* is therefore an act of staging [*mise en scène*], ordering, and putting into speech.

The Space of *Palabre*

The *palabre* is not held just anywhere, and since choosing a place is the object of a miniature *palabre* in its own right, the space of *palabre* becomes highly symbolic. The space of *palabre* marks the transformation of extension in space. By virtue of its continuity, extension presents a "substance which, once informed and transformed by humans, becomes space, i.e., form, suited for the purpose of signification by virtue of its articulations."[6] An ordinary place is thus built up into a signifying space, converted into an arena where the same and the other, the here and the beyond, confront each other through and by means of human beings. A place signified in space is truly polemical, insofar as it allows the sacred to be distinguished by opposition to the profane, and the private as counterpart to the public. In *palabre*, signification first passes through space: for space is what expresses the relations between the subject, the law, and what is forbidden, or between culture and nature.

Relation to the Law

In certain cases, a *palabre* is held in the chief's house or at the home of the eldest person in the highest age class, or, finally, at the home of the eldest member of the lineage.

Among the Beti of Cameroon and the Fang, the *palabre* takes place in the *abââ* (the large house for men, which serves both as living room and as courtroom) and never in or in front of a kitchen. The site of the *palabre* obeys the law of the father and indicates in a nutshell the preeminence of patriarchal ideology. In all these societies, filiation is patrilineal and the father is the true symbolic figure representing the law. The *palabre* could not take place under feminine symbols and auspices without raising a juridical problem. According to the laws of exogamy, the wife does not live with her own clan, the land she cultivates does not belong to her, and consequently she is not an owner of space. Since the masters of space are men, it is "normal" that *palabre* should unfold in the *abââ* under male leadership. This raises two problems: on the one hand, that of the very masculine character of the juries in a *palabre*, and on the other, that of women's access to landed property in traditional Africa.

Relation to the Forbidden: The Limit and Space

The *palabre* often unfolds in a border region between two ethnic groups (this is so among the Odjukru of Ivory Coast, for example). This site is strategic. It expresses a certain neutrality, but also a certain contradiction, insofar as, belonging to neither one side nor the other, it allows each to engage with the other. This figure of the border symbolizes law itself in its double function of forbidding (a breach of the limit) and of authorizing (the exercise of action within a certain frame).

The Subject and Nature

Palabres often take place under a tree (especially in West Africa). "If trees are so frequently part of the judicial décor, this is because they attract divine charisma and transmit it to the magistrates . . . seated in their shade. . . . In Israel, the Book of Judges (4:5) evokes justice delivered under a palm tree."[7] The tree symbolizes rootedness, and extends a symbol of collective life over the conflict. Relations interior to this space must be developed in the larger context of a study of the *proxémie* of judicial space in Africa.[8]

The Time of Mediation

The form of mediation instituted by *palabre* follows a well-established procedure, varying according to each society.[9] Often overlooked by observers, the procedure's initial moment is very important because it establishes relations between speech, the subject, techniques for domesticating violence, and above all, the precautions subjects must follow to present their demands in public. Yielding to procedure is a detour signifying the subject's submission to the symbolic, and this is what distinguishes *palabre* from a simple, spontaneously convened debate. The public space of discussion created by *palabre* presupposes this structured detour. *Palabre* does not organize a visual confrontation between parties but establishes a symbolic mediation with many entry points. With *palabre*, we leave the immediacy of relations in order to enter a web of mediations that are infinitely nested within each other. In this *mise en abyme*, each mediation opens out onto another mediation, which in turn gives rise to new ones.

Jurisdictions: Who Convenes Whom?

Thanks to its playful, theatrical, and rhetorical aspects, *palabre* has much in common with a jurisdiction.[10] It is the very composition, organization, and competence of this legal authority. The composition varies according to the society. In strongly hierarchized state societies, the court [*juridiction*] is composed of members of royal families, "champions" of initiatory tests, and often the eldest in an age class. If the jurisdiction covers a small territory, it is composed of the eldest, but on the occasion of an appeal or a very serious case, the family heads refer it directly to the sovereign. Thus among the Mossi of Burkina Faso, we find *kasma* for the small jurisdictions and *naaba* for large ones.

Among the peoples with centralized governments, the composition is very carefully arranged. The Badia (or Wadia) of Zaire, for example, have courts composed of judges, who are split into three groups: the *ntieme*, the *kebin*, and the *lengomo*.[11] To constitute a tribunal, the *lengomo* convene the *ntieme* and the *kebin* to collectively arrive at a decision. The place of *palabre* (*izobele*) welcomes both civil and criminal cases,[12] the goal being to repair any damages. One also finds the equivalent of judicial police officers (*mviemva*) and the plaintiff can have recourse to the services of a "lawyer" chosen from among his or her family's orators. The authority of jurisdictions may depend on geographic criteria (ranging from a single village to a whole region) or anthropological criteria (for a lineage, a clan, or a group of tribes). These competences can multiply because they depend more on the kinship system than on political coercion.

Before the *palabre* session properly speaking convenes, there are pre-*palabres* during which the people who consider themselves wronged open up to a third party whose influence is equally recognized by accuser as well as the one accused.[13] Among the Beti, this complaint is made in several stages including a warning (*mbémé*) and earnest advising (*évui sòn*). Often, a discreet inquiry is undertaken by mediators who, by trickery and experimentation, manage to gather information from both sides. Among the Gimbala of Zaire, these mediators are called *ngenzi*.[14] This pre-*palabre*, frequent in the case of landed property conflicts and sorcery disputes, is unnecessary if the culprit is caught in the act.

Evidence

The search for evidence is essential in the agonistic type of *palabre*. The purpose of evidence is to remove arbitrariness from verbal discussion and to give more substance to the jury's final verdict. Evidence forces the debates to undergo a second detour and demonstrates that sanction and deliberation are not immediate. They are also acts through which the deliberating society looks at itself from a distance and asks about things that are beyond the *palabre's* immediate scope: destiny, the ancestors, nature—in short, the other. The court is instructed by five sorts of evidence—oracles, oaths, ordeals, testimony, and the exercise of the judicial duel. Not all of these are brought in at the same moment: sometimes one requires evidence in the course of instruction during the pre-*palabre,* and sometimes during the hearing.

The oracle, always announced by a seer, takes diverse forms: the bale of straw, the spider, the test of sticks, the cobblestone (among the Gbaya) or plants (among the Sara)[15]—the most formidable oracles being the consultation of cadavers or of individuals said to be possessed.[16] Oaths may precede ordeals and often involve foodstuffs.[17] Among the Sara of Central African Republic and Chad, "one cuts a tree branch . . . and one attaches it to an ear of red millet . . . the suspect must hold this little bouquet in the right hand and swear."[18] One can also take an oath on the blood of an animal or on the head of one's ancestors; the most important is the oath taken on the honor of one's family. Far from being the epitome of terror, the oath calls up the notion of honor, because nothing—even one's own life—is more important for traditional Africans than honor.

Ordeals constitute the most violent way that the accuser and the one accused face the gravity of discord, putting their very lives at stake. "The ordeal combines the effects of the oath (religious character) and those of torture (primitive character)."[19] The first form of ordeal requires the suspect to ingest poison after having sworn.[20] If he dies, he is considered guilty, while he is innocent if he vomits it all. The same test can also be carried out on a chicken. The second ordeal is by boiling water; if one is burned after taking the oath, one is guilty. The third involves the injection of a blinding substance into the eyes: if guilty, one's sight is lost, whereas otherwise one's eyes simply tear up.

Anyone can be a witness if they have gone through the work to acquire relevant knowledge. One also needs occult vision, because if judgment bears on what is visible, it also does so on the basis on the invisible. One should not testify unless one's gaze can see the invisible as well as the visible. The judicial duel, finally, sets the plaintiffs and accused to grapple with each other in a public place: victory will designate those who are "just." All these tests, especially the last one, reveal that spectators at debates often have a voyeuristic and sadistic side.

Criminal Trials [Assises]

At *cours d'assises,*[21] individuals outline the facts and engage in verbal struggle by wielding scorn and insults. The language is often quite metaphorical, given participants' frequent recourse to proverbs and to riddles. Such trials are an occasion for violence to be displayed before the whole world. The public demonstration of verbal violence can call the jury's competence and authority into question. "*During a judicial hearing,*" considers Katik Diong Bakomba, citing André Jolles, "*the judge is the one who should know, and meanwhile it is the accused who does know. . . . One of the two has a vital duty, a vital necessity, to elucidate the other's knowledge. It is the accused who poses the riddle and if the judge cannot manage to guess it, he ceases*—hic et nunc—*to be a judge*."[22] To be a judge implies authority based not just on the sacred but also—and above all—on knowledge.

The assizes are also characterized by continual consultations with the plaintiffs or accused parties, as well as with the jury. The presentation of complaints and the defense reveal more than the point of legal contention: they also reveal the state of the jury's knowledge. The assizes are therefore a test for everyone, defendants and judges alike.

Sentences: Punishments, Appeals

The sentence is delivered after long deliberation by a jury. The sentence is read either by the chief—in the framework of societies with traditional states like the Ashanti, it is the *ashantene* (king) who pronounces the sentence—or an orator judge (the *mbaku* among the Pende populations of Zaire).[23] It could also be done by the great orators belonging to the oldest age class of the lineage—the *odadu* among the Odjukru of Ivory Coast[24]—or, finally, by a notable known for his uprightness.[25] The latter is the case among the Beti of southern Cameroon where the judge is called *ntsig ntol,* the "elder-carver." The sentence can also be pronounced by a member of the secret societies or by a "village-mother" who plays the role of judge between two villages (among the Akoué of Ivory Coast, this role has fallen to the Akandje village-mother).[26]

As for sanctions, they may consist of compensation and reparation, of a fine (the *mokwana* among the Basakata of Zaire),[27] of slavery, and more rarely of the death penalty (except for slaves). When this was required, as among the Bobo of Burkina Faso, the condemned person's animals and goods might be executed in place of the culprit him or herself and thereby become sacrificial beings. There also exist psychological sanctions such as shame, the gods' vengeance, and particularly, exile. Among the Bantu, exile always takes place in the home of maternal uncles. There, the condemned man's rights are reduced, because he will never again have a full right to the use of landed property. Prison remains rare, but present—especially in Islamized regions. Meanwhile, let us note that punishment changes someone's status but does not exclude them: one tries to find a group to welcome the culprit. The possibility of appeal is relatively rare.

Reconciliation

After the sentence, however, the *palabre* does not stop. The goal is not just to compensate or to sanction, but to restore the human relationship. *Palabre*'s true function is to achieve peace. For the sake of peace, truth is sometimes sacrificed, and therefore certain truths can be hidden to preserve social harmony. In *palabre*, the *ratio cognoscendi* is a servant of practical reason. This is because "the social order has been shaken even by the innocent, by the one who is right."[28] Of the three Kantian questions: "What can I know?" "What must I do?" and "For what may I hope?" *palabre* cannot answer the question regarding knowledge. But *palabre* does respond to the question concerning action at the heart of a community and, especially, allows one to hope for peace. "What must I do?" Maintain social bonds. "For what may I hope?" To have peace! This provisional peace will not be like the one wishfully envisioned by the Abbé de Saint-Pierre and after him, Kant.[29] Reconciliation holds one in a delicate, fragile state of connection. "[What is at] stake, in fact, is not the justice one applies on behalf of an individual, but the harmony to be established at the heart of a community. . . . This assures a justice which goes beyond the juridical order, or the letter of the law."[30]

Three essential moments continue the celebration of reconciliation: the oath, honor, and the follow-up. The oath, which expresses an existential commitment, tries to guarantee peace for the future. Among the Odjukru of Ivory Coast, the *palabre* (*emokr*) ends with the *pia pia ok,* a ceremony during which each person comes to "pour out his bitterness" in tasting a bit of salt.[31] Following the oath, there is forgiveness. The wrongdoer requests forgiveness, but to prevent him from being humiliated, the winner "lifts up his fallen brother" by asking the audience for pardon as well (the Beti of Cameroon use the same word to mean being wrong, losing a trial, and falling: *ku!*). Moreover, if the loser must repay the plaintiff and give him a goat, the latter must kill it and give part to the loser's family. Sometimes, forgiveness is requested by the reconciling party who conducted inquiries during the pre-*palabre*, to avoid inflicting excessive hurt on those who were dishonored by losing the trial. Forgiveness here is not an activity destined to lower the person but to reinsert him into a relationship with the other. It does not imply folding a guilty conscience into its *for intérieur* to restore a relation with abstract transcendence through remorse, but an opening toward others, which exteriorizes and reestablishes a bond with immanence.[32]

A follow-up is initiated after the *palabre*; the hearing is not the end of it all. *Palabre* must continue, for which reason the Odjukru often designate several members of the age class of both plaintiff and accused to verify if *peace has really come about*.[33] Often, one does not assign blame to anyone but attributes the conflict to a bad spirit. Everyone knows that this is a way of talking to avoid hurting the accused party.

Ways of Saying

Palabre is played with words and plays off of words. Enunciative processes are equally complex in the agonistic and the peaceful genres of *palabre*. In both cases, the word introduces an ethical and legal relation between actors, constructs roles, and implies changes of attitude. Indeed, *palabre* shuffles different types of statements whose status is ambiguous. What is assured in any case is the performative character of all the statements employed in the course of the *palabre*. *Palabre* is not a place for just any kind of speech, but for speech that induces a change in behavior. This exchange refers to the subject (who to speak to?), to the object (what to speak about?), and to a modality (how to speak?). The subject, the object, and the manner of speaking situate *palabre* as a network of "language games."[34] The latter leads to the notion of a "participatory space" that implicates not only those who speak and those who remain quiet, but also those who observe them.[35] This interaction indicates that during the *palabre*, the destiny of language is at stake, and that "the verbal event reflects not only what persists but what changes in things."[36] In the transformations constituting *palabre*, how does communication take place, what psycho-linguistic components are involved, and how is speech theatralized through gesture?

Communication

Here we aim to show the diverse ways one can take the floor in the course of a *palabre*.[37] The rotation of speech organizes the aggressiveness of debates and reflects the status of each participant during linguistic exchange. It implies an obligation (to be quiet or to speak at a precise moment), a rule (to speak in turn), a hierarchy (certain people direct their speech while others receive it), and constraints (one must observe rules of propriety). Rotation of speech manifests the notion of order. It signifies not only when each interlocutor may speak and the degree of verbal violence he or she is authorized to use, but also how he or she can mobilize the audience's emotional capital using rhetoric. As structured and mastered violence, the taking of turns exorcizes everything unforeseen from the *palabre*. Thanks to alternation,[38] the present speaker permits the listener, also a potential speaker, to construct a role and to anticipate his or her next intervention. Thus, the rotation of speech constitutes the speaking subject as a transitive and transitory subject. The only serious prohibition in *palabre* is against monopolizing either the conversation or the space where it occurs.[39]

Because the rotation of speech brings order in its wake, it also contains the principle of its own subversion. In a *palabre*, there can be "failures" in the taking of turns such as simultaneous comments or silence. An example of the first case is found in Guy Menga: a member of the accused's family, to whom the session leader had not given the floor, took it upon himself to clarify some information in the trial.[40] The taking of turns transforms *palabre* into a game, in the double sense of "game" (observance of the rule) and "play" (being cunning with the rules and inventing new rules). The *palabre* is an intermediate zone between the frivolous and the serious. Despite this ambivalence, *palabre* actually divides the court into two camps: the "distributors" and the "receivers" of speech.

The "distributors" of speech are supposed to be on the jury's side. They might be the eldest of the age class judging the concerned parties, the chief (in societies with centralized power), or a *griot* or a hero who, out of respect for the jury, does not permit its members to assume the thankless task of "serving" speech to those on trial. The distribution of speech is linked to the *palabre's* opening rites, which may vary considerably. The jury in whom authority is incarnated is a "servant of speech" in the double sense of one who, by mastering language, makes him or herself its assistant (he must prove his ability at the risk of being discredited), and one who gives this language to others. The distributor of speech is also charged with announcing the end of the debates. It is the same "distributor" who closes the *palabre* . . . albeit rather provisionally, since the crowd has a voice in this chapter in addition to the plaintiff and the accused. Here law [*droit*] is linked to the gaze: authorization to attend a *palabre* grants someone the right to speak (except for slaves) even if he or she is not directly implicated in the case: there are no passive spectators.[41]

The Psycho-Linguistic Component

The psycho-linguistic component determines the speaking roles in any given situation. These roles depend on the situation of the exchange, and not on the topic in question. Partners are bound by an implicit speech contract dividing those who question from those who must respond. We will leave aside the analysis of the "principle of cooperation"[42] during these skirmishes in order to focus on the enumeration of tricks used by questioners and the strategies of respondents. First we must identify the forces at work; above all, the character of the "influencer."

In *palabre* sessions, there are always opportunists who are there less to pacify the conflict than, on the contrary, to stir it up (in Beti, one calls them *mfòngòlò*). These pit the parties against each other using ironic comments. Their role is that of *tertius gaudens* (the third party who profits from or enjoys a conflict). Drawing on proverbs, their interventions utilize the *thrène,* which is a trope consisting in lamenting over the death or disappearance of an important figure in order to provoke either sorrow or anger in those who remember him or her. The *tertius gaudens* will express regret over some ancestor who has nothing to do with the conflict, in hopes of inciting the jury to conclude that those who are in conflict have not followed the example of the valiant ancestor. The *tertius gaudens* can be hidden as easily on the side of the jury as on the side of the crowd.

As for the questioners, they employ three sorts of tricks—always in imagistic language—to confuse those who are "on the stand." First, the "communicational trope." This is produced "each time the addressee—posed as the direct addressee by allocutionary indexes—is in truth only a secondary addressee."[43] Often, one member of the jury poses a question to another, in order to speak either about the plaintiff or about the accused. Afterwards, questioners employ the rhetorical figure called epiplexis.[44] This interrogative figure is designed to blame the addressee, posing trick questions whose goal is to reveal whatever the speaker considers to be his or her faults. Epiplexis is backed up by cataplexis.[45] This tactic intimidates the accused by reminding him of the menaces that threaten him. It is a sadistic practice, making accused parties suffer psychologically by predicting the evils that inevitably await them.

In turn the respondents use many stratagems. The first, during the discussion, is the *retorsio argumenti*, which consists in turning an argument back on the one who proposed it, using his own terms. In Africa, proverbs serve to prop up a line of argument: one proverb put forward to support a claim will be followed by another whose aim is to neutralize the first. The second rhetorical trick—the *mutatio controversiae*— consists in turning aside from the debate in order to orient it toward an uncertain destination, to bewilder listeners with "red herrings," as one would say today. The third—*refutatio ad auditores*—allows the one being interrogated to circumvent a question from the jury by turning toward the audience and provoking laughter, pity, or indignation.

Gestures

In *palabre*, gesture allows individual identities to be designated for the sake of promoting communication. Putting a discourse into place also means putting it into gestures. First there are communicative gestures, among which we will distinguish paraverbal behaviors tied to the rhythm of speech. For example, it is forbidden to have a rapid speaking rhythm on the stand (in the *palabre* of the Beti). As for intonations, someone may clap his hands or shake her head even when he or she has not yet been given the floor. Next, there are authorized illustrative gestures, among them the deictic gestures that designate referents (among the Beti, unless one is on the jury, one may point out something with a finger), and kine-mimetic gestures imitating an action in space.

In addition to communicative gestures, *palabre* puts extracommunicative gestures into play. First of all, there are gestures that express comfort of position and of posture. Those who appear before the court are always standing while the jury and audience are seated. Next, there are gestures centered on one's own body. For example, it is forbidden to scratch oneself or to spit when one is "on the stand," but this luxury can be allowed to the jury. Finally, there are playful gestures centered on objects. It is always permitted to hold a flyswatter or finger a rosary, no matter what place one occupies. On the other hand, toothpicks are not tolerated for those who appear before the court. Among the Beti, it gives supreme offense to address an authority with a toothpick.

Justice between Ethics and the Law

Bringing Justice Closer

Palabre brings justice closer to the trial participants, because contemporary Africans who consult the official legal system often fail to understand the language in which justice is rendered. How to make a Beti of south Cameroon understand that there is a distinction between terms with a precise juridical meaning such as contract, understanding, protocol, treaty, settlement [*concordat*], and covenant [*pacte*], when in his language, all these terms are subsumed under the single notion of *oyili*? The trial participants have just as much difficulty identifying the author of law who has "a thousand mouths, corresponding not only to the formal sources of the law properly speaking (law in its texts, custom in its formulations, maxims, and adages) but to all the voices which mix in the creation of law."[46] How to ensure that this plurality is grasped in a culture habituated to the anonymity of custom?

In the Western criminal trial, debates are concentrated on procedural points and neglect the basis for the case. How will an African villager understand that a legal decision can be reversed on account of a "technical error" [*vice de forme*]? The law distinguishes at least five stages in the introduction of a motion or petition [*requête en justice*]—*la demande, la prétention, l'allégation, la preuve*, and *la justification juridique*.[47] How will a Bantu be able to distinguish *la prétention* (what the litigant asks for) from the *allégation* (the statement of a fact that founds the *prétention*)[48] when, in his traditional justice, the two steps are almost identical? One need hardly multiply these examples to grasp the immense value of traditional mediation techniques like *palabre* for conflict resolution. All the more since the everyday character of words is not what prevents justice from having its due.[49]

Offenses are not identical [between the two approaches]: noise pollution and aggression, for example, are not yet perceived as offenses. It is possible to "identify an offense without being able to qualify it."[50] The customary age of majority used by *palabres* is often very young (fourteen years for girls) while legal majority is later (twenty or eighteen years). How then to implement prohibitions on "corruption of minors"?

Other obstacles are added to these linguistic or juridical difficulties. These include the rather high cost of court fees and the slowness of judicial procedure: a trial can last several months while the informal resolution of conflicts takes no more than half a day. A criminal case lasts on average twenty-four to twenty-seven months in Senegal; a commercial case, fifteen months. In Niger, preventive detention can run from one to seven years.[51] Courts can be located very far from the parties because of the immense African distances, but the most difficult distance to conquer is of the psychological order. What difference does an African trial participant perceive between the robe of a lawyer, that of a judge, and that of the Protestant pastor who has broken his "idols"? The "judge's robe" can be an unexpected cause for fear.[52]

Even more than the visual setting, the African on trial fears the "solitude in the crowd" that plaintiff and accused often experience during hearings. Analyzing the solitude of the accused during the criminal trial, a ritual that is almost sacrificial, Garapon thinks that "the ritual is what constructs the social object one calls the accused."[53] Having already symbolically taken impurity onto himself, the latter finds himself stuck between a public of ordinary people and a curtain of black robes that are going to judge him. What is he doing there, in the middle of the hall, with his back turned to the public and facing his judges? How can he stand up in that firing range of a witness box? How does he live the limit between the space of the initiated and that of common people? How does he inscribe himself in this space? As a "stray, a dissident, a culprit"?[54]

In *palabre*, the accused is not left alone. He is often surrounded by his family, and it is not rare to see someone rise and speak in the place of the accused. Guy Menga gives us an illustration: Vouata, who accuses his wife of infidelity, has the chief, Kitengue, organize a *palabre*. The wife, Loutaya, asks for a divorce during the trial and, according to the custom, her family must return the dowry to her husband Vouata. At a certain moment in the trial, a member of Loutaya's family stands up and pleads as if he himself were the accused.[55] The one who speaks in the place of the accused is more than a lawyer because he will participate materially in compensating the plaintiff. Since the accused never feels this guilt-producing solitude associated with courtrooms, it is understandable that he will often prefer a *palabre* where he can have company.

There is also a moral difficulty in going to court.[56] In family disputes, every denunciation is perceived as tattling and gives rise to shame. In a case of rape or incest, people prefer to have a *palabre* and to treat this "in the family," where honor can always be secure. During the *palabre*, individual responsibility will be detached from the subject in order to condemn the outcome: "He did not do it on purpose, one will say, he acted in the grip of a tragedy."

All these obstacles underscore the urgency of reestablishing a justice of proximity in Africa, one with a simplified procedure and clear language to put flesh back on the concept of justice.[57] These informal modes of conflict resolution restore the subject's dignity. As the law is part of the subject's cultural imaginary, he will know what he is being reproached for. Moreover, conflict resolution through *palabre* consolidates a sort of social pedagogy: the solution to a piece of litigation is not separate from the litigants themselves. What is important is neither the execution of an obligation, nor the serving of a sentence, but the preservation of future relationships between the litigants. One must save a relation, not satisfy vengeance. The *palabre* is an *entretien* in the double sense of "conversation" and of "making something hang together."

After the sentence and before the actual act of compensation, *palabre* requires forgiveness. This consists less in humiliating than in preserving honor. The party who yields must first ask for pardon from the plaintiff, who then solicits forgiveness from the community in order to save his or her adversary's honor.[58] Compensation is sometimes symbolic because what counts is substituting a constitutive, living, and fragile relationship for an already constituted and defective one.

Against a Penal Vision of African Society

Palabre discourages an excessively penal vision of society, such as the one whose emergence in the West has been so well described in Michel Foucault's history of the prison. In contrast to "discipline and punish" [*surveiller et punir*], *palabre* would be better characterized as "discuss and redeem" [*discuter et racheter*]. But this penal vision of society is spreading in contemporary Africa because, among other factors, of Islamic and Christian religions and their particular conception of wrongdoing. Missionary Christianity presented God as an accountant/legislator/prison guard, which favored a Manichean vision of reward (for the good) and of punishment (for the wicked). The notions of inquiry, admission, and guilt used by African penal law refer curiously to the procedure of confession. Used and readapted in Africa, the law and its respective codes preserve their Catholic background, along with the reflexes of pontifical rhetoric. Moreover, the majority of African judges suffer from the illusion that the discourses of their codes (civil and criminal) are self-referential; they do not imagine that this discourse, particularly in criminal cases, preserves "its distant reference to the Decalogue" and sometimes to Islamic law, even when it has been reorganized.[59] These factors contribute to a very guilt-invested vision of society.

The relation to the other, which is never more on display than in the law, becomes a relationship of interest and of fear, because a demand placed on the justice system can have no outcome other than compensation or penalty. The immediacy of commercial exchange, which is the paradigm of every legal relationship, dissolves the symbolic. The penal vision of society was certainly encouraged by colonial repression, in which the administrative police and military police often did the work of judges. In a recent inquiry regarding informal justice, Pathé Diagne observes that "participants in a conflict never begin by calling on the representatives or auxiliaries of the justice system . . . but [rather] the district head, the police commissioner, and the military police."[60] Fear of the military official is what drives conflict resolution. To evade this primitive and punitive notion of law, one would have to encourage the installation of "*palabre*-based" courts from which no litigant will leave dishonored. The importance given to these courts will reduce the frequency of recourse to immediate justice (public lynching, for example) and will give justice its true place between the ethical and juridical orders.

In today's Africa, the everyday handling of the concept of justice in positive law suffers from lack of a political philosophy that could provide a frame of reference for interpreting and implementing it [*dire le droit*]. *Palabre* was once supported by such a political philosophy, prescribing not just law but also social ethics. Among the Yoruba of Nigeria, the judges of Ibadan mediated conflicts under the direction of the *olubadan* (king) but did so within the framework of a political philosophy: *omoluabi* (code of good conduct). Here, *palabre* is proposed "less to distribute sanctions than to convince, to reconcile, to restore peace in the community perturbed by conflict. The frame of reference is constituted by the philosophy of *omoluabi*—code of good conduct, of sociability, of honorableness and of loyalty . . . that every Yoruba is supposed . . . to put to work in his social practice."[61]

Currently, the mediation being effected by *palabre* indicates a specific relation to the social base: whether in elaborating diverse enactments of justice, or in interpreting and carrying out the law, it never forgets the seemingly negligible and fragile moment of mediation. The spontaneous character of the sketch (informal mediation) must never be suppressed in the final work (codified law). Like "being" in Aristotle, justice will therefore be said in many senses.

The problem is that Africa seems likely only to consider a single sense in the foreseeable future. In practice, European jurisdictions employ informal procedures of conflict resolution similar to *palabre*: arbitration, mediation, and reconciliation. In Africa, a few countries have institutionalized either mediation or reconciliation; others admit them without institutionalizing them as such, and still others have no recourse at all to informal proceedings.[62] The general tendency is to minimize these mediation procedures, considered as "subjustice." Sometime justice and mediation are dissociated: "It is right for justice to be different from mediation. The promoters and users of mediation expect characteristics such as proximity, originality, flexibility, rapidity, participation. . . . Justice, moved by a different principle, institutionalized at the highest level . . . neither can nor should by nature conform to all these efforts. . . . Justice comes from above, while mediation grows from below."[63] And to better reduce its importance, one evokes the fragility of mediation in the West and cites the reasons advanced for this relative failure: the prominence of the legal model in people's minds, absence of confidence in the mediator, and the *habitus* of magistrates and lawyers that makes them reluctant to use such procedures.[64]

Palabre *between Ethics and the Study of Customs*

Palabre substitutes words for brute violence and often, in this way, reveals a forgotten social bond. Sometimes *palabre* delivers justice outside the strict frame of the law, and even when it uses law, goes beyond it to touch on morality. In *palabre*, one interprets and implements law when provoked by "nonlaw" and goes beyond it to achieve justice. Perhaps, in privileging *palabre*, one empties out the political dimension; and it could be objected that "there is no politics to be drawn from nonlaw (such as palabre). . . . And it would already be an achievement if our politicians agreed to consult a few maxims. . . . *Between two solutions, always prefer the one which requires less of law and leaves the most to customs and to morality.*"[65]

Given the "uncertainty of norms,"[66] the loss of collective social reference points, and strategies to reduce responsibility in the public sphere—ranging from the "withdrawal of law" [*repli de droit*][67] to the "illusion of transparency"[68]—the restoration of the legal subject's right to speak is urgent. This right was first confiscated from the subject and then delegated to people who will never be able to think in his or her place. Contrary to received ideas, *palabre* is not the antithesis of law and of the individual. In its opacity, the word reveals the subject, and to a certain extent the strategies and imperfections of *palabre* constitute the legal subject: "to be a subject of law is to envision that speech is intended for oneself: speech that separates, speech that accompanies, speech that reconciles."[69] "The way to language"[70] through *palabre* is a preliminary step toward the constitution of the legal subject in Africa and one model for interpreting the political dimension.

2 A Political Paradigm

IF CONFLICT CANNOT be eliminated, how can we live together with it? How should we contemplate a form of consensus that does not revert to the demand for unanimity found in so many totalitarian regimes? How to make consensus and pluralism cohabit in a single public space? As an uninterrupted dialogue, *palabre* embodies dissensus in a peaceful social space. It establishes the limits between the tolerable and intolerable, allowing one to evaluate and strengthen the connections between them.

Palabre as Dissensus

Palabre can generally be defined as a movement that brings violence to a halt after heated debate. It leads conflicting individuals toward consensus. In *palabre*—according to this perspective—one exorcises disagreement in order to foster unity, and create a people united and indivisible. *Palabre* would therefore give a society the opportunity to achieve a symbolic order and "develop" into a new state.[1] The authoritative article on this notion is by Benoît Atangana, entitled "Actualité de la palabre?"[2] This article views *palabre* as a contradictory process inexorably leading to the restoration of harmony. The important thing is not so much the opening created by discussion as the final benefit: reconciliation. Atangana asserts that "the deliberation of whites aims at establishing a system of justice, while that of blacks seeks to reestablish harmony and unity."[3] And yet such emphasis on consensus harbors three illusions: that of transparency, of unity, and of power or ability.

By insisting on the restoration of unanimity, these authors make *palabre* into the site of transparency: since the discussion is public, nothing can be hidden. To listen to them, word and speech would be entirely transparent, which is contradicted by all research in pragmatics. To the contrary, such scholarship shows that words are opaque and can—in certain cases—form a screen between the subject and reality. The same applies to speech: a well-placed word has a displaced meaning. In its flight, speech draws us toward an elsewhere in which transparency cannot be grasped. This rush to retain nothing of *palabre* but its result cheapens the dynamic of conflict. Through its "openness" [*publicité*], *palabre* plays with misunderstanding more than with consensus. This is why it effects a continuous shift of meaning/perspective and proves itself rebellious toward any closure in communion. It is dissensus that creates distance and that allows society to find another terrain.

The illusion of unity was also one of the reasons put forward to exclude African societies from history. Because they were fundamentally repetitive, consensual, and conformist, they were thought to be incapable of producing the famous "movement that displaces lines."[4] These are cold societies whose concern is simply to maintain order, which *palabre* could restore but not create.[5] Africa maintains "a society of conformity and consensus that leaves no room . . . for dissatisfaction and therefore for contestation. Meanwhile, it has efficient conflict resolution mechanisms at its disposal, which allow it to reduce all elements of disagreement."[6]

Too much emphasis on rediscovering consensus denies conflict a constitutive place in the social realm. Dissensus becomes nothing but a temporary moment that culminates in reconciliation. In fact, dissensus should be an all-encompassing element that frames every relation to the political, because beginning from the existence of desire—in the double sense of affirmation in Being (as in Spinozist *conatus*) and greed—subjects return to divergent relationships at the heart of a common political space. Consensus-driven *palabre* develops into aporetic *palabre*, which displays a society's founding symbols while simultaneously staging misunderstandings about them. Rather than harmony, this kind of *palabre* contributes to *compromise*, temporary agreements that respect particularities and alterity. Such a compromise implies a "concrete utopia": the promise. Compromise signifies a confirmation of this promise—namely, to resume discussion. The compromise is both an appeal and a reminder: "As promised . . . , I . . ." The compromise is moreover an appeal to our memory and our responsiveness, and, finally, to our resurgent activity. In the ideology of consensus-driven *palabre,* one proceeds toward a "resolution of conflicts,"[7] whereas in aporetic *palabre*, conflict is only suspended.

Palabre as Tolerance

Palabre implies the concept of tolerance. A form of tolerance that usually runs from "Why not?" to "Leave them alone" [*laissez-faire*] does not fundamentally threaten its participants' regime of truth. But this is the concept of tolerance that prevails today in the course of Africa's Westernization. In all areas of life, it was clear that this process only tolerated African traditions when they left unquestioned the different regimes of truth on which the West relies. Passive tolerance, which is what we confront in Europe's relation to its other—"leaves alone" while leaving each other's prejudices intact. Here, tolerance encourages parallel monologues rather than an encounter: speak your truth, I will speak mine, and let's not bother one another! In this case, how can we conceive of a real encounter with the other? This form of passive tolerance is an evasion of face-to-face confrontation and its risks.

Palabre, quite to the contrary, draws our attention to the possibility of an active form of tolerance. *Palabre* points out that human being is the being of a relation before it is the being of a substance. In such a relation, each individual experiences a "little death" of selfhood. In the *palabre*, I surge up and exist through my own shattering (deriving from my economic, political, ideological, and other roots). I only enter into relations through "loss." To accept one's own loss requires active tolerance. The intolerant one—like the one who is passively tolerant—preserves him or herself, saves him or herself. He or she lives from herself/himself and with herself/himself: like a petty salesperson who makes money from the great product of his/her *self*. He or she is a being of the "penal administration,"[8] a prison bailiff whose prisoner is simply his or her own self: *ipse!*[9] Active tolerance means that one accepts being torn so that the other can see him or herself in one's own wound. "Human beings are never united with each other except through tears and wounds."[10] Active tolerance is perilous because it is the passage from one modality of being to another: it is a "going beyond the self." Tolerance does not leave the self intact, but feels itself—and is felt—in relation.

The active tolerance that makes the spirit of *la palabre* possible leads to a *docte ignorance*.[11] Posing the question of validity and truthfulness in conflict-laden dialogue means revising the concept of understanding and therefore the status of knowledge. Since any relation to another results in loss, I first have to "lose knowledge" with all its self-satisfaction and its confidence in order to accept not-knowing. Such a situation is uncomfortable insofar as it is in suspense, waiting to discover something not yet given. The situation of real communication gives rise to conflicts of its own insofar as that is where we speak without escaping the limits of our short-sighted timeframe and our prejudices. Since the other stands before us with the same faults, conflict is inevitable. A *palabre* will not be possible unless we recognize our fallibility and our limitation in space and time.

This awareness brings with it an important political attitude. *Palabres* among major social institutions (states, tribes, churches, etc.) must agree to a "loss of sovereignty." Conceding the possibility of error and even, if the occasion arises, a change of opinion, brings temporary peace to the political and social realm. One can only exercise one's civic duty in a democratic space if one is aware of these limitations, and above all, if one answers "I," doing so in a responsive/responsible way. The Hebrew language has three terms for saying "I": "Ani *corresponds to an 'I' that is keenly conscious of its own presence.* ... Anoki *implies a more dialogical notion of the 'I.'* ... Its

self-consciousness is not privatizing, but is already relational. Hinéni . . . *implies an 'I'
that does not take the initiative to assert itself but responds to a 'you' that questions/
challenges it.*"[12]

Palabre as a Social Bond

In Africa, the institution of the state has broken off *palabre's* "thread of tradition," as
Arendt called it,[13] by installing an elite that never learned the "loss of self-sovereignty."
The state has established a mode of collective life [*vivre-ensemble*] that fails despite
all the constitutions, obligatory solidarity, and decrees. This is because the capacity
to promise or give one's word is lacking, along with self-recognition and recognition
of the other, all of which would have reinforced collective life in another era. Political
relations in Africa have become synonymous with the relation to the state, as if politics
could be reduced to this. This confusion is evident in the discussions of African political scientists and Africanists. In their view, political criticism means nothing more
than denouncing the "postcolonial state." The fascination that the African state exercises over them, the love they devote to this staged reality and its features, is expressed
on the theoretical plane through militant and aggressive rhetoric, which proposes a
bad object, even a new scapegoat: "the post- or neocolonial state." There is actually an
air of sacrifice to their militant criticism of the postcolonial state—overwhelmed by
every evil. The African intellectual must accomplish a rite of passage in order to earn
the title of "political analyst," and he cannot carry out this transformation without sac-
rificing something. In the wake of colonization, the lamb of sacrifice will be "the state."
This reduction of politics to the state stifles current African political thought since it
prevents us from thinking about the problem of collective life.

This is the central political problem in Africa today. It is against the mystery of
collective life that all questions of the state, of institutions, of intermediate institutions,
of action and of the subject run aground. "What does it mean to live together?" implies
questioning the constitution of the self and of action. The difficulty of responding to
this question contributes to the psychological disorganization of Africans, who are
torn between nostalgia for a past they will never see again and a present that shines
for everyone but them. It also renders the international context facing Africans more
fragile. Finally, the disintegration of social reference points complicates the question:
What can one rely on? On religion? To Africa's traditional religions are added Islam,
Christianities, and Asian religions. This overlay of religions engenders dependent personalities, insofar as these religions bind Africans with an impressive display of material power. Could the state stimulate collective life? No, because in its foundation, it
lacks any *palabre* and because, moreover, it seems to have been built for an alienated
African elite! Must we return to ethnic groups? Not only do they no longer guarantee
collective life, but they are factors of division.

This question of what guarantees African collective life remains unanswered. *Palabre* allowed society to be reflected in its order as well as in its disorder. Above all, it

prompted people to rethink the problem of the social bond between them. One cannot build a democratic state in Africa, promote the advent of a legal subject, and conceive a plan for society, if one does not first answer this question of social ties. Establishing a social space where discussion can take place is the necessary, if not sufficient, condition for responding to this question of social ties. Such a public space will not lead to a weak consensus but will produce a spacing that links together and separates. As Arendt said so well, it is "an area in which there are many voices and where the announcement of what each 'deems truth' both links and separates men."[14] This space will be the frame within which subjectivities can challenge each other concerning definitions of the true, the legitimate, the permissible, and the forbidden.

What everyone—colonialists, African states, churches, and African intellectuals—have failed to supply is a reflection on the conditions of possibility of a public space in Africa. On the contrary, the *secret* was the preferred mode in which the exercise of power was cultivated. The colonist kept his real motives secret, just as the state in Africa cultivates secrecy in its affairs, just as the churches conceal the economic forces making them so powerful, and just as African intellectuals keep their real political and economic stakes discreet. If it is helpful not to give in to the illusion of absolute transparency in the public space—which would still be the dictatorship of transparency!—one can at least establish a principle of openness [*publicité*] applying to all matters that affect the collective destiny. Because, as Kant reminds us, "a maxim which I may not *declare openly* without thereby frustrating my own intention, or which must at all costs be *kept secret* if it is to succeed, or which I cannot *publicly acknowledge* without thereby arousing the resistance of everyone to my plans, can only have stirred up this necessary and general (hence a priori foreseeable) opposition against me because it is itself unjust."[15] In renewing the spirit of *palabre*—rather than the form, since African society changes—Africans will reacquaint themselves with the virtues of this principle of publicity. The fact remains that the tribal model has already realized what contemporary African states are still incapable of achieving: a public space of discussion. *Palabre* as the formation of a discourse, of codes, and of networks constitutes the place where human coexistence is made concrete. It does not define collective life, but draws a frame around it. The idea of *palabre* as elaboration of a public space "implies both the notion of giving meaning [*mise en sens*] to social relations . . . and that of staging them [*mise en scène*] . . . we can say that the advent of a society capable of organizing social relations can come about only if it can institute the conditions of their intelligibility, and only if it can use a multiplicity of signs to arrive at a quasi-representation of itself."[16]

This "quasi representation" of African society comes just in time since it allows us to reflect on the "figures of catastrophe" in Africa today. The wars and genocides of this continent have been facilitated by the absence of *palabre*. *Palabre* produces possibilities and its participants enter a horizon of possibilities through the speech of the other and the speech addressed to him or her. Each human being participating in *palabre* bears a horizon of possible meanings, and connections with others signify that the other is an alterity that I can neither seize nor master in a definite fashion. Henceforth, the other becomes not a simple presence but a future, an on-coming event, and the connection with the other, a connection with the future.[17]

Palabre will not resolve all of Africa's political problems; it is only an "imperfect mediation," according to Ricoeur's expression, which, by giving rise to mediations, tries to translate the misunderstanding that is constitutive of our utterances. The subject's incompleteness, an inevitable effect of being represented in others' minds during the *palabre*, reveals its finitude. This finitude is registered in a demand for justice; although justice has not always been done to *palabre*.

3 Convergent Suspicions

PALABRE EXORCISES, CHANNELS, and sometimes authorizes the use of social violence. Its function is to stage public confrontation, a spectacle in which the self grapples with its other. And yet, there are institutions in Africa competing equally with *palabre* in the project of reducing alterity. These include traditional powers, colonization, single-parties, and the false pluralism of present-day regimes.

Traditional Powers and *Palabre*

The primary competitor to *palabre* is found in traditional societies' existing forms of domination. We are not talking about one group's submission to another after a military victory, where an essentially physical form of domination is founded exclusively on force. Rather, we are interested in forms of domination whose foundation is metaphysical and on whose popular support authorities can rely without needing constraint: in other words, those forms originating in myths, symbols, and customs. These forms of authority are derived from genealogy and sexual difference, aristocratic systems, secret societies, age classes, and age hierarchy. These factors can govern *palabres* but are never vulnerable to their judgment.

The Order of Generations and Sexes

Let us take the example of matriarchy and the valorization of masculinity. Matriarchal regimes vary because relations to the land, to time, to the subject, and to action depend on myths as well as on the particular history of each ethnicity. However, what unites the different matriarchal systems is the recognized power of femininity rather than that of woman as such. This becomes the source of the right of life and death over men. Among the Makhuwa of Mozambique, women "control access to sex, progeniture, the production and the distribution of food."[1] The Makhuwa accept exogamy: a man leaves his clan to reside with his wife. A foreigner to his wife's clan, he is rented a plot of land for cultivation. And before being accepted by his future wife, he must prove his docility and his competence through work. In this way he will be "assessed" by his mother-in-law.

Even when married, the produce of his fields does not belong to him, since, according to customary law, this cultivated plot does not belong to his clan: just as the seed is given by the mother-in-law, the harvest also escapes him. Contributing economically, but also making their wives fertile, men lack authority over the children, which belong either to the wife's brother if he is not yet married, or to the older women (*ashi maama*). Given that among the Makhuwa, the one who has rights over the children is the one who feeds them, and since the wife controls access to the granary, children consequently belong to her. As for access to sex, men are refused mere sexual pleasure: "foreigners' access to women is not tolerated for mere sex. What one expects from sexual union is a child. Men must make fertile, and if they do not, they are excluded."[2] The man has therefore neither a right to land ownership, nor to parental authority, nor to sexual pleasure. Being the object of exchange, of production and reproduction, the man has no rights but only duties.

This domination is legitimated by a mythical image of woman. In her role as producer of milk and children, she transmits life, and in transferring all one's rights to her, one acquires life. Everyone accepts a certain degree of domination by women, which is why no *palabre* would be allowed on this subject. Such a force is propped up by a metaphysical menace: every infraction of the maternal order is paid for through an interruption of the lineage, because only the mother assures the continuity of generations. To generate, to leave a trace, a name, is to inscribe oneself in Being. One does not negotiate this inscription in Being: we are there, and that suffices.

Secret Societies: The Invisible and Consensus

Secret societies rest on a consensus that no *palabre* can break. Even if, in certain aristocratic societies, the secret societies act as a counterpower, they generally confer a recognition that no *palabre* can disturb. Their influence is of a symbolic nature and is usually based on myths and sacrifices. Secret societies may call for and lead a *palabre* but do not tolerate *palabres* pertaining to themselves. One cannot convoke a *palabre* over those who convoke the *palabre*, since they represent tutelary powers, not simple individuals charged with maintaining the social order. In the Gabonese secret society *ndjobi*, one says that "the ndjobi sees and hears everything." Collective support is therefore founded on a mystical menace: it is necessary to defend the institution of *ndjobi*, because the latter protects against sorcerers. In reality, the constraint exercised by secret societies is most often physical and clandestine. Those who provoke the *ndjo-bi*'s authority are secretly assassinated to assure that the profane continue to believe in the force of divinities. Consensus becomes repressive.

Age Classes: Solidarity, Hierarchy, and Consensus

Nor does one discuss the symbolic relations ordained by age. In these complex systems the "age group"—the set of individuals having around the same age at a certain moment—is distinguished from the "age class," which includes everyone of the same generation who went through their initiatory tests together. "We are the same age" does not necessarily signify being born the same year, but having experienced the same initiations. An obligation of solidarity rules at the heart of a single age class. This solidarity is not chosen but imposed by political menace. It is better to be "protected" by one's group of brothers[3]—one never knows!—even if they may oppose one's desires. The brothers of a single age class can call a *palabre* on any topic except one that challenges the ties binding them together.

Nor is the authority of the eldest open for discussion in a *palabre*. One can have a dispute with someone older on condition that one does not question the rights given to him or her by relative age. Among the Mossi of Burkina Faso, the youngest group (*cadets*) work for the older ones in order to acquire a wife and some land.[4] The older beneficiary of these services must, in return, aid his *cadet*. At the lineage level, it is the eldest (*kasma*) who commands. The only authority capable of defying the institution of age hierarchy in Africa is royal authority.

Among the Mossi, the *naaba* (holder of royal power) has authority over the *kasma* even when the *naaba* is young. At this level, however, one cannot institute a *palabre* to discuss the slippery relationship between the *fact* of being older and the *right* that comes from this status. The same consensus is observed in the aristocracies that found their power on origin myths. These aristocracies provide power with legitimacy and permit chiefs/leaders/heads to break in during *palabres*, but no *palabre* can legitimately address the mythic foundation of their power. Habermas would say that myth paralyzes *palabre*'s ability to pose questions and reinforces "colonization of the lifeworld."

Colonization and *Palabre*

One cannot continue this inventory of repressive forms of consensus in Africa without spending a moment on the colonial adventure, whose consequences are still being felt today.

Justifications

Colonization relied from the outset on an economic alibi. Outlets had to be found for the new products of the industrial revolution.[5] It was necessary to develop capacity in those parts of the world that—it was claimed—would perish if left to themselves.[6] In the end, colonization would offer a solution to certain political problems internal to the Western countries such as the exile of undesirable citizens (i.e., the Communards in France). "Colonization," considered Ernest Renan, "is a political necessity. . . . A nation which does not colonize is necessarily doomed to socialism, to the war of rich and poor. There is nothing shocking about a superior race conquering a country of inferior race."[7]

The second reason was supposedly politico-juridical. Africa, which had never left the state of nature, found itself in the grip of tribal wars. To remedy this situation, colonization was going to export the constitutional state [*état de droit*] and thus impose stable borders along with tolerance and liberty—in short, the path toward "civilization."

The third argument is ethico-humanitarian. It was necessary to help Africans acquire "Western values" of honesty and hygiene, to push back sickness, abolish slavery, fight against polygamy, and reduce paganism: in a word, to make them achieve modernity (in the Western sense).

The final justification is of the philosophical order. Africa escaped from the movement of history. Colonization must therefore reintroduce Africa into history. Africa was "an inert and passive bloc."[8] In addition to movement, colonization would bring it equilibrium.[9] The philosophical justification was reinforced by a juridical argument: Africa is the domain of nonlaw, from whence the imperative to colonize it.[10]

Two different anthropological presuppositions were at work in the colonizer's mind. The first was stamped with evolutionist conceptions. The history of all humans had to follow the model progressing from "savagery" through "barbarism" before reaching "civilization." Thus, European nations had to colonize Africa in order to tear it out of a frozen relation to time. The European present became the future of these child-peoples, whom Europe was obliged to lead to maturity.[11] In the context of French colonization, this evolutionist prejudice supported the assimilation of colonized people. To assimilate Africans meant to reduce their alterity, so that they might be forced to enter history.

Elsewhere, the functionalist influence of Radcliffe Brown can be observed. In this model, primitive societies were compared to living organisms in which each element, fulfilling a precise function, cooperates in perpetuating the system. Because this equilibrium must not be broken, British colonizers adopted *indirect rule*, which granted traditional heads a certain autonomy to avoid overly affecting traditional social structures. Sometimes the occupation unfolded in a peaceful way (the former trading posts negotiated investment in the hinterland) but most often it came about *manu militari*.

This occupation divided European public opinion. In the metropolis, it inspired the constitution of colonial parties as well as great hostility. At first, opponents of colonization relied on an economic argument: basically, the colonies turned out to be an economic sinkhole.[12] The second argument was juridical: right must take precedence over force. In defending this idea against Jules Ferry, Clemençeau stressed that "conquest is the pure and simple abuse of force. . . . It is not justice, it is the very nega-tion thereof!"[13] The last reason for opposing colonization came from anarchists and from certain socialists who saw in colonialism a "pretext for maintaining permanent armies. . . . The armies themselves offer employment to a whole series of idiots . . . who, once decorated, become its most fanatical supporters."[14]

In Africa, resistance to colonization took many shapes. In Senegambia, the French conquest confronted Islamic movements, and above all those of Latjor, the religious head of Kayor. Among the Toucouleur, El Hadj Umar defended his kingdom. Samory Touré fought against the French in the vast region that extends from Mali to present-day Guinea. Similarly, the Ijebre in Nigeria and Gbehanzin, king of Abomey, put up wild resistance to the English governor of Lagos. In Kenya, the Nandi and Akamba pushed back the English momentarily; and in Tanganyika, German penetration encountered the resistances of the Hene and Makonde. But let us leave this enumera-tion;[15] what is essential is that the colonizer's manner of governing had the effect of repressing *palabre*.

Despite their divergences, French, English, and Portuguese colonial systems shared a fundamental methodological postulate: that of the indigenous cultures' infe-riority. Their technological and military superiority could not help arousing an infe-riority complex among the colonized peoples. Domination also affected the economic domain (the goods they found must be exploited), the religious domain (Judeo-Chris-tian monotheism), and the political domain (new ways of conceiving authority, power, and justice) as much as it affected their relationship to the world itself (i.e., a new con-ception of Being, space and time). We will restrict ourselves to examining some of the interesting legal consequences for our topic.

Juridical Consequences: Equality versus Equity

Colonization brought several consequences that can still be seen in contemporary Africa: the religious acculturation of Africans, unequal economic distribution, and a transformation of the African personality toward neurosis, aggression, and timidity. Colonization imposed its own reference points, its own way of making history, and an aggressive relation to Being (Being-oneself, Being-with-others).

The colonial system also promoted a specific kind of equality. Even if the British sys-tem left traditional hierarchical structures standing in certain places[16] and colonization created elites in others (the *évolués* in the Belgian colonial system and the *chefs de cercle* in the French one),[17] the African heads and their subordinates were equal in the eyes of the colonizer—equal in servitude. They all had the obligation to obey and submit to the colonizing power. Colonial authority had a monopoly on the conception and execution of "penal politics," which is to say that it had the right of life or death over the colonized. All colonized people were equal before colonial law, which in certain respects was a vio-lation of the principle of equity. Dominique Manaï reminds us of Aristotle's definition of equity: "a sort of honesty rectifying rights that have been overlooked."[18]

If equity is supposed to be the "bridge between positive law and its supporting cultural base,"[19] colonization negated justice in scoffing at equity. Aimé Césaire gives a good summary of this relationship between the colonizer and the colonized, a relation that could tolerate no *palabre*: "*I spoke of contact. Between colonizer and colonized there is only room for forced labor, intimidation, pressure, the police, taxation, theft, rape. . . . No human contact, but relations of domination and submission which turn the colonizing man into a classroom monitor, an army sergeant, a prison guard . . . and the indigenous man into an instrument of production.*"[20] Colonization was therefore the negation of *palabre* par excellence, a negation enduring even beyond the establishment of independence.

One-Party Systems and *Palabre*

It is difficult to reconcile political pluralism with a community—or a society—that structures itself around several values that on which there must be consensus. If there is one consensus over the right to difference, there exist others—unfortunately, more numerous—that level opinion and stifle all creativity. This is what the single ruling parties did in Africa for thirty years (1960–90). Sometimes quite brilliantly, the *parti unique* succeeded in maintaining a false consensus that, by disintegrating emotions and social space, pushed Africa to repress the tradition of *palabre*. The reality and recognizable logic of the single party had consequences at all levels of society.

The primary foundation of the single party is racist and colonialist. The establishment of one-party systems symbolizes a moment in African history when the African lost all confidence in his or her institutions and might have been vulnerable to an unconscious self-hatred. The interiorization of this racism engendered "self-hatred" among the colonized.

Peace was mentioned among other political justifications for colonization. The very Western- and Christian-inspired ideology of the *pax coloniae* explained why the colonizer had to venture forth among peoples demonstrating a warlike atavism. Moreover, the occupation of colonized territories was called "pacification." This formulation of the project rested on the prejudice that ethnic groups were incapable of getting along with each other, and that only a strong centralizing authority capable of imposing cohesion could prevent these populations from being annihilated by tribal wars. At the urging of colonial advisors, African rulers took up this argument about "interminable tribal wars" to justify the *partis uniques*. It is quite revealing of Africans' loss of faith in themselves: having let go the values of *palabre*, they no longer believed in their capacity to live pluralistically.

Another goal of one-party government was to stifle threats of fragmentation and tribalist particularism in the name of grand national ambitions.[21] The *parti unique* justified its existence by the need to protect minorities. The argument was as follows: the vote being ethnic in Africa, minority ethnicities were at risk of not being represented, since their leaders could not hope to gather a sufficient number of votes. Only one large rallying party, in which all citizens would be likely to find themselves, could effectively protect minorities.

The second argument in favor of a one-party system[22] was derived from the need for national integration, on the one hand, and from the ideal of a classless society, on the other. The problem of the young African states was essentially that of constituting themselves as nations. The single party was supposed to channel all energies toward the country's full development. Mobilizing people for development required a strong party with which they could identify, and that would, in turn, lead them to surpass themselves. Some believed that only a single party would be able to assure the passage from an ethnic consciousness to a feeling for the nation. With neither a common history nor language, the ethnicities making up African states were considered major obstacles to unity.

Regimes that claimed to represent socialism or Marxism had to refuse multiparty politics for the sake of a society without class. In this case, "the Party expects to guide the whole people, to overthrow the natural passivity of the masses, and to mobilize individuals under collective supervision in order to give them not only a national consciousness but also a blind belief in work."[23] This mystification did not value discussion and the Guinean Sékou Touré affirmed "that there is no place for an opposition whose tactics would only serve to divert popular energies."[24] As for the Tanzanian Julius Nyerere, he considered that "multiparty politics is a gratuitous pastime that we, in Africa, cannot permit ourselves: we are pressed for time and have more serious things to do."[25]

In Francophone Africa, the *parti unique* was also influenced by the constitutional history of the Fourth and Fifth French Republics. It can be explained by the instability of the former as well as the authoritarianism of the latter. After the 1946 constitution in France, multiparty politics was implanted in Africa. Most of the African parties, moreover, were only local sections of metropolitan parties: the SFIO [Section Française de l'Internationale Ouvrière] partnered with the party of Modibo Keita in the French Soudan (today's Mali) as well as the socialist party of Léopold Senghor in Senegal. The RDA [Rassemblement Démocratique Africain] of Félix Houphouët-Boigny of Ivory Coast was affiliated with the Communist party. After the Loi-Cadre Defferre of 1956, territorial governments were formed under the patronage of French high commissioners and nothing resembled the pitiful image of governmental instability offered by the African parties so much as the Fourth Republic itself! From 1957 to 1960, most of the countries had changed government at least once.[26] If multiparty politics functioned poorly, this was not because of African tribalism, nor what Maurice Duverger called the "uneducated popular masses,"[27] but because of the mimicry of *évolués* who reproduced the vices of the Fourth Republic's governmental practices in Africa.

The ungovernability introduced by the instability of these governments eventually added to the persuasiveness of single-party politics; advocates of such a system were redeemed by the 1958 Constitution. Everything helped them out: the presidential regime, the weakness of parliament, election by universal suffrage. The party had to drive every wheel of the state and civil society. In this system, the role of leader (incarnated by one person or by a collective entity, the party) and of his ideological substitutes is central. On the administrative and political plane, the party machinery monopolized all talk of national unity. Like all forms of power, it drew on the register of the sacred: for example, one was forbidden to "pronounce the name of the leader thoughtlessly" except in metaphors and for the purpose of praise; otherwise, one faced public sanctions or, given that the prohibition was so thoroughly interiorized, simply a dull anxiety of the religious type. The leader was not an ordinary individual.

Social life reproduced the model of the leader in an analogous way. Apart from its institutional violence, the *parti unique* encouraged socialization through imitation of the leader.[28] The leader was an object of fascination for his people's desire and eventually gained a monopoly on glory, as well as hate. The *parti unique* created an artificial consensus running completely at odds to the African tradition of *palabre*. The nation, the general interest, and the common good, which the definition reduced to a single good, were nothing but excuses for renouncing the pluralism represented by the tradition of *palabre*.

The socio-political consequences of the one-party system were multiple. The *parti unique* had ceased to think about alterity, which is still an essential given of politics, understood as the organization of human coexistence. It also fostered new social fears, by giving a very imprecise definition of the enemy (who is just as often a political opponent as a neighboring country). It condemned the subject to being only an echo of authoritarian power, incapable of any autonomy. The other could only be perceived as a commander or one who carries out orders. The upsurge of the self and the other and their reciprocal fertilization were purely and simply eliminated.

The one-party system installed an authoritarian mentality that penetrated every level of society. Even when one contested the *parti unique*, one did it in an authoritarian manner. After all, is not totalitarianism defined by its ability to contaminate everything, even the most unlikely antibodies? Critics of the one-party model have not sufficiently noted this assault on the human personality even outside of institutions. These critics have confined themselves to the register of power—talking about its capture, its reorientation, its strategies—and have generally missed the social pathology engendered by the *parti unique*. Before being a political phenomenon, the disintegration of society was first and foremost felt emotionally, because affect is the register to which the single party primarily appeals. This explains how the single party could find its most fervent defenders among the disadvantaged classes.[29] The authoritarian personality is not only characterized by an extreme violence in human relations and in administration (the minor leaders) but also by the "the very willingness to connive with power and to submit outwardly to what is stronger, under the guise of a norm"; this, for Adorno, constitutes "the attitude of the tormenters that should not arise again."[30]

Because it neglected *palabre's* essential procedure for "going outside oneself," the epoch of the one-party system risked giving birth to an unprecedented personality type: the unstable African, withdrawn into himself and only capable of expressing himself in an aggressive way. This personality confuses political action and activism, revolution and aggression. Perhaps this also explains why the contemporary African is so anxious. He was made to believe in an exclusively "organicist" vision of power that could only be found in the state, even more specifically in the government, and therefore to believe that all problems could be resolved if the state's head were severed—from whence, perhaps, the proliferation of coups d'état in Africa. This sadistic drive to "decapitate power" is prettied up by the care, so evident in African culture, to "get along" with power. In reality, this zeal represents an effort to get oneself recognized or named, in which it is not hard to see the old mythical-feudal reflex to seek a totem's protection. The influential person has taken the totem's place. This desperate quest for a great protector has four consequences: insecurity, phobia of all openness, reciprocal manipulation, and finally, depoliticization.

When pluralism is reduced to simple chattering, the citizen experiences an insecurity that recalls the state of nature: "If something happens to me," he thinks, "I am lost!" Self-preserving instincts give rise to the search for protection, plunging each person into the permanent anxiety of having to depend on a single person's whims rather than on the law. This vital need distorts all publicity in Kant's sense, since the real motor of political activity is never spoken about. After having found some protection, one must hide the identity of one's "benefactor" at all costs, in order to humor him and preserve that protection. Dissimulation thereby becomes the political virtue par excellence. But this is not the only vice of the system, which also encourages manipulation. The protector needs his dependents in order to feel empowered; his divinity comes from the fawning gaze of another person whom he manipulates with promises. But this manipulation is reciprocal insofar as the dependent's obedience also has a "hold" over the protector and guarantees the latter's grandeur.

The final result of all this is depoliticization, which can take two forms. First, there is total defiance regarding the law: the law will never protect one as well as an individual can (which explains why one often turns toward the latter rather than to the former). We can add to this a total loss of the idea of general interest. Further, the system takes away the individual's sense of responsibility since, no longer being protected by rules of play that are external and visible, he or she will do nothing but censor himself, stifling anything that is not authorized by his or her protector. If, on the other hand, the latter covers his back, then he is allowed to do everything including transgress the law.

Thus, the *parti unique* has disintegrated the black African personality by forcing it to undertake an apprenticeship in lawlessness. Everyone, whether or not they are protected, agrees on one point: it is more advantageous to have a powerful totem on one's side than to have the law.[31] One could not be further from *palabre*.

Pseudodemocracies and *Palabre*

Following the multiparty politics of the colonial period and the era of single-party states, Africa seems to have chosen multipartyism once again in the 1990s for a whole host of reasons: the new international situation created by the end of the Cold War, the exhaustion of African dictatorships that, materially, could no longer maintain their machinery (armies, special services, etc.) and finally, the pressure of unions, associations, and more generally, of African civil society.

Stakes

Multiparty politics in present-day Africa were founded with the famous "national conferences," which one can group into two categories: the sovereign national conferences and the others. The sovereign national conference was a vast forum haphazardly bringing together associations, corporations, not-yet-legalized political parties, representatives of the executive branch and the legislature and, finally, judges. Debates were public and sometimes rebroadcast by audiovisual media, as in the Republic of Congo. The national conferences took on the task of elaborating new modalities of democratic life. Their first act was to suspend existing constitutions, then to authorize the—verbal—prosecution of prior regimes. Thus, corruption, assassinations, and clientelism were denounced.

During these hearings, the functioning of the state was assured by governing bodies from the conference, among whose members one often found Roman Catholic bishops and archbishops.[32] Transition governments were installed and pluralist elections organized. Sovereign national conferences took place in Benin, in the Republic of Congo, and, to a certain extent, in Kenya. As for the nonsovereign national conferences that took place elsewhere—for example, in Gabon and Chad—they embraced the phase of airing grievances and vast *palabres*, but sometimes refused, as in Chad, to let the executive branch be controlled by the conference while it was led by archbishops. The executive, on the other hand, sometimes considered these conferences constitutional "coups d'état."

Each African country called for its national conference. This was interpreted as a huge *palabre* instituting a new African-style democracy. What was it exactly?

Reception

Africans gladly lumped together multiparty politics, democracy, and technological development, which allows the experiments to be sorted into four groups.

1. For the first group, multipartyism is nothing but a forced transposition into the South of a development model that comes from the North, heavy with its interests and values. Pluralist democracy allows the West to do business in good conscience with regimes whose democracy is far more apparent than real. For Lawyer Kafureeka of Zambia, the change of international stakes at the end of the Cold War pushed

Westerners who supported dictators to review their strategy and to encourage multi-partyism: "Now you see why democracy is defined simply as multipartyism, a democracy of the status quo, a democracy that does not question unjust structures deserving of change."[33] Kafureeka ends by qualifying this movement of democratization as "Western fundamentalism." The West, according to him, wants to forge the world in a single image using this model of "democratization": its own.

2. The second group mistrusts "democratization," not just because it is presented as a typically Western product, but also because of its intimate link with a notion of economic debt that democratization refuses to challenge. Democratization, which also means liberation of prices, promotion of private enterprise, and opening to international trade, leads to a new form of colonization when Northern capital is injected into countries that will neither impose heavy taxation nor prohibit child labor.[34] These critics also denounce complicity between the process of Africa's democratization and the real controls exercised by the World Bank and IMF,[35] as well as the symbolic and ideological control coming from NGOs.

3. The third group criticizes democratization and multiparty politics on the purely political plane. For the Ghanaian Maxwell Owusu,[36] there was first multipartyism, then the *partis uniques*, then multipartyism yet again, but always with the same constitutional structure, which reproduced the vices of Western systems and learned nothing from the African symbolic.

4. The last group is composed of Western Africanists like the historian Basil Davidson for whom multiparty politics represents a non-African history and who suggests that, so long as it involves democratic forms of participation, the formula of the *parti unique* is not so terribly bad after all.[37] For Jean Copans, multiparty politics is only meaningful when human rights are really guaranteed by the state; and, in their absence, democratization remains nothing but a distraction.[38] One finds a similar argument in Andre Gunder Frank, for whom multipartyism and democracy require liberty and therefore economic power—yet to be found among many African countries.[39]

Questions

Negligence with respect to the elaboration of a democratic public space has brought about a particular kind of apoliticism. After the sovereign national conferences, an expiatory apoliticism took the place of ordinary apoliticism. In this new case, "the apolitical attitude is not, as one might believe, a passive psychic state, but a very active stance."[40] The liberation of speech produced a flurry of meaningless talk, and the discussion of meaning, collective life, notions of community, and of the social bond were smothered in procedural quarrels over votes, the future constitution, the status of new rulers, and the fate their predecessors deserved. Liberalization translated into the multiplication of parties whose reality and reach sometimes went no further than the scope of an extended family (each clan being tempted to turn itself into a political party). In this cacophony, public opinion became an anonymous "one."[41] As soon as one dissociates politics from meaning, and above all when political debate no longer turns around anything but organization (of elections, legislative houses, and state chancelleries), one begins sliding toward a subtle depoliticization. This is because politics, as Arendt said regarding the Romans, means to conserve "the city's foundation."[42]

The politics of *palabre* would go beyond organizations and procedures, not just to liberate speech, but also to ensure that the foundations of ethnic collective life were handed on. Political forms of action and speech that hesitate to reformulate the problem of foundation, even in the context of party pluralism, degrade into a fussy "apoliticism." This is not so much a refusal to take part in political life but a dissociation between the claim of rights and the search for meaning. For a legal subject, according to Marcel Gauchet's apt expression, has a "debt of meaning" when it comes to politics.[43] In Africa, infatuation with politics has become a way to expiate one's prior compromises with the one-party regimes. The political space is reduced to the single aspect of making claims. Permission to discuss—and to criticize—is transformed into populist impatience that demands everything and demands it right away.

The critique of *partis uniques* during these national conferences rested on another unfortunate consensus: failure to show how the present system of political parties in Africa developed out of patriarchal systems of domination. Approaching politics from the angle of meaning implies not just promoting the legal subject's expression, but above all revising and revisiting traditions. Now, during these national conferences, the critical relation to tradition was not broached, smothered as it was by the settling of scores between intellectual, industrial, juridical, and religious elites.

In *palabre*, we always participate in a double movement. On the one hand, we decide problems with an eye to the management of power at the community's core. On the other hand, we define new guarantees of transcendence through the public use of speech, by reactivating certain symbols associated with time, space, and the subject. Thus, *palabre* rests on problems relative to *power* and to *authority* in a movement minimizing discontinuity with the past. As reflection on the relation to power and to authority, *palabre* is open to imitation by "sovereign national conferences" whose great weakness was talking exclusively about the state.[44] Democratization was understood in a restrictive sense, limited to the state and its mechanisms without extending toward *society*. Like the political, ecclesiastical, and intellectual African elite, the political scientists only focused on instituted power, while failing to reflect on the instituting authority. Authority refers to something that, without immediate coercion, nevertheless makes us subscribe to and obey transcendence, meaning, the social bond, and constructed belief [*faire-croire*]—in short, to whatever holds things together.

What are the new figures of transcendence in Africa today? How does African society represent its "outside" to itself and how does it exploit this "outside" when exercising justice? Meaning is what permits us to hold, to stand upright, to pull through in adversity, to stand before other people. As for the social bond, it permits us to think through the relationship with power, with authority, the law, and community. Here we are not just considering mediation from the agonistic standpoint, as a way to resolve conflicts, but as that which reminds each of us that there is a "you," [*tu*] a gauge of intersubjectivity, internal to the self-affirmation of every "I" [*je*]. Life in the public sphere is only possible if the demand for intersubjectivity is posed a priori and promoted a posteriori.

The context for laws, duties, and obligations used by the subject to orient him or herself in the city is a sort of constructed belief [*faire-croire*]. This phenomenon includes all the representations that frame the community, as well as problems of "face-to-face" interaction raised by symbolic exchanges. Political reflection on democratization in Africa has thus bypassed real debate on the meaning of collective life. What won out, instead, was simple public debate on the seizure, preservation, distribution, participation, and control of power. The common, public, and contradictory task of redefining the *je ne sais quoi* that holds together a given society constitutes the most fundamental topic for political reflection in Africa today.[45]

Evading this question of meaning put a very consensualist spin on a debate that was supposed to be democratic and pluralist. Absent was any "political pathetics" whose role might have been to analyze the principal political passions and mechanisms of mobilization. The national conferences occupied themselves with the efficacy of power and not with its affectivity. Political analysts did not bother to examine the passions expressed during these national conferences. How are political passions, emotions, and collective sentiments put in place? What affective devices are at work in the implosion of this or that regime in Africa, and why is a dictatorial regime put back in power by the very people who swept it away several years before?[46]

Montesquieu formulated a hypothesis according to which each political system had a corresponding dominant passion, which contributed to its stability and regulation.[47] What is this passion in Africa? This is not the question on people's minds! One phrase is heard again and again: "respect for the law." But how to promote such *respect* in a democratic context among citizens habituated to charismatic power, where the leader incarnates the visible law? For whom, moreover, the constitution is an abstract construction? How to make citizens who demand a "visible presence of the law" respect justice and the constitution?

Marx was right to identify three fundamental traits of political passions—ecstatic enthusiasm, malaise, and revolt[48]—to explain why the oppressed classes are sometimes the ones most opposed to change. If the observers of democratization in Africa were more interested in political passions, they would probably have done a better job identifying the means of emotional persuasion and the sites where this "ecstatic enthusiasm" is propagated. How are liturgies of power constructed in Africa? How do these liturgies produce unbreachable thresholds and borders? How do the liturgies of sovereign national conferences "stage" power?[49] As with *palabre*, the problematic of power comes down to the role of the body. Power is invested through bodily discipline, something that has escaped many scholars who would have been well advised to follow Foucault's analyses of "politics from below."[50] How does corporeal *héxis*[51] participate in the "language games" that have performative value in the African political arena? Taking corporeal language into consideration could explain how people decide between two candidates standing for election who—as is repeatedly the case in Africa—belong to the same party, come from the same ethnic group and clan, and have almost the same level of affluence. Above and beyond ethnic explanations like those of Jean-François Bayart[52]—which consist in reducing the political action of African parties to an alimentary and ethnic competition, in which the granary-state is the object of hatred and envy—reflection on the body may offer a key by returning us to considerations of communication (the body is a sign and the site of sign-creation), of the subject, and of Being.

Another error has been the failure to bring the social base together. The gap between rulers and people has carried over from the time of the one-party systems. This goes some way toward explaining the fact that the chatter about constitutions and the rule of law has not been understood by the people. Political reflection in Africa forgets about the phenomenon of "nonsimultaneity" described by Ernst Bloch,[53] which consists in a population's finding itself out of sync with time: it lives in a so-called modern period while its consciousness remains completely attached to past forms of thought and to a past mode of production. Living in a more and more differentiated society, the African preserves a communitarian mentality. The discourse on African democratization thereby becomes a "luxury" for an African elite that turns around on itself. The public use of speech such as it existed in traditional *palabre* has been confiscated.[54] The free speech promoted by multiparty politics is an illusion: "In reality, the speech in question here is not available to all: it is the speech of an elite, of those who are educated, the speech of those who can preoccupy themselves with grand principles, regardless of whether this preoccupation is legitimate."[55]

Despite multipartyism, African countries—or better their political regimes—are "democratures." No longer outright dictatorships, but not yet democracies, and lacking autonomy for themselves, these regimes do not create a favorable environment for autonomy. There is no democracy without autonomy; a people can only give itself a democratic regime if it can give itself its own law. Now, the true power in Africa is in the hands of foreign investors, bankers, and financiers who can make and unmake regimes. Moreover, in this new economic game, support from the IMF and the funding agencies is a major electoral argument.[56] To be "the friend of Western ambassadors" and investors, or to demonstrate overtly one's future networks of dependency, constitutes a serious trump card for getting oneself elected in Africa today.[57] Thus the persistence of an old colonial complex, which consists in expecting everything to come from the colonizer.

These "democratures" do not encourage autonomy. Moreover, the political and intellectual elites are not challenged. They demand the maximum transparency through the development of the so-called independent press while concealing the reasons that they push for this transparency. Further, there is no question of recommending a social ethic that would encourage the formation of individuals capable of taking on citizenship.

Last but not least, the political debate in Africa has failed to pose the question of secularism in political institutions. The "sovereign national conferences" were led by Catholic bishops. The problem of the state's secularism is immediately apparent. What role have apostolic nuncios really played?[58] What will their position be concerning the problems of euthanasia, cloning, frozen embryos, abortion? The same problem of secularization is posed in a pluralist democracy like Senegal, where we know that the imams and marabouts of the two great Muslim brotherhoods (Mourides and Tidjanes) issue voting orders to their members and direct Senegalese political life from behind the scenes. When it is not a matter of Christian or Islamic intrusion, appeal to the invisible forces of traditional beliefs[59] suffices to show that this problem of secularization remains untouched in Africa, from whence the importance of *palabre*.

4 A Difficult Place in Political Thought

THE COMPREHENSION OF political mechanisms in Africa—the cost, exercise, transmission and control of power—must be the object of a second anthropological reading of symbolic systems structuring the collective and the subjective, the institutional uses of rhetoric, and the specific conflicts they engender. Where does *palabre* fit in here?

Palabre and Pan-Africanism

Pan-Africanism was supposed to be a political, economic, and cultural movement to restore the dignity of blacks at the geostrategic level. The protagonists of this movement, which stretched between the Americas, the Caribbean, and Europe, were African-Americans and Jamaicans as well as Africans. Pan-Africanism was born during the colonial period and still survives in weak form in the Organization of African Unity (OAU). To grasp how Pan-Africanism drowned *palabre* in the mystical celebration of a black people, let us briefly recount the evolution, protagonists, and objectives of Pan-Africanism.

Born in America, Pan-Africanism was meant to be a continuation of the "back to Africa" movement of freed slaves who had founded Liberia. This tricontinental "pan-Negro" movement sought to end slavery and colonization by returning deported blacks to their mother Africa. One of the first protagonists was H. S. Williams (of Trinidad), followed by Marcus Garvey, another Jamaican who wanted to unite all blacks in a single people.[1] W. E. B. du Bois, another leader in the United States, distanced himself from Garvey.[2] On the African continent, the great figures of this movement were the

Nigerian Adeoye Deniga; the Ghanaians Casely Hayford and later Kwame Nkrumah; Isaac Theophilus Akunna Wallace-Johnson in Sierra Leone; Raphael Armattoe in Togo; Ras Makonen in Ethiopia; and Jomo Kenyatta in Kenya. As its conferences evolved, Pan-Africanism was gradually transformed into nationalism: the liberation and development of Africa had to happen under the banner of mysticism concerning the black community.

The one who put Pan-Africanism on the path to real institutionalization was Nkrumah, who made the project concrete by withdrawing his country from the British Commonwealth and inaugurating a process of continental integration through his union with Liberia, Mali, and Sékou Touré's Guinea.[3] Nkrumah mistrusted the model of the nation-state,[4] whose problems he wanted to circumvent by recommending that the whole of Africa oppose the superpowers as a bloc by engaging in common economic planning, defense, and diplomacy. These ideas were brought to a halt by the leadership of Francophone countries.

Nkrumah's Pan-Africanism integrated two elements of *palabre*: *cooperation* and *partial renunciation of sovereignty*. Nkrumah recommended that elites go among the people, debate with them, and listen to them so as to not be cut off from their base of support;[5] likewise, believing that Ghana was destined to disappear in a United States of Africa, he wrote into the Ghanaian Constitution that the principle of sovereignty should eventually be abandoned. To engage in *palabre* is to be willing to listen to others and, if necessary, to give up part of one's own sovereignty. But Nkrumah destroyed the spirit of *palabre* with his obsession to achieve African unity from above: he insisted that central institutions had to control and bring about the unity of governments according to the American [federal] model.

Few followed Nkrumah in his Pan-Africanism, and the creation of the OAU eliminated the idea of a continental government. This organization outlined the terms of mediation for cases of conflict, but in a bureaucratic and juridical fashion (organizing itself as a forum and body of international criminal law).[6] The essential motivations represented by age classes, tribal and matrimonial alliances, relations between people and land, and notions of prohibition and authority were not employed. Here politics was conceived in terms of administration, not signification; in terms of summit meetings, not grassroots discussion. In part because it neglected these anthropological parameters, the OAU was neither able to maintain peace in Africa nor to prevent genocides.[7]

After having failed to communicate Pan-Africanism, Nkrumah finally took refuge in a philosophy of praxis: consciencism. This is defined as "the map in intellectual terms of the disposition of forces which will enable African society to digest the Western and the Islamic and the Euro-Christian elements in Africa, and develop them in such a way that they fit into the African personality."[8] This philosophy mixed dialectical materialism and religious spirit, a dimension Nkrumah was well aware is essential in Africa. Consciencism did not accept party pluralism[9]—any more than it would reserve a place for *palabre*.

Like most integrating movements (Pan-Arabism, Pan-Germanism), Pan-African-ism sinned by underestimating the resistance posed by singularities: everyone had to comply with the vision of an elite. The African peoples were not consulted. Such logic, which tries to mold reality according to the fantasies of an upper class that celebrates itself through summit conferences and meetings (as the privileged link from the colo-nial system), postulated a kind of African Eden prior to colonization that became the scapegoat for all evils. All that was needed was to *reestablish*—and not to *invent*—an original harmony by returning to consensus and solidarity, by emphasizing unity and suppressing the conflictual elements that also structure every society. Through this mythical vision of Africa, Pan-Africanism encouraged a regressive step toward unity. For Pan-Africanism, beyond all political and geostrategical justification, the return to an undifferentiated, would-be-originary Africa (without colonial borders) meant a return to the One, a unique foundation from which solidarity and African communi-tarianism would naturally flow.

Such an absorption of singularities in an overarching identity (Pan-Africanism, the OAU) and such insistence on the communal bond placed too much value on the notion of race. We must unite, not because we have had defined interests, aspirations, significations, and common utopias, but because we are blacks. To believe Pan-Afri-canists, traditional African society would be the only society where communal soli-darity takes precedence over disagreements. Without knowing they do so, and cer-tainly without intending to do so, Pan-Africanists exclude African society from the concert of societies when they insist on the communal and racial bond. All societies simultaneously produce communal bonds and factors that dislocate these bonds, and this is why politics consists of instituting mechanisms for the prevention, control, and resolution of conflicts. For Pan-Africanism, African society would be protected from that process, which is to say it would lack stories, and finally—exist outside of history.

We must focus on this imaginary that results in the opposite of what it seeks; first and foremost, on this hypothesis of original solidarity. The fact of sharing a common juridical and symbolic space does not automatically imply solidarity, and as in every society, the defense of neighbors happened only rarely [in Africa]. We have been given an example by the Lobi subclans of Burkina Faso, who were not generally obliged to help each other in adversity and in case of external attack, but only when agreements had been concluded between lineages, and exchanges effected on the matrimonial level. Solidarity was not immediate and mechanical but resulted rather from media-tion—that is, an interaction putting the symbolic, the imaginary, violence, and desire into play.

Moreover, the African communitarianism praised so much by Pan-Africanism is not grounded in the facts. One finds extremely individualistic societies such as the Kiga in the north of Rwanda and in southern Uganda. The institution of *ikyivugo* among the Kiga—the act of reciting one's own genealogy and thereby inventing a personal epic that precedes every public speech—does not exalt the group's great deeds but those of the individual speaker.[10] Through *ikyivugo*, the individual could claim rights against the collective; he confirmed his existence as a legal subject by saying "I." The anonymity of communitarianism on which the partisans of African cultural unity rely removes Africa from real history in making it a society without antagonisms, a stranger to the work of differentiation and internal domination. Pan-Africanism describes African societies essentially as passive, capable only of consensus and cooperation without the possibility of competition, which is to say conflict. This is indeed to misrecognize Africa. In reference to the Kiga, May Mandelbaum Edel emphasizes their individualism and their taste for private property and competition.[11] Individualism and the conflicts it engenders have even given rise to a particular political role in several East African societies whose only function is to mediate conflicts.[12]

Why have Pan-Africanism, and its legacy, the OAU, not thought about the continent in terms of *la palabre*?

In fact, the OAU has had great difficulty maintaining African unity. It found juridical solutions for most problems (border conflicts, authority crises, dislocation of populations), deciding very diverse situations in an abstract and uniform manner, and putting African societies with very different approaches to law, authority, and other legitimation procedures on the same footing. This complexity immediately forces us to consider conflict as a normal factor inherent in all social interaction. Such considerations could have led Pan-Africanists to draw an original conflict resolution method from the forms and procedures of *palabre*. *Palabre* is a product of tribal reality, but it could nevertheless have constituted a method of interstate conflict resolution, supplementing the state's juridical instruments insofar as it makes room for the other's appearance in an Africa where multiple states and ethnicities coexist. Rather than dreaming of a vast empire supported by the mysticism of African communitarianism,[13] Pan-Africanism would have done better to think about emancipating Africa using the paradigms of diversity and difference. The question is not: How to reestablish the primitive unity and solidarity shattered by colonization? but, starting from the foundation of new states: How to manage internal diversity and the conflicts brought into view by the reality of statehood? How to think through the African way of being different, rather than African identity?

Traditional society was not homogenous, for instance, in regard to the *occupation of space*. Residences were highly concentrated in some societies—such as the Yoruba in Nigeria—who developed a state-like power for this very reason; in others with a dispersed habitat like the Beti in Cameroon, the model of government did not develop in the direction of a state. *Mobility* was another factor of diversity, since nomadic societies did not demonstrate the same attachment to the political notion of territorial occupation as sedentary societies. What does the juridical notion of border mean to a nomad? As for agricultural communities, their attachment to the soil led to the establishment of authorities based in cults of the earth. The *residential factor* also differentiated African societies between those that were patrilocal (dwelling next to the father or the paternal family), matrilocal (dwelling in the maternal family), uxorilocal (dwelling with the in-laws), and neolocal (dwelling in new villages according to age).[14] Each type developed a different relationship with authority.

Homogeneity did not even exist within a single ethnicity, given that the *political status of the subject* was constructed in light of the possible forms his or her tribal integration might take: Is he or she part of a group assimilated by alliance or by conquest? Is he or she a former slave who was freed? Differentiation [between societies] also appears with respect to certain aspects of "civil law"—that is, the regime of goods and the whole inheritance system, as well as with respect to "criminal law."[15] Where the acquisition and exercise of power are concerned, categorical norms to control the abuse of power can be distinguished from conditional norms, which control access to power and dictate procedure for removing a leader. In terms of *ways in which power is passed on*, one notices a great diversity of factors linked to sex, wealth, and initiatory knowledge. The relation to the sacred, finally, is not the same in an Islamicized society and an animistic society. So many reasons to rethink Pan-Africanism beginning from the notion of diversity.

Palabre and African Socialisms

Socialism exercised a great popularity among young African states.[16] They adopted the ideology of nonalignment at the Bandung conference (1955). Certain countries such as China and Yugoslavia pushed African leaders to take the path of a nonaligned socialism that would be African. Among the different socialist options in Africa, largely influenced by Pan-Africanism, we will only consider two: the socialist *Ujamaa* of Nyerere and the African socialism of Senghor.

Nyerere and Ujamaa Socialism

The doctrine of this form of socialism is found in the famous Arusha declaration of February 1967 and in other writings by Nyerere.[17] These texts advocated a form of politics that would bring about a new kind of man: a socialism founded on psychological,[18] political, ideological, and economic independence. In order to make this kind of person a reality within a violent world, Nyerere approached African tradition, not to exhume a lost past but to valorize one of its important traits: *interdependence*. Africans only conceive of themselves in community and, within this, they must be united. Community and solidarity thus form the first article of the Arusha declaration, which postulates the right of all beings to a dignity founded on equality. The structure of *Ujamaa* (fraternity and extended family)[19] made Tanzania a simultaneously socialist and African society. *Ujamaa* socialism derives its particularity as well as its universality from a vision of humanity, society, and history. Three points merit attention: the distribution of wealth, cooperation, and discussion.

The system of distribution and the importance of wealth, the function of work, land ownership, social relations, and the individual's place in the community: all prove, to Nyerere, that African society was socialist before its time. Socialism being in essence distributive, African society was socialist because it watched over the individual, over "his widow, his orphans. No one saw him or herself deprived, either of food or of human dignity, by simple lack of personal dignity; he could count on the community of which he was a member."[20]

In turn, cooperation within the community rested on three notions: love, ownership, and work. Love concerns interpersonal relations. The traditional family framework requires respect for the other. Each individual in an extended family adopts an attitude suited to his or her age and sex, and in return, the family softens the inevitable inequality of tasks by means of equal rights recognized for all. This love for others was not a mere sentiment but an obligation.[21] As for ownership, it was shared collectively and the systems of giving and inheritance suppressed anything that could tend toward individual appropriation. Work, finally, was an obligation for all. African hospitality, often regarded as parasitism, actually implied an obligation: work for those who welcome you. Nyerere cited a well-known Swahili aphorism: "Treat your guest as a guest for two days, on the third day give him a hoe." There was an obligation to work for the community because, Nyerere believed, no conflict of interest existed between the individual and the community.

Discussion within the community is supposed to be open because every member in the big *Ujamaa* family who pays tribute through work must have the right to speak. Moreover, Nyerere speaks of "African-style-democracy," not necessarily multiparty but inspired by the model of *palabre* "where the elders sit down under the big tree and discuss until they have the same opinion."[22] This discussion, which evolves to the point of unanimity, implies equality and perfect freedom of expression among members of a single community.

Distribution, cooperation, and discussion are fundamental notions in all democracies. Since they already exist in the African traditions, Nyerere wonders what end would be served by adopting a two-party democratic model like the United Kingdom or a multiparty system as in other places? Since *Ujamaa* socialism makes individual interests coincide with those of the community, and since the principle of distribution is accepted, why choose multiparty politics? The latter would only make sense in a society torn by selfish interests, whereas for Nyerere the *terms "class" or "caste" do not exist in African society and languages.*[23]

Based on this egalitarian concept found in tradition, *Ujamaa* socialism joined Nkrumah's consciencism in recommending Pan-African unity, because the prosperity of a single country is meaningless unless it extends to neighbors. After the Arusha declaration, Nyerere recognized that "despite our politics and all the democratic institutions, certain rulers would not listen to the people; too often meetings were only monologues."[24] In reality, *Ujamaa* socialism—like most ideologies from the period of

African independences—turned out to be incapable of thinking African society in a dynamic way by insisting on internal motivators such as *palabre*. Once again, reflection failed to include the notion of *conflict*, essential to all political societies. Nyerere was unable to understand the originality of *palabre*, which is its ability to bounce off of discord. Taking the unanimist option of *Ujamaa* socialism required him to construct a consensual axis that did not consider the diversity of African society.

Nyerere had populations displaced in order to create villages. This forced "villagization" in the name of communitarianism was derived from a false premise: spontaneous African solidarity. Gathering in the traditional villages did not automatically imply solidarity. Solidarity was conveyed through kinship relations, the obligations of matrimonial pacts, and one's rank on the social ladder of caste societies. Nyerere did not understand that it was not so much the place that created the bond of solidarity in traditional African societies as it was the quality of the connection. Traditional political organization was based first and foremost on a system of personal connections in which authority was exercised *intuitu personae* rather than *intuitu loci*. Powers were recognized according to preestablished responsibilities that an individual held in a defined social group and particular affiliations that bound him to that group. When the colonial state instituted administrative conceptions founded on the anonymous character of power, blockages sometimes arose: How to make members of a group agree to obey a judge or a subprefect belonging to a group traditionally submissive to their own? This is the same problem raised by these Tanzanian "socialist villages": How could you obey a leader of an *Ujamaa* village (installed by the ruling single party)[25] whose original group, lineage, or clan was ordinarily dependent on yours?

Here we find the great problem encountered by postcolonial African states: the lack of fit between the possession of a real power that can be exercised and recognition of the symbolic legitimacy that all power implies. In the case of *Ujamaa* socialism, the village (similar to the kolkhoz or kibbutz) dragged behind it like a ball and chain the paradox of leaders who had power but no authority.

This conflict between power and authority could have been surmounted if *Ujamaa* socialism had instituted an ethic of mediation drawn from *palabre*. This would revive the place of the symbolic within a community, redefine its identity, recall its origin, take on violence, and set up solutions to consolidate collective life. For one must not freeze this connection between authority and power that birth and religion bring about so spontaneously: a contract of reciprocal interest forged through *palabre* could guarantee their alliance just as well. The Anuak in Sudan are divided into autonomous villages under the authority of chiefs who can be removed. Groups subjected to the chief are composed of families from his lineage and others who are not related to him. Each family can escape the chief's authority by migrating. Now, the nearby Nuer tribe carries out punitive raids among its neighbors. The Anuak will thus envision authority as a contract of mutual interest: the groups need a chief in order to defend themselves from the Nuer and the chief needs a larger number of families if he is to govern and resist the Nuer. If protection is no longer well assured by the chief, and if the families' loyalty is no longer guaranteed, the contract is either broken or renegotiated through *palabre*.

This aspect of the exercise of authority is extremely political because it is not mixed with any familial or religious element. Access to politics happens here through *strategies*, *interests*, and *contracts* as opposed to a vague notion of African solidarity and communitarianism. Conflict is the chief idea that could have allowed reflection on politics in Africa to move forward. With the appearance of the state, new African political powers adopted a vision of conflict that was oriented either too much toward punishment or too much toward crisis management because it repeatedly forgot that conflict constitutes a point of access to the symbolic. Through conflict, society redefines its normative regimes, structures new expectations, produces and revises its procedures of interaction, probes heteronomy in the midst of its institutional order, and, finally, puts some of its foundations back into perspective. Before symbolizing reconciliation, conflict allows society to step back and take a look at itself. This mirroring function of conflict can be found in the implicit drama of *palabre*. The great weakness of this first form of socialism was that it pasted the African family—a communitarian structure (*Gemeinschaft*)—over the problems related to society (*Gesellschaft*). Now, can one conceive of the state, which reconciles multiple interests, as a family?

Senghor and African Socialism

The roots of Senghor's socialism are found in his thoughts on *Négritude*, in Teilhardisme,[26] and, finally, in certain ethnological theories.

The essence of being African, for Senghor, is emotionalism: "Emotional sensibility, emotion is black as reason is Greek."[27] Senghor creatively reappropriates the idea developed by Lucien Lévy-Bruhl that the principal black attribute is a primitive and mystical mentality. Perhaps the affective and emotional predominance of the black should be sought in his or her relationship to nature. This last is a "being of open senses, permeable to all solicitations, to the very waves of nature, without an intermediary between the subject and the object."[28] Senghor finally adds a fundamental difference between the African and the white: "the European white distinguishes himself from the object, he keeps it at a distance . . . he dissects it with relentless analysis . . . the black-African does not see the object, he feels it. . . . He lives with others in symbiosis, he is born-with [*con-naît*] the other. The black-African could say: 'I feel the other, I dance (with) the other, therefore I am.'"[29]

Senghor then borrows from Teilhard de Chardin's concept of evolution. The evolution of the universe according to Teilhard comes from cosmogenesis, passing through biogenesis and noogenesis only to culminate in "Christogenesis." Christ is thus the center of evolution. That Teilhard identifies God as emerging from the internal necessity of the organization of matter comforts Senghor, for then he can also have African cultures emerge from it. Senghor finally references the inheritance of psychological characteristics: "What strikes me about the blacks in America is the permanence not of physical but of psychological characteristics, despite the mixing of heritages, despite the new environment."[30]

Senghor's socialism is articulated on three levels: national, Pan-African, and global. On the national plane, socialism is a humanism that seeks human happiness above all else. Marxism also seeks to improve humanity—that is why one must return to Marx, but only for his method, because one must preserve African religious values and the gains of Christianity and Islam.[31] One must reject class struggle, communism (though not communitarianism), and atheism, "this short-sighted logic"; and adopt an African socialism in which religion will remain "the most solid foundation of ethics."[32]

In this undertaking, the state offers the best means for realizing the nation. For Senghor, socialism and nationalism go together, the latter being surpassed by federalism. But before realizing the final step of federalism, one must plan not just on the economic level but also on the social level.[33] This requires the professionalization and the Africanization of managers, and the distribution of investments with an eye to agricultural reform. Here, however, Senghor recognizes one of the contradictions of his socialism, which is supposed to be African and independent while unceasingly pursuing help from foreign capital.[34]

This socialism is not exempt from criticism. At first, refusing the notion of class struggle allowed Senghor to leave intact the traditional caste system in Senegal. If socialism refers to the—perhaps abstract—notion of equality, how can "African socialism" be achieved at the heart of a Senegalese society secretly governed by the Islamic aristocracy of two large brotherhoods, Mourides and Tidjanes? How does he conceive the notion of equity? Could there be equality of treatment between an ordinary Senegalese citizen and a marabout? Senghorian socialism does not take into consideration the interactions in society: What happens when an "I" and a "you" exchange norms in this African society? How to articulate, describe, and examine conflict and negotiation? In short, how to engage in *palabre*?

Palabre and *Négritude*

Now we turn to another aspect of Léopold Sédar Senghor's thought, shared with Aimé Césaire: *Négritude*. Many topics are developed within this political and literary variant on the great theme of emancipation for oppressed blacks: the renaissance of a black culture rendered inferior by colonization and enslavement,[35] the return to the sources of African culture by way of its artistic, mythological and religious elements, and, finally, the fight against political, ethical, scientific, and humanitarian justifications associated with the colonial adventure.

Négritude originates in the colonization against which it is the intellectual reaction. It was born among the African and Antillean groups that had formed around the review *Légitime Défense* (René Menil and Jules Monnerot), and then the review *L'Étudiant Noir* (including Senghor, Césaire, and Léon Damas). Its definition is variable, and depends in large part on what discourses these thinkers were engaged with, but all of them recognized each other in a *political definition* that made *Négritude* into "the effective instrument of liberation."[36] A more anthropological approach makes it into "the cultural heritage, the values, and above all the spirit of the black-African civilization."[37] From a psychological point of view, *Négritude* is the specific behavior of the proud black.[38] In short, from the start it was tied to the omnipresent idea of the black race, to an existential definition: the black person's being-in-the-world.

The Concept of Speech in Négritude

For Senghor, the word [*verbe*], above all the poet's word, is demiurgic: it makes things spring from primordial chaos.[39] But, according to Senghor, language and speech can either be understood in terms of the opposition between black-African and French poetics, or in the use of neologisms. Concerning French, Senghor vaunts the merits of "clarity and distinctness in this language of mathematicians and diplomats,"[40] but marvels at African languages in which "the arrangement of a sentence's propositions obeys sensibility more than it does intelligibility."[41] Senghor pushed the opposition all the way to the level of syntax: he compared written French and the structures of unwritten African languages. According to him, French possesses an analytical structure with a syntax of subordination whereas the African languages, expressing a synthetic thought, have a syntax of juxtaposition and coordination.[42]

This conception of language does not allow Senghor, obsessed with creating an opposition to whites at all costs, to study the poetic oral creativity specific to conflict. How could this syntax of and for coordination express the noncoordination found among diverse members of the black-African social fabric? The only conflict in which *Négritude* was interested was the one between the colonizer and the colonized. Now, conflicts existed among precolonial Africans. How could *Négritude*, which liked to consider itself the liberatory speech of the colonized, verbalize antagonism and demonstrate the power of social bonds except through the notion of race? Césaire does not respond to these questions, any more than he thinks about *palabre*. What interests him is the creative power of words.[43] How do speech and the word verbalize relationships and how can one test the solidity of social connections, beginning from the word?

The *Négritude* movement, which mythologized black people, lacks substantial reflection on *palabre*. Certainly, one must represent the experience of suffering to the world to preserve it against forgetfulness, one must plead in the lingua franca before history's tribunal, but this suffering no longer suffices to justify the life of the victim before his or her catastrophe. The cultural practices of black people need not find their justification in suffering. The first mystification of the discourse of *Négritude* is the valorization of sadness and *ressentiment*. Everything in African cultures that the colonizers rejected was revalued without discernment. It is difficult for a discourse that throws all "poor oppressed blacks" into an undifferentiated mass to elaborate a thought of alterity on which an ethics of mediation could be founded. *Négritude* was too occupied with reviving a wounded African "identity" to search in the past for those combative elements that encouraged movement in the African social fabric.

The second mystification proceeds from a polarization of relations with the other. *Négritude* works by couples: white/black, oppressor/oppressed, alienation/liberation. The foreign is a synonym for alienation. To adopt foreign values is in itself proof that identity has been corrupted, a sign of treason. These oppositions generate a split notion of human relationships that is organized in a space divided between inside (the apparently homogenous, familiar, secured and securing African culture) and a fundamentally dominating, threatening outside (foreign cultures), a source of peril promising death. This Manichean imaginary presents an African subject who is frightened and aggressive in his or her encounter with the other. This victimization paradoxically culminates in a certain narcissism, which protects the subject from ever being called back into question.

Négritude was criticized. First, as an intellectual form of the African elite, expressing itself without authorization on behalf of African values, even though the revaluation of African cultures cannot be done without African peoples themselves. From whence this unhappy suspicion that *Négritude* may be a discourse by blacks about blacks, for the benefit of the West. "The African people does not feel involved in this affair at all, it is not even going to take part in the sacred meal to which . . . *Négritude* invites it."[44] On the sociological plane, *Négritude* legitimates traditions en bloc. The frantic notions of solidarity and compassion glorified through *Négritude* were eventually critiqued by other African writers, the wisdom of old people mocked, the community created by blood connections criticized,[45] along with the notion of family authority.[46] Finally, at the practical level, *Négritude* would be dangerous,[47] since it privileges emotionalism that then becomes the black's only attribute: it is a vast tautology, a rhetoric of poignancy[48] and an "antiracist racism."[49] Even more violent, however, was the critique of *Négritude* as imprisoning the black in an outdated past and engendering a narcissistic inward turn. *Négritude* thus became the "soporific of the black. It is opium. It is the drug that allows there to be 'good blacks' at the moment of great divisions."[50]

These critiques, however, did not register that *Négritude*'s focus on redemption by means of the "black race" allowed it to sidestep reflection on the notion of *palabre*. The "black race" is the suspect notion preventing thinkers of *Négritude* from reflecting on conflict, on ruses, and on styles of mediation. Now the notion of race, referring at once to biology and to psychology, is ambiguous. *Négritude* was a political and cultural response to colonial racism based on a denigration of the psychological and physical personality of the black. From the cephalic index, to the form of the nose, the muscles, and the quality of hair, one concluded that this was an inferior race doomed to the pursuit of pleasure. *Négritude* was influenced by this alliance between the biological and the cultural, created by a certain colonial ethnology. *Négritude* takes back the same language of race and reverses its meaning by exalting the beauty of the black person, his or her originality, his or her intuition. The "refuge of race"[51] is therefore supposed to support politics, poetic creation, the struggle and the teaching of Pan-Africanism as a doctrine. *Négritude* is a racialism that has not managed to liberate itself from the presuppositions of colonial ethnology. It was unable to consider relationships between the individual and the collective in African societies.

Négritude—Senghor in particular—invented the vague notion of "cultural mixing" [*métissage culturel*], which was nothing but a symbiosis between his African values and "Christiano-Greco-Latin civilization." In this mixture, how will contact be made, according to what procedures, on which terms, and for what ends? What place will be reserved for violence? *Négritude* did not consider translation and mediation, two key notions of *palabre*. Does not *palabre* represent the transformation of one state of society into another? Is it not simultaneously schism (parties are distinct in the discussion) and relation (an attempt at reconciliation/liaison)? What does this relation show, if not precisely that a society reveals its real relations and interactions through separation? How can one speak about a "black renaissance" without addressing the discordant interactions within African society itself? Does getting rid of colonialism and revalorizing African culture license us to forget that dialogue also contains conflict? Can the triumph of the "black race" and of its authentic values (the dubious theme of racial redemption is often repeated by Senghor and Césaire), work without a philosophy of relation? What does "living-with" mean for Africans?

Négritude is a compensatory response to colonial frustration, a defensive reaction that exalts the black race and African tradition without discernment and without any precise transmutation of all those things in it that can put a human being down. This defensive attitude is assisted by an offensive reaction, interpreted in light of an overestimation of the black person's cultural personality and an unexamined scorn for Western values. This frustration behind *Négritude* sometimes led to dangerous identifications: Western equals colonial, and the poets—starting with Senghor—are identified with great African leaders such as Samory Touré in Guinea and Shaka in South Africa—leaders who were, despite their resistance to colonial penetration, real tyrants to their own people.

Négritude wanted to be the advocate for the ensemble of the black world's cultural values, but why then did it fail to mention *palabre*? Maybe because it was a movement of well-to-do black intellectuals within the colonial system, more worried about getting recognized by Europeans than by the peoples in whose name they nevertheless spoke. *Négritude* is a ruse of the colonial system that fostered its own criticism—by channeling it. Senghor's and Césaire's concern was not to engage in *palabre* with their peoples, but to debate with the Westerners in an exchange where the theoretical and symbolic weapons (the mastery of speech) were furnished by their own adversaries. The connection with their people was only political and administrative. Through *Négritude*, the African intellectual measures his degree of integration into the dominant academic language and culture. Reflection on *palabre* has once again disappeared.

Palabre and Evangelization

Christian missionaries venturing into Africa found themselves grappling with Islam, as well as with African beliefs and traditions. Some clashes with Islam occurred, but the real conflict remained the one between local cultures and Christianity. How to express the Christian message, which claims to be universal, in a non-Western culture? How to escape the danger of an evangelization that would be mere Westernization? How to speak while respecting difference? Evangelization[52] was hampered by its alliance with the colonial adventure[53] and the rivalry between the Catholic and Protestant Churches.[54] So fully and strongly that it was no longer African culture that posed a question for missionary work but the mission itself that had become a question.[55] The politics of evangelization in Africa have followed two paths in Africa: conversion and adaptation.

The circles urging conversion insisted on the destruction of paganism and on bringing colonized and evangelized cultures into line with the model of Western Christianity. The instructions of the "Propaganda Fide," for example,[56] insisted on the fight against superstitions, return to the Tridentine catechism, the reinforcement of Thomistic teachings, the Romanization of the clergy, and rigorous conformity to the rites of the Roman Church. The Protestant confessions were equally aggressive in regard to "paganism." This political strategy met African resistance, which in many cases led to the formulation of African messianisms with black prophets and Christs.[57] The tendency opposed to adaption—whose concrete expression was inculturation—consists of respecting non-Western cultures that come into contact with Christianity. Faithful to the instruction of "Propaganda Fide" dating to 1659,[58] the missionaries submitted themselves to non-Christian rites that would not hurt the faith and, in this sense, they engaged in *palabre* with African culture. The missionary would have local catechists charged with introducing the catechism to future converts under the model of *palabre*. The missionary would become "polygamous" (he would reimburse the dowry of the women in polygamous unions who thereby became "the priest's daughters or wives"), a "slave owner" (he would buy back slaves to free them and to Christianize them), and he would invest himself in the strategies of *palabre* in his relation to African cultures.

Inculturation was taken up once more by the African clergy shortly before and then again after the Second Vatican Council[59] out of concern that the Church might become a foreign body in African society. This, then, required Christians to reappropriate certain rites of African origin. This orientation has been understood in various ways. Some assumed the "conversion of African culture to Christ,"[60] and others, the mutual transformation of Christianity and African cultures.

What is inculturation? This word reminds one of the theme of the incarnation of a message, the conversion and the adaption of God's Gospel. On the theological plane, inculturation follows the tradition of "contextual theologies" that mistrust deductive universalization, wherein the theological principles developed in particular historical circumstances tend to be universalized to the point of becoming the unique and supreme norm for all religious practices. Each cultural, social, and political context therefore founds its own theological discourse, necessarily local and limited to a particular kind of experience. This contextual theology aroused great debate by questioning the universality of the North's theological discourse, its traditions, and its modes of thought. Inculturation sees itself as close to Latin-American liberation theologies insofar as it insists on the material and practical liberation of suffering beings.

In Africa, the theological debate over inculturation took a political turn and, to advance their discourse, African theologians drew inspiration from one component of *palabre*: the use of archaic symbols and images that generate consensus and structure the community's identity. In their choice of themes, African theologians utilize the method of "representative anecdotes"[61] involving theological notions of the Exodus, the suffering servant, and the Last Judgment. They have brought these themes into relation with African realities and thereby reformulated lived experience in a theological language utilizing political, anthropological, and juridical references common to Christian theology and African culture.

The Exodus allows these theologians to develop a terminology for oppression (the Egyptians subdued Israel, as the West did Africa), an incentive for rebellion (Moses becomes the head of a rebel movement against the Pharaoh just as one insists on the African resistance to dictators), and all hopes for liberation (God saves the Hebrews from oppression, as he will save Africans from their current oppression). On the other hand, the image of the "suffering servant," which comes from the prophet Isaiah and became the image of Jesus for theologians like Dietrich Bonhoeffer, establishes an identity between the destiny of African peoples and that of a God who has taken on the face of the humble man, the weak and suffering one. The theme of the Last Judgment, finally, makes the humble God into one who will recognize his own people (the humble and the oppressed). Are not the Africans the "wretched of the earth," to refer to the title of Frantz Fanon's famous book, the ones whom God will take first? This image serves to reassure an African culture despised and inferiorized by the colonial adventure. Inculturation thus becomes the workshop where images linking the African situation and theological themes are fermented and folded together.

The *palabre* between Christianity and African cultures modified the church's management of power. Once again, we must meet on the imaginary plane of anthropological referents capable of opening Christian discourse to African acceptance. One begins with a semantic change in Christian missionary terminology. At mass, or during rituals, the reading of the epistle that appeared in the old liturgy as a one-way injunction becomes a "liturgy of the word." Africans easily recognize themselves in an association between the terms liturgy and speech, since orality is one of the pillars of their culture. When it comes to representing prohibitions and processes of internalizing guilt, terms such as "confession" or "sacrament of penance" have been transformed into "sacrament of reconciliation." It was hard to make Africans accept the idea of a genetic culpability that humankind would have inherited from Adam's curse. The moralizing discourse of missionary Christianity always failed as long as one talked to Africans in terms of condemnation, penitence, contrition, and absolution. The theologians of inculturation assumed that the term "sacrament of penance" automatically implied the idea of condemnation, whereas with "reconciliation," derived from *palabre*, the notion of condemnation is not necessarily present. Often we are reconciled due to a misunderstanding in which neither party is wrong.

Palabre often insists on the affective dimension. The notions of filiation and genealogy, the extreme value placed on speech, the dialectic between distance and proximity, and the notion of welcoming the other were reclaimed by the advocates of inculturation. Concerning genealogy, the church is presented to Africans not on the imperial and pontifical model but as a family.[62] Jesus is no longer a Lord—who might have power, but without authority—rather an "older brother," an "ancestor." With these two terms, Africans capture the notion of a social bond.

In Africa, and notably Zaire, "just ancestors" were added to the saints and angels who received prayers on behalf of the pope and bishops during the "canon" of the offertory. This allows Africans to understand that their ancestors are not excluded from the "communion of saints" and allows the church to realize its "universal vocation." As for the extreme valorization of speech,[63] the famous "In the beginning was the Word" may be invoked. This idea is much appreciated in the context of Africa's inferiorization for lack of writing, for it is seen as the revenge of orality against writing.[64]

The notion of proximity is visible in the nomenclature of the Roman Catholic hierarchy. Despite having patterned itself too closely on the imperial model and borrowing the terminology for certain ecclesiastical titles from the medieval order,[65] Rome recycles the symbols of African authority. The denominations here are much more intimate and familial. In the archdiocese of Yaoundé in Cameroon, the Pope, the bishop, and priest are designated as "great-grandfather," "grandfather" and "father." (*Tara*: father, also stands for priest in the Ewondo language; *mvamba*: grandfather, means bishop; and *emvemvam*: great-grandfather, designates the Pope[66]). This slippage toward the familial and the affective is intended to reduce the psychological distance of an overly imperial terminology.

Finally, welcoming the other constitutes one of the goals in a well-led *palabre*. The theologians of inculturation revive this notion for an apologetic and polemic reason. To those who complain about the heterogeneous character of the Christian religion in Africa, one retorts that good African tradition implies hospitality. This must thus go beyond the tribe[67] and integrate concepts coming from elsewhere.

Liturgy is still the domain in which the staging of *palabre* is made concrete. The principal event in staging the *palabre* between African cultures and the Gospel is the transformation of mass into a huge *palabre* whose most remarkable example is still the Vatican's approval of the Zairian rite of the mass.[68] The latter is an example of what the Zairian bishops call "the Africanization of Christianity,"[69] which implies a change in preaching style, in the church's government, in sacred oratory and finally, in the symbolic. The mass becomes *palabre* on four levels:

1. *The deferral of the penitential rite until the end of mass.* In the Latin rite of the mass, one begins by purifying oneself with water (the famous *asperges me*). One then asks for forgiveness (the "I confess to God"; *confiteor dei*) by imploring God's pity (*Kyrie eleison*). To Africans, this procedure appears demented. One does not ask for forgiveness without having explained oneself; first it is necessary to speak, explain oneself, and establish the wrongs. Speech precedes condemnation. The explanation must precede the sentence, repentance, and remorse. The Zairian archbishop explains: "It is basically inconceivable in the African tradition that in order to meet, one must begin by asking for forgiveness. The first priority is to indicate the meeting's purpose, so each may proceed by expressing him- or herself and presenting his or her point of view. It is only at the moment when one knows what happened, what provoked *palabre* to be called—in short, after being mutually listened to, that one can ask for forgiveness."[70] What led the Zairian mass to put the Act of Contrition at the end was the primacy that *palabre* gives to speech.

2. Modifications are also introduced at the level of the sermon. In the Latin or Orthodox Church, and in most Protestant denominations, the preached word is unidirectional: it is delivered by the priest, the Pope, or the pastor, since only he can examine its secrets and evaluate their importance. The worshippers receive this discourse and have nothing to say, since the arrangement of the scene and the distribution of roles do not recognize the faithful as having a "say in the matter." But in the Zairian mass, by contrast, the sermon takes a "dialogical" form: "It is thanks to the dialogical character of African *palabre* that we have encouraged homilies in a dialogical style: the priest who preaches, speaks and prepares the Christians' response."[71] In this exchange, he seems not to effect a unilateral transmission but a collective construction of the truth.

3. In *palabre*, bodily expression is fundamental, since speech is inseparable from style in African traditions and the body is inseparable from meaning. Speaking is not simply the expression of breath or of a sound with performative value, but above all a bodily disposition. In other words, in *palabre*, the recognition of nonverbal aspects indicates that communication is part of a total interactive movement whose instrument par excellence is the body. These considerations led the Zairian "*palabre*-mass" to privilege "bodily liturgy." Dance, play, and bodily display are Africans' response to the austerity of the regular rituals (offices) conducted by Catholic and Lutheran churches. From the point of view of interaction, this dance that goes from the faithful to the officiating bishop plays the role of synchronizer; pointing fingers and mimicry reinforce the phatic effect whose function is to maintain contact between celebrants and the faithful.

4. In *palabre*, the one who has sinned is never totally excluded, and even if he has been chased out of the village, the tribe finds a society to take him in. Among the Beti in Cameroon, someone who is banished due to a scandal is "put back" with his

maternal uncles. This unwillingness to totally exclude any wrongdoer is picked up by theologians because it echoes the famous Christian theme: "God does not want the sinner's death but his conversion" and even his or her continued presence among the circle of God's children. The discourse of inculturation also places a high value on this theme, since it rejects the guilt-inducing rhetoric of colonial Christianity.[72] Inculturation also relies on the therapeutic dimension of authority. Since chiefs are sometimes healers in Africa, Christian theology insists on Jesus the *thérapeute* who cures the ill (lepers), from whence the pastoral importance of public exorcisms and charismatic movements that insist on possession and trance.[73]

Inculturation uses the forms of *palabre*, but manages to miss its spirit. Evidence for this can be found on multiple levels:

1. *Predisposition.* Every *palabre* presupposes that groups or subjects will be ready to put their truths at risk through confrontation. This implies that absolute and assured positions will be worn away. To engage in *palabre* means to consider the possible relativization of one's "absolutes." This play between an absolute that becomes relative and the emergence of "relativity" as a sole absolute is a component of *palabre's* movement of verbal appropriation and dispossession. Here the possibility of rendering truth relative is not a simple epistemological matter, but also affects the juridical domain of legitimacy. To engage in *palabre* is to risk questioning its reference points—in a word, its power.

To engage in *palabre*, finally, means to be *disposed* to let the justifications of our actions and values be shaken. As an attitude of openness to dispossession, whether it be epistemological (relative truth), juridical (relative legitimation), or axiological (relativized values), African *palabre* is not found in "inculturation of the Gospel." Inculturation involves a clarification and adaptation of positions, not the elaboration of dispositions to do this or that. One "positions oneself" in front of a counterpart; one "does not put oneself at the disposal of" (or "in the mood to"). Christianity poses absolute references prior to all discussion (dogma for Catholics, and the Bible for the different Protestant denominations). The object of *palabre*, the very thing one must debate, is the incarnation of dogma and the ways it is presented. Dogma in itself and the Bible as such are withdrawn from relativization. For the Christian side, dispute can involve the diverse ways of presenting doctrinal substance and not the substance itself, while for African culture one could just as well discuss its substance as discuss its manifestations. In the end, can one think without absolutizing . . . even what we think is relative?

2. *The principle of equity* is sometimes problematic in this *palabre* between the Gospel and African cultures. Good *palabre* respects the principle of equity between the parties, which is the reason why preparatory *palabres* were held prior to the "hearings" of a *palabre*, to verify that the principles of equity would be respected. Now in this dialogue with African cultures, Christianity enjoys a strong position that does not place it on an equal footing with African cultures.[74] In René Luneau's opinion, the evangelical message

and the (historically dated) cultural forms of its expression did not have equal advantages at the outset, given the absence of a genuine respect for the cultures encountered.[75] It is not correct to say that there was *palabre* between the Gospel and African cultures, since their relation appears distorted by relations of force in which missionary Christianity benefited from its association with Western technological supremacy, which inculcated an inferiority complex in other cultures.[76] *Palabre* is a game of reciprocal recognition, and this does not seem to be the case in inculturation, since Christianity only recognized the elements of African culture that fit with its own vision of the world. In this case, Christianity only recognizes the identical and ignores the different.

This partial recognition is reinforced by the Pope:[77] it is the African culture that must be regenerated by the incarnation of the Word and not the reverse. And to better avoid the risk of a genuine encounter, the conservative fringe of the Roman Catholic hierarchy used a cultural argument drawn from African cultures themselves: the right to follow and learn from elders! Relying on the notion of age groups and the juridical primacy of the eldest, the Pope recommends that young churches return to the good old African tradition of respect for the elders, and the right of the elder to instruct and transmit knowledge.[78] In the name of this right, the young African churches must follow the Roman teachings and the Westernization of European churches, for they are "elder" churches [vis-à-vis Africans]. The categories of "youth" and "age" play a very powerful role in African societies: they assign to each person his or her place and role. They are thus recruited for a certain political strategy. Because what is at stake for the Pope is rendering Vatican politics acceptable using the very terms of the black African imaginary. What African will call into question the predominant role of eldest person's right to educate? A new religion has been substituted for the genealogical religion of tribes, that of our "genealogy in Christ."[79]

3. *The absence of the third.* Inculturation has been a distorted *palabre* because it never had a third party. The notion of the third party serves to guarantee a minimum of objectivity between the parties in *palabre*. There must always be someone not directly involved in the *palabre* but whose moderating and strategic role consists of not allowing the parties to wrong each other. By this very fact, he also channels any overt verbal violence. "An Ashanti king or chief . . . remains strategically outside of the debate: it is his staff-bearer [*porte-canne*] who leads discussion in his place. . . . The speech of a chief must be filtered by the staff-bearer. . . . The chief therefore listens therefore without concluding."[80] And yet, in the kind of inculturation that claims to present itself as *palabre*, we do not find this notion of the third party who channels violence. Who will be the third here, Christianity or African cultures? Who will arbitrate and in the name of what legitimacy recognized by both discussants?

4. *The desire to engage in palabre.* Inculturation appears to be a distorted *palabre* inasmuch as the shared desire for *palabre* is lacking. In *palabre*, the entire community (those who demand compensation and those who are accused) shares a need to hear one another's self-explanations in order to restore the equilibrium broken by a

wrong. Now, who poses the question of the Gospel's inculturation? On the one hand, it is the Western Christian hierarchies, and on the other hand, the African clerical hierarchy, enraged that it cannot benefit from the advantages its rank deserves within the "universal church," which is primarily Western. The way the discourse of inculturation is staged conceals the social and institutional system organizing it from above. The discourse of inculturation says nothing about its premises. It is subject to a theological teaching—the African theologians who hold this debate were educated in the West—that obeys the organizational restraints of the Northern churches and the socio-cultural models imposed by the respectability of a theological discourse. The discourse on inculturation carried out by African Christians hides its connection to the socio-economic system, organizing it on the basis of the West, for the training of the theologians of inculturation is really framed materially by the latter. The discourse on inculturation remains quiet about what makes it speak (the financial institutions) as well as those in whose name it speaks (the African peoples). The famous *palabre* between African cultures and Christianity is thus unfinished. For *palabre*, meaning must always be constructed by several people before it is shared: meaning is neither sent nor presupposed by anyone.

All these doctrines, political or religious, have denied *palabre* as a mode of access to the symbolic. At most, they have recuperated it to profit an abstract communitarianism or an ambiguous evangelization.

Conclusion

THE GOAL OF reflection on *palabre* is not to impose a mode of thought coming from tribal society on the organization of the state. Nor is it a matter of making *palabre* a panacea that will resolve all the problems raised by the present organization of African societies. *Palabre* unlocks the trigger of historical reflection. It does not offer Western societies, often in love with exoticism, an "access to the primitive forces of human evolution, but rather a confrontation between types of becoming."[81] By *palabre*, we understand the African person's becoming-subject within his or her social space. The politics of the word and the words of politics that make up *palabre* preoccupy every reasonable being, because *palabre* is the path by which one raises questions about culture, becoming, recognition, the common good, and above all, action. Today's political structures have suffered a great loss of confidence, to the point that democracy—which is the least bad system—is often discredited as a whole. The very notion of practical politics, not just reflection on the political dimension, has been flattened following the ruin of contractualist theories and the reduction of political practice to domination. *Palabre* allows us to get beyond this damage; it lets us discuss politics in terms of acting rather than in terms of the state, laws and legislature. What is at stake in *palabre* is the possibility of once again finding a real theory of action.

Right away, this last thought underscores the permanence of conflict in the socio-political space: conflict (and bond) between action and ethics, conflict (and interpenetration) between ethics and morality, conflict (and copenetration) between the sphere of law and that of politics, conflict between justice as the good and justice as the rule. Conflict—whether it is expressed under the form of brute violence or under the form of competition—indicates for starters that there is mobility and therefore an unstable equilibrium within every society.[82] The problem is then to redefine the forms of coexistence.

The negation of conflict led Europe either to propose perpetual peace as a utopian culmination of the social process (Kant) or to bet on the rationality of an ethics of discussion (Karl-Otto Apel, Jürgen Habermas). In Africa, the first way to negate the permanence of conflict is usually by retrojection. One claims a common kinship for all Africans. The most tenacious of myths is the one tying all Africans back to pharaonic Egypt. The kinship of Africans would render conflict impossible; because society is founded on the One, conflict would always come from elsewhere. This very origin and the communitarianism it implies allow Africans to look in the mirror and imagine an eschatology that automatically justifies flight when confronted with very real divisions. Refusing to think politically when admitting the reality of conflict as a dimension inherent in society leads contemporary Africa to proliferate fundamentalist mystical groups. The subject integrates these nonconflictual spaces into his personality and makes them into a "home" wherein he can escape the reality of conflict. An overinvestment in the private sphere is supposed to compensate for having deserted the public space of speech. Although these groups may conflict with the rest of society, in their own hearts they inhabit an illusion of peace.

Meanwhile, if conflict is permanent in the social body, there is a possibility of resolution. This does not mean the reconciliation of society with itself, but requires society to see itself from a distance. The public space of speech that clears the way for *palabre* is constituted by what Ricoeur calls "conflictual consensus." This notion—as Ricoeur formulated it, beginning from the experience of Western democracies—introduces ethics and morality as constitutive dimensions of every reflection on politics.[83] How to define the goal of democracy at the moment when it tends to be tarnished by violence and lies? How to reconcile "the kingdom of ends" (Kant)—in which each would be simultaneously citizen and sovereign—with the permanence of conflict in democracies? To answer these questions, Ricoeur gives us the following definition of democracy: "With respect to the notion of conflict, a democratic State is that State which does not propose to eliminate conflicts but to invent procedures allowing them to be expressed and to remain open to negotiation. A State of law, in this sense, is a State of organized free discussion. . . . If this free discussion is to be practicable, it must also be recognized that political discourse is not a science . . . but at best an *honest opinion*."[84]

Democracy requires two tools: procedure and right opinion. *Palabre* is the place par excellence for procedure. Everything in it is the object of a negotiation, of a meeting, of a consultation with other people. A single *palabre* can involve up to seven or eight other pre-*palabres*, and each step is equivalent to a procedure. Procedure is the modern form of mediation that allows for distance and passage through the symbolic. *Palabre* also takes right opinion in hand. To accomplish this, it is urgent that democracy undertake an archeology of the law in order to disrupt the mythical and ethical prejudices on whose basis it is nourished. Finally, these two essential dimensions of *palabre*, procedure and right opinion, assume there are citizens.

In Africa just as in Europe, there is often withdrawal if not outright defiance with respect to citizenship. In Africa, politics is reduced to a vast "victimology"—one only reflects on the state in the role of victim; one only examines relations to the West, Christianity, and the other in general as a victim. Real political reflection, on the other hand, would not evade evidence (of victimization) but would also transcend it in order to analyze the passage from individuality to citizenship. All procedure implies the idea of passage. In Europe people also give up on citizenship in many ways, first and foremost through "moral idealism." When individuals desert the public space of discussion for the security of private life, or refuse to "get mixed up in politics" by the shorthand that translates all questions about the political into variations on the *lie of power*, they also refuse to consider themselves as citizens. The individual who did not grow up as a citizen persuades himself that there is an abyss between him or herself and political problems. And private "ranting" against this or that political decision becomes the only form of political intervention. These habits make it hard for political reflection to analyze the transference of the religious dimension into political practice. How is this religious transference assumed by the passage from individuality to citizenship? As movement, does not the act of transference also imply going through some sort of transferential procedure?

The anthropology of action implicit in *palabre* makes the very notion of "narrating" into a constitutive element of democracies. Like *palabre*, democracy tells its own narrative, it is a narrative and an act of narration, a nest of intrigues and an "overlapping of stories."[85] Democracy can only constitute its public space by telling itself stories about its own reference points—overlapping stories about what is just, what is desirable, what preferable, and what counts as the common good. And the public space is the arena where an individual narrates his or her story, a story that is part of the tragic story of all the others. The condensation between these stories inscribes the subject in public space as a historical being. At the risk of becoming abstract systems, democracies must learn to tell themselves stories about their origins, their fears and phantasms, and their points of reference—which implies, as in *palabre*, that one can only enter society insofar as one is "mixed up with" a story.

In the end, by putting the act of narration into form and on stage, *palabre* leads to practical wisdom: "The art of storytelling is the art of exchanging *experiences*; by experiences, he means not scientific observations but the popular exercise of practical wisdom."[86] Is not the great problem of democracies, apart from their "rational" organization, the problem of rediscovering a "practical wisdom" that, as Ricoeur contends, can equally include "care of the self," "care of the other," and "care for the institution"? Then, of course, it would be necessary to hold a *palabre* on the procedures by which this "practical wisdom" is given a shape. . . .

Translated from the French by Laura Hengehold and David Stute.

OTHER ESSAYS

Rationalities and Legal Processes
in Africa

About the Encounter . . .

Taking together place, time, and manner, it would be possible to describe "the encounter" as comprising at least six modes: fragility, temporality, activity, integrity, causality, and disparity.

1. Whether it is a collision or a harmonious synthesis, the encounter consists of a rather *fragile* balance, since two realities (cultures, or forms of rationality) in contact will never be arithmetically proportionate; asymmetry is a necessary part of the encounter with the other, as Emmanuel Lévinas would say. Hence that fragility, which is indeed the expression of the encounter as a place and moment of instability and thus reversibility.

2. The fragility inherent in the encounter is associated with *temporality*. The time of the encounter mobilizes expectation, tension, and retention[1] at the same time: expectation of the unknown, tension between going toward it or resisting it, and holding back at the very moment when the need for giving (giving to others and giving oneself) is at its strongest.

3. And so during the encounter, an entire *activity* takes place: the encounter is deliberate or provoked. Within this activity are inscribed the *structural element* (an encounter may be imposed by the socio-politico-economic structures), the *intentional touch* (the encounter is desired or not), and the *trick of unpredictability* (the encounter happens all the same, belying our predictions and those of the structures surrounding us).

4. The encounter also raises the issue of form, which itself refers to that of *integration* and *integrity* when two or several realities meet and merge. When the forms interweave one with another, what will be their eventual form and what is the fate of their original forms (disappearance or transformation)?

5. The encounter, insofar as it is destined to take place in the history of our human condition, insofar as it sets out to be an event, often reveals or conceals the *causality regime* it belongs to. What determinisms do certain types of encounter belong to?

6. Finally, the encounter is a confrontation that expresses the existing division and disparity between the parties being combined. The joining together implied by the encounter is possible only because there is division and disparity of the elements at the base. The encounter is the site of tenuous relations that resist reductions. An encounter is not a *bivocal/univocal* relationship between realities, it expresses neither their complete integration nor their integrity.

Between Rationalities . . .

How does one recognize a rationality? From the way it sets out its modes of effectiveness, you might reply. A rationality is the ordering in a discourse, representation, or practice that gives logic to both processes and results. If we stop at that point, the reply seems very general and vague. And it is precisely in that vagueness that we may have to look for the sense of rationality. It assumes several meanings, the widest of which makes it generally *coextensive with the term culture*. "The meeting of rationalities" would in this sense mean "the encounter between cultures or the forms of expression of civilizations." "Rationality" can also have the sense of its *practical activity and explanatory logic;* at this level the "meeting of rationalities" would imply the various executive and explanatory modes of different practices either within a particular culture or between different cultures. If we look at the etymological domain, rationality is associated with reason—and we do not know whether that is a reality or a montage of explanations to account for certain behaviors!—which itself leads us to problems of *constitution, basis*, and *use*.

What does a "rationality" comprise? If it is composed of practices, they are legitimated by narratives. So who decides which are the "scientific" elements of a narrative and which the mythological fictions? Is mythology therefore part of rationality? At this level of analysis, the encounter between rationalities means a "meeting of narratives" that each have a pragmatic and a fictive element. *What is a rationality based on?* History, which is the site of both violence and cooperation! The historicity of a rationality is also evaluated at the level of the *uses* subjects and communities make of it. But in order for a rationality to be revealed to others, it needs a *language* capable of expressing it. Thus the issue of language is inseparable from that of rationality. The latter presupposes intersubjectivity and communication that institute the subject as a speaking being and an animal that manipulates symbols. This communicability is, as it were, an a priori in the exercise of reason (Habermas). Rationality, insofar as it also claims to be communicative, is "a hovering cable-car."[2] This implies that the "encounter between rationalities" is a risky exercise in which we have to allow for misunderstanding. In this wavering encounter, how should we judge, if it is the case that we are limited in our respective enunciatory processes by our history and geography?

In places and moments of "encounter between rationalities," we may need to take into account, even if we do not accept all its consequences, the philosopher Alasdair MacIntyre's observation that what "we now need to recover is . . . a conception of rational enquiry as embodied in a tradition, a conception according to which the standards of justification themselves emerge from and are part of a history in which they are vindicated by the way in which they transcend the limitations . . . of that same tradition."[3] So, is the encounter between rationalities not a meeting of competing traditions? The fact that there is no *rationality* other than a *narrative* one—every kind of rationality is embodied in a narrative—indicates that rationalities as an *ordering* of knowledge and practices appear first as a *staging* and *narrating* of the function of institutions. Here it is the *issue of institutions* that will provide the context for the question of the encounter between types of *legal rationality* in Africa: How should the law be instituted? How should we experience and represent normative systems when each one within its field of definition and determination tries to impose itself by "communicating by way of enigmas, silent demonstrations that force our hand"?[4] What happens when those normative systems that "combine" within a particular history attempt to combine with other systems?

The Encounter between Legal Rationalities in Africa

How should we approach these rationalities? Through usage, observing how a culture's legal *processes* are built up by changing others? Focusing on processes has the unfortunate habit of making us think the problem of the law is bureaucratic and rational, and so it ignores the actors in this area. Should we stress the *actors* and especially the way people who come before the courts perceive the cross-fertilization of legal rationalities and practices in Africa? If we stop there, we would give the impression that legal rationalities are purely structural systems and conceal the fact that legal *phantasms* play on guilt, taboo, genealogy, transmission, and symbolism. How do these different elements build up when normative formulations enter into competition with one another in Africa? To give a partial answer to this question, I shall take not two extreme paths—one that bases law on problems of the unconscious and one that situates it at the purely rational level—but the path that consists in interrogating legal systems in their threefold aspect, which Gérard Timsit defines so admirably: predetermination, codetermination, and overdetermination.[5] "The before-saying law" (Jean Carbonnier), the embodiment of predetermination, is as important as the text, processes, and social consequences of law.

Thinking about the encounter between legal rationalities leads one to say, after analysis, that the creation of the law is a multidirectional phenomenon that neither state nor civil society nor custom can monopolize in Africa. Thinking about *identities* provides the context for the encounter between rationalities, since when we reflect on this encounter, we in fact assume two *identities* coming into contact. But what if we were to abandon that paradigm of *identity* to think again about *traversing*—that is, interfaces, shifting environments, transitions, and transformations of the law in Africa? Three themes will claim our attention: first, the *ethos of the judge* (a), which then leads us to the *division between form and content of the legal act* (b) and finally the distinction in the *figure of the Third Party,* torn between conciliator and arbitrator (c). The issue of the judge's ethos relates to the judicial actors' *perception*; interrogation of the judicial act is connected to *procedure*; and examination of the ambiguity of the Third Party figure falls within the domain of *anthropology*. Our suggestion is that the law exists in Africa today only in the tension between old and new and between imposition and negotiation. The question at issue is the *possibility of thinking* "*between-two-realities.*"

Judge and Ethos: The Judge's Symbolic Effectiveness and Its Failure

In Africa, traditional judges used to have at least two skills: first the *linguistic competence* by which, through the interplay of the to-and-fro of speech between a pronouncing party and a receiving one, the *figurative frame of the speakers* is constituted in the speaking space that is the trial; then the *figurative skill* by which judges, those appearing before them, and the other members of the jury panel *all construct at their own level an image of themselves* in the discourse of the law and *an image of others*. Two problems arise: first of all, the place of subjectivity in the judge's discourse, then the impact of the effectiveness of this discourse on those appearing before the court. To answer these questions we may need to look at the interaction ritual that structures the linguistic interchange between speech users during the trial. How do people move from *interlocution* to *interaction?* "Speaking is exchanging, and it is changing through exchanging. . . . As any communicative exchange unfolds, the various participants, whom we shall therefore call interactors, bring a network of mutual influences to bear on one another."[6]

How does the judge's "face" appear in the interaction at a trial in Africa; in other words, how is the interplay of *figuration* played out? We should explain that here the "*face*" means "the totality of the valorizing images that one attempts during the interaction to construct of oneself and impose on others."[7] In the traditional trial the judge used to bring his ethos to bear, which is no longer the case with judges in postcolonial states. Defined interactively, ethos is, as Barthes says, "the character traits which the orator must *show* the public (his sincerity is of little account) in order to make a good impression: these are his 'airs,' . . . the orator gives a piece of information *and at the same time* says: I am this, I am not that."[8] If we go back to Aristotle, ethos as compared to pathos "may almost be called the most effective means of persuasion he possesses."[9] Why is this? Quite simply because ethos in Aristotle implies two orientations: a moral sense based on the notion of honesty (*epiéikeia*), encapsulating attitudes and virtues such as honesty, propriety and equity; and an objective sense (*héxis*), which includes habits, behavior, customs, and character. For traditional judges to be credible in African societies, they had to show their ethos in speaking the norm—in other words, both honesty in content and especially uprightness framing their words. In this way, traditional law produces an effectiveness that present-day positive law no longer has. In their relation to articulating the law, contemporary judges most often seem just to stick to technicalities without getting involved in "speaking the law." They are merely interpreters who try as far as possible to make facts come into line with the law. The judge is "only the mouth that speaks the words of the law."[10]

Ignoring the judge's ethos obeys a kind of syllogistic strategy among judges in present-day courts in Africa. What is at issue here is the problem of the legal definition of facts. The juridical text must be applied; in other words, the case we have before us must follow the norm that preexists it. And so, with this in mind, judges would simply repeat, reiterate the text of the law to be applied. Their judgment must not depart or differ from the legal text. The relationship between the norm articulated and the verdict announced must be one of transparency; here the judgment re-produces the law. From the methodological viewpoint, this path followed by the judge is subject to a dualist metaphysics. "The text of the law represents the norm . . . the verdict is always prejudged already in the norm for which the (legal) text that represents it is given. There is a continuity that runs from the (invisible) norm . . . and ends in the decision that applies, expresses the norm . . . in this process the judge is merely an effectively inanimate being . . . the judge's prejudgment would distort the prejudgment of the case in the law . . . the verdict occurs at the junction between the perceptible world and the intelligible world. In this model the verdict is inscribed in the dualist structure of metaphysics."[11]

Application of the law and nothing but the law: this is the guarantee of objectivity. An interpretation that departs too far from the norm seems dishonest. "In justice the danger lies in straying away in language."[12] In this enterprise judges must never express their ethos as was the case with traditional judges. Present-day judges in an African lower or appeal court are not asked to make a good impression, to combine self-presentation with precision of speech and honesty of character; they are expected to *interpret the text* and restrict themselves to that intellectual operation that will make the text become meaning. On one hand, we have a verdict influenced by the *judge's ethos,* and on the other, a verdict constructed by the *judge's technical competence.* In Africa the so-called customary courts that were established during the colonial period threw out the dimension of ethos that was in some sense the basis for the relationship of trust between subjects and justice. Who is the judge who does not display his *narrative identity?* What narratives does his discourse stem from? What founding taboos and original phantasms does his legal text express?

Through the writing of the law, the dramatization of the establishing operation is phantasmically played out. How in Africa—in an environment of orality—did the technical nature of the legal written text provide another way of conceiving the estab-lishing act? How, via the law, are these various theatricalities constructed? In Africa the body of modern law remains quite silent about the various ways it was put together. It appears to have fallen from the colonial sky almost fully formed; European coloni-zation in Africa concealed the processual character of every legal system that is both "imposed and negotiated."[13] How have the various codes that constitute the African states maneuvered so as to appear almost perfect while remaining silent on the *enunci-atory theater*, the *enunciation ritual*, and the initiating violence that presided over their advent? How does any codification of a norm arrange both *dramatization* and *textu-alization*? How should we evaluate fairly the fact that the different bodies representing the texts of legal discourses are collages; a collage of customs with myths, a collage of phantasms with fears, and a collage of the taboo with the acceptable? "*Corpus juris*, the body of law, body of doctrine, etc., these formulae . . . indicate the relative simplicity of the mode of social regulation that is known as *establishing*. Establishing institutions means manufacturing written collage."[14]

The issue of the judges' ethos, insofar as they stage the presentation of themselves (their body), character, and language, brings us to the scientifico-administrative tech-nocracy that sometimes takes hold of the law in Africa. A law that, through denial after denial, conceals its strange relationship both with myths (which it does not consider it represents) and with the bureaucratic rationality it claims to regulate. "It is easy to see, in all the places where modern management is effectively implemented, that it works to produce a series of written documents where the subject is absent. In these places everyone takes the necessary precautions never to be suspected of being identi-fied with what they write. Keeping your distance, as far away as possible, that is the rule."[15] The postcolonial state, which operates *in the name of the law*, and civil society, which appeals *in the name of the law*, get along fine with this idea of a legal system that, textually, has become a mechanism whose language is just as bombastic as it may be complex. A language that is cleverly maintained by a few legal experts, who have become a priestly caste in Africa and a substitute body for totems. Love of procedure, proliferation of committees, inflation of "decisions at the top," and repetition of checks are all practices that, by appealing to efficiency and "rapid study of files in the interest of plaintiffs," make us forget that wrenching legal texts out of the imaginative source that nourishes them results in their being simply "management doctrine, clinging fanatically to the government's beliefs."[16]

The relationship of the law to *the image of the self*, the continually repeated produc-tion of the place of the confrontation, the maintenance of the scene of speech where what the law says meets both the old and the new, the same and the other, raise the problem of the "space-between": How can one produce and interpret the legal text in Africa, knowing that it is a "space-between"? If we wish to restrict it to the justification that the lawmakers give for it—that the legal text indicates it is already an allusive varia-tion—if we wish to reduce it to what is called the "traditional core of the law" composed of nomogonic and etiological myths, it already eludes us and shows us that it remains first and foremost a rational construction. Through the judge's ethos we need to examine the production of subjectivity and the status of the image in African legal space.

When judges in Africa, according to jurisdictions, use their ethos (in the traditional courts that exist alongside the state courts) or, *a contrario*, use *technical expertise* on the hermeneutic level (by emptying their decisions of any self-implication), what is at issue—and what by that very fact relates to this encounter between rationalities—is the production of *legal subjectivity*. What is a subject in law when it is an *intermediate subject*? The subject in law, that autonomous entity that in a democratic space is subject to the law it has given itself, is in fact a subject implicated in the tension between the *speaking-the-law* associated with ethos and another speech that refers to technical expertise. How to make a subject emerge from that tension? How should the subject in law be thought of, no longer within the certainty of constitutions (fundamental laws) but in the uncertainty of tension?

As far as image is concerned, traditional judges most often started from confusion (they worked in a space that did not separate legislative, executive, and judiciary), whereas African judges, who have studied Western law, set out from a *division* (executive, legislative, and judiciary). The image of the judge in Africa today emerges from a contradictory background (both confusion and separation of spheres). This contradictory model of the judge's image has gradually become predominant since the colonial period. Except in societies that have a strong central power, other African societies with lineage structures bring together in a single person the power to judge and political authority. But with colonization two kinds of dualism were introduced: the first is associated with traditional jurisdictions and professional magistrates, and the second embedded in African societies the institution of traditional judges turned civil servants.

> The dualism that existed in African countries throughout the colonial period as regards the structures of jurisdictions also existed in relation to their composition. Schematically it could be said that the main legal order was characterized by the professionalism of judges and the separation of administrative and judicial functions, whereas the opposite was true of indigenous jurisdictions.[17]

But within traditional power, colonial administration was turning traditional judges into administrators. A manual of French colonial legislation states that

> we are counseled by both logic and experience to use natives to assist our domination ... that is the best way to get people and their natural leaders to support us in the common task of material and moral development which we are pursuing in the colonies. ... In French West and Equatorial Africa the native leaders, from the most to the least important, are our assistants and receive in some cases fixed honoraria and in others rebates on their personal taxes.[18]

The consequence of thus bringing some traditional leaders into the colonial judicial apparatus was on one hand the presence in the same judicial space of *magistrate-judges* and *nonmagistrate judges* (a first dualism) and on the other hand the presence in the village space of the *traditional judge* with authority and the *nonmagistrate judge appointed by the administration* (a second dualism). Among the Mossi, on a limited scale, the *bud' Kasma,* who is the eldest, and judge of a segment of agnatic lineage, had complete power over those in his *budu* (segment of patrilineage); after colonization the *bud' Kasma* was assisted by the *Kombere,* who was the chief of the locality appointed by the administration. "The *bud' Kasma* lost his particular penal powers, except the right to pronounce banishment of the *budu* who had committed repeat theft ... it seems that the death penalty could be pronounced only by the *Kombere* and carried out by his men."[19] But after independence African states reduced or changed these courts presided over by nonmagistrates. "Because of the general movement of integration that was taking place within the judicial apparatus in most states, nonspecialized personnel was to decrease substantially in jurisdictions."[20]

This transformation and fragmentation of the judge's image encouraged people to rethink the relationship between image and the law. With this fragmentation of the *judge's image, what was left* of the representation of the judge in the minds of those who appear before him? An image always leaves something behind, so what has happened to *what remains* of the perception of the law after the encounter between Western legal systems and traditional African ones? What is the image of the law in postcolonial states? The image is both a *trace that preserves* and also *what establishes* something different. How, in the encounter between judicial rationalities, can one both *preserve* and *establish*?

Abstraction of Form and Downgrading of Content: Misunderstanding of "Technical Irregularity"

Where Western judicial rationalities (particularly the Latin tradition) emphasize the form of the act, African legal systems pay more attention to content. After the warning (*mbémé*) in a traditional trial among the Beti of Cameroon, the charge (*sòman*) and the appearance (*nkat*) attend to the substance of the case. Why this stress on content over form? Quite simply because the opprobrium and offence do not harm one person alone but also "sully the earth," poison the air we breathe, and compromise the ethical pact with the ancestors. The content of the offence is more important than the manner, which is why the vindicatory system used to follow a certain order and did not tolerate private revenge.

Let us look at a few examples of penal customs from Chad, most of which, we should remember, have connections with Muslim law. Among the Masalit, a deliberate wounding "which does not result in inability to work does not give the victim any right to compensation."[21] The case of woundings that give the right to claim incapacity for work confers a "right to compensation set by the village Djemaa."[22] In pre-Koranic custom, a wounding resulting in "loss of both testicles was worth two cows, loss of a single testicle—one cow, loss of both eyes—two cows, loss of one eye—one cow, ... loss of a hand (or foot)—one cow, loss of a finger—a heifer."[23] For the rape, for instance, of a "married woman, payment of compensation of a cow to the victim's husband . . . of a girl payment of compensation to the girl's father; the rate was set at half the dowry. In this case if the seducer was accepted as husband, he would have to pay the normal dowry on top of the compensation as set out above."[24]

When compensation is decided upon, traditional judges consider the seriousness of the act in its materiality and not the process of the rapist's arrest. However, in the procedure according to Western judicial rationality, the rapist would have been arrested, he would have been brought before the court, there would have been questioning while he was in custody. This period of custody had to conform to certain rules that are part of what is called "drawing up the dossier." Here the time element is very important. A period of custody that goes beyond the regulation time can lead to the simple release of the prisoner. He will be released because of a "*technical irregularity*"—in other words, the *form of the charge* determines the content. How could a Masalit from Chad understand that someone who has cut off his hand should be released simply because he was held for longer than the period of time allowed? How could he understand that kind of rationality that always separates *form* from *content* and is the result of both idealist philosophy and judicial positivism, as understood by the Austrian philosopher and jurist Hans Kelsen?

Without going back as far as Aristotle, who in his theory of causality distinguishes efficient cause, material cause, formal cause, and final cause, let us pause at Kant. In the classification of an act's morality, he emphasizes the fact that an act is moral if the *form of the act*—that is, the intention—is moral. For example, an accountant who does not steal for fear of the supervisor and prison is not then performing a moral act by not stealing. Only someone who refrains from stealing out of duty, in other words, someone whose act is intentionally good, where the *form of the act* coincides with duty, performs a moral act. We know Hegel criticized this separation of form from content as an abstraction—form being a moment in the development of content—but we can look for the origin of this distinction in the dualisms that come down from Plato, with his distinction between a formal intelligible world and an ephemeral unreliable world of the senses. The latter only drew its solidity from the former; in other words, for Plato *the forms of things* (their ideas) are more important and determine *the content* of things. Today this rampant Platonism still conditions the various codes of civil and penal procedure in Africa. It is a form of abstract judicial rationality where the form of the act—and thus the bureaucracy that establishes it—becomes the driver of justice.

On the epistemological level, this *emphasis on form* is a translation of the judicial philosophy of Kelsen, who to a greater or lesser extent influenced French-speaking African jurists raised "in a Romano-Germanist tradition." In Kelsen's view, the law is defined as a collection of norms and institutions and is external to the social reality it is intended to regulate; consequently, judicial science is itself external to the law it aims to study. For this to happen, the content of the norms must be placed between brackets and only their formal aspect studied. Legal theory has to be purified of foreign elements like psychology, sociology, ethics, and political theory.[25] In distinguishing the law as a collection of legal norms (*Rechtsnormen*) from the science of law, which expresses the law's propositions (*Rechtssätze*), Kelsen goes on to make another distinction between the "function of the will," with which law is associated, and the "function of truth," to which the science of law refers. Kelsen gives more emphasis to the function of knowledge and the law's formal aspect than to its content as such. This move, together with the fact that for Kelsen there is no true law except where there is a state, harks back implicitly to Kant. "And so Kelsen transposes to the legal domain Kant's famous distinction between form and content."[26] What interests us is this emphasis given to the form of acts, doctrines, and epistemological approaches.

Reconciling and Arbitrating: Two Images of the "Third Party"

Conflict is the site where we discover how the social bond is coming apart. It is not only the site that is at issue but also the ability to judge. Tying, untying, and judging make us think of the position of the Third Party. There it is a question either of compensating the person who has suffered the wrong or of repairing the bond. *Compensating* and *repairing* correspond to two quite distinct regimes, which are implicitly connected to very different forms of justice. Compensation refers to *the past* and its link with *the present*. Compensation estimates the damage suffered by one of the opposing parties, recalls it, and puts an end to the grief or suffering. Here the relationship to time is two-dimensional, it is about focusing on the present in evaluating the relation between wrong and compensation and finding a *position of equivalence*. On the other hand, reconciliation has a threefold link with time: a reminder of what took place (the wrong suffered), concern with the present, and a project of hope and patching up the broken bond. After compensation, which more often than not is an arithmetical relationship putting a final end to the dispute, reparation is there to allow the group to survive after the trauma of conflict.[27] Whereas, on the side of compensation, there is a struggle for *symmetry in the idea of a distributive justice*, with reparation it is *asymmetry* that reigns; the essential thing is neither in the number of objects brought into reparation, nor their importance, but the *action* and *initiative* of the subject who caused the damage. What is crucial lies in the rehabilitation of the other. Thus reparation is conjured out of anything; often the object symbolizing reparation is trifling compared with the wrong done.

Western justice as it has been applied in Africa has fashioned a new image of the "Third Party." In it the *Third Party* is today the one who decides the dispute without demanding both compensation and reparation. The antagonism between a judges' justice that *arbitrates* and a nonjudges' justice that *reconciles* reminds us nowadays of the great challenge facing justice in Africa, because reconciliation and arbitration conform to different judicial philosophies and in particular different anthropologies. On one hand a distributive justice that is not really concerned with rehabilitation when it punishes, and on the other hand a justice that each time rehabilitates the subject by getting him to understand that he is greater than his unfortunate act. On one side the stress on *equality* and on the other on honor: that seems to be the opposition in Africa between the justice that arbitrates and the one that reconciles.

Nowadays there is a kind of return to reconciliation in Western societies. The French legal philosopher Bruno Oppetit, a specialist in codification, notes that there "has developed in the last few years, and not only in France, a very keen enthusiasm for spreading [alternative modes of resolving disputes, and particularly] extrajudicial conciliation. The disaffection on the part of the public as regards the state apparatus of justice may proceed . . . from the same reaction of rejection as the one that the social body manifests towards what is here called legislative inflation. . . . This trend has found its expression in the institutionalization of conciliators . . . whose task is 'to facilitate the amicable resolution of disputes outside any judicial process.'"[28] This return to conciliation is theoretically based on the reconsideration of the concept of equity: first by the very mobile character of cases in dispute, then and on a practical level by new state interventions that give rise to a "legislative inflation."

Conciliation revives a conception of *the just as the equitable* and not just *the legal.* It was Aristotle who long ago reminded us that "the equitable, while it is just, is not the just according to the law but a corrective to legal justice. The reason . . . for this is that the law is always something general, and there are specific cases for which it is not possible to lay down a general statement that applies to them with rectitude."[29] Thus equity is a corrective for the law when its generality does not include a solution for a specific case, hence the need for modes of conciliation not provided for by the law. Jean-Étienne-Marie Portalis, the editor of the French civil code in 1804, took the same view and said that a "code, however comprehensive it might appear, is no sooner completed than any number of questions occur to the judge, since once the laws are written they remain as they were drafted; but people never rest . . . , and this ceaseless movement . . . produces . . . some new combination."[30] The mobility of human reality escapes the constructions of the code, which is why it is important nowadays to produce an alternative mode of dispensing justice in Africa.

Finally, the form of postcolonial state justifies this urgent need for conciliation. When the state wishes to intervene in all areas of the social order by issuing legal regulations (for example, legislators frame rules designed to protect consumers and regulate the behavior of drivers), this "legislative inflation" ("orgy of law-making") leads us to seek alternative modes of making law.[31] In general this is what international commercial law does: "being friend[s] of the concrete and the particular, they [those who operate international commercial law] have always wanted to escape from general state provisions and submit their disputes to examination case by case by an arbiter or conciliator."[32]

On the strictly philosophical level, Paul Ricoeur seems to come back to this idea of a justice that restores the social bond. For him the act of judging (in the legal sense of the word) consists of arbitrating,[33] but the short-term aim is to decide the dispute in order to put an end to the uncertainty caused by the conflict. In the long term "the ultimate finality of the act of judging . . . the horizon of the act of judging is finally something more than security—it is *social peace*."[34] This is what takes us back to the conflict between a *distributive rationality,* which talks of compensation, equal shares, and is the result of a society of distribution, and a *cooperative rationality,* which stresses reparation and a social peace that is not based on distribution alone but, as Ricoeur says, on "recognition."[35] This is why honor and reputation (*fama*) were more important than arithmetical equality in the development of traditional African law.

Rationality between Time and Hope: The Issue of Space-Between

What is the goal of the encounter between rationalities? To bring humanity together in a common hope? If that is the objective, hopes will turn to despair, for a common hope to which the various kinds of rationality must submit would lead to a sort of dictatorship of hope. For the meeting of rationalities, it is rather a matter of interrogating socio-politico-religious structures to discover how systems of meaning are built up. In other words, how codes find representations that organize the subject's and communities' action, and how, in a world with different rationalities, *structures, meanings,* and *processes* intertwine to give each type of rationality that mobility and uncertainty that will determine its logical form, program, and systems of intelligibility. To evaluate these rationalities, which are mobile (they circulate) and tactile (they touch something else), we need to return to the "space-between."

How should we—accustomed as we are to thought that identifies, that assigns predicates to each type of rationality—conceive of what "space-between realities" is? How should we read those in-between texts that require our eyes to be attentive and trained in a particular way? The space-between assumes three ideas: "the paradigm [of the] interval . . ., interaction, [and] inversion."[36] The issue is to know how to rethink the *interval,* in that it is what brings together but separates. What is an *interval* in the transcription of the law in Africa? In the area of activity, what is *interaction?* Applied to law in Africa, how have interactions, on the twofold level of handing down and reception of law, occurred in Africa? As for *inversion,* how do changes in stance and permutations of positions take place in an encounter? How does one "cobble together" (Lévi-Strauss's phrase) meaning when there is a conflict of norms? What is the judicial norm in the final analysis and why?

To think this mobility, at least two conditions must be fulfilled: (a) *evaluation of time;* (b) critique of a *"form of bivocal/univocal alterity."* Since we do not have a single model for the future, the requirement for the "meeting of rationalities" obliges us to think in future time. Thinking the future would mean "seizing favorable opportunities" and "propitious moments" (*kairos*): "Let us risk that derision . . . and what if 'seizing the moment' today meant 'taking one's time'? And what if, in an environment of speeding up and radical change, the true alternative was the ability to go slowly? . . . [O]pposing the tyranny of urgency and the culture of impatience, we must take our time and especially think of the time and moment for the encounter in the 'dissonance of times,'"[37] and not the "consonance of times," which we are invited to strive for by globalization, that system that is entirely without love and humor.

Finally, we need to reflect on what I call the practice of "bivocal/univocal alterity," which is a form of monotheism. Bivocal/univocal alterity is the frame for the discourse about the encounter of Africans and students of Africa. When people use the expression "the other" in Africa, they often mean the Westerner! For over forty-five years the writings of African philosophers on "the other" just conjure up the figure of the West (either to criticize or to praise it), or at best monotheisms such as Islam. The struggle of philosophers, the meaning of their action, their hatreds and loves, their dreams, their model of humanity, and their picture of freedom can be conceived of only in a *bivocal/univocal* context (West>Africa>West). For them, the "meeting of rationalities" of course becomes the encounter with the West. When *the sacred coagulates the divine* into *the One,* which is called monotheism, and when the African merges *alterity* into *the One,* into a single figure (the West), it replays in a roundabout way the game of monotheism; it practices a "secularized monotheism." This marking of the African consciousness shows how far our narratives on the encounter between rationalities are masked by this *misrecognition* of a "secularized monotheism" that works on the underlying thread of our options.

What have we done in this paper? Study the relations between African and Japanese legal systems? Work on deliberation among the Maya and the Beti? Assess what a confession is for a Papuan and a Breton? Not at all! We have subscribed to the "secularized monotheism" by working on the relations between the West and Africa in order to focus attention on the fact that Africans who ask questions about the encounter between rationalities are "bogged down in stories,"[38] complicated stories, among them this particular type of monotheism.

Translated from the French by Jean Burrell.

Strategies for "Constructing Belief" in the African Public Sphere

"The Colonization of the Lifeworld"

NONIDENTITY HAS BEEN perpetually stifled in Africa by discourses and practices of repression. Research is needed to show how the political dimension affects the concept of possibility in Critical Theory and in the confrontation between African modernity and its possibilities. Further, the epistemo-political importance of such an inquiry must be demonstrated. Finally, given the multiplicity of parameters that may be generated by every discourse on the political domain or political practice, we must identify the *site* from which our own interrogation of African political reality will emerge.

What would justify an analysis of African politics with respect to the concept of possibility in Critical Theory? For starters, the major task of critical theory (by contrast to traditional theory) is to connect the discriminating mission of reason, emptied of its formalist/instrumental aspect, with the historical content of human actions. The relation of reason to history requires an inquiry into the ways rationality is deformed in political life. Moreover, speaking about rationality in politics supposes putting into perspective the multiple rationalizations by which repression appears and becomes permanent. Critical Theory occupies itself with thinking about domination, beginning from the domination of the concept, and through the immediacy of relations, it reveals the multiple mediations by which law is elaborated, inscribed, subscribed to, and proclaimed.

Critical Theory aims to break down surface coherence so that a future both on-coming and be-coming can sprout from between the cracks. But if such an analysis of African political reality is so meaningful, this is only because the scrambling of codes, the debasement of language, and the inflation of texts have become normal practices in Africa. These problems result from the heritage of Western bureaucracy, but also from longstanding attachment to dogmatic practices. To think the problem of the possible and to ask how subjects relate to the law seems in keeping with the lines sketched out by Critical Theory.

But we must note a paradox that risks seducing us into collusion with the eradication of possibility in African politics. Our research is oriented by a working hypothesis—namely, African political reality is invested with the discourse of identity. But we confront a question: How can politics, the art of the possible par excellence, at the same time be a discourse of identity—how to resolve the paradox that possibility is *lacking* in an art of the possible? There is an opportunistic use of the term "possible" that justifies profit-seeking and last-minute social climbing, in addition to a dialectical use that makes the term into a heuristic category for pursuing what is not-yet developed or thought. Once this distinction has been noted, it becomes legitimate to circumscribe the site of our interrogation.

The imposition of self-generating and regulative texts, bureaucracy and its corridors (where all the conscripts learn to lie easily to themselves), the myth of the rationality and asexuality of laws invite a political analysis of Africa from the point of view of its participants' psychic investments. This analysis will be, more specifically, a *pathetics* of politics, examining in large part the forms of pathos by which people enter into the process of becoming-slave. In other words, our interrogation is not situated on the plane of constitutional analysis, but on the plane of reading African politics from the angle of the imaginary. It will be a matter of seeing the relationships between politics and the problem of *desire*. Relations within which one can examine the reproduction of power; but "how could power reproduce itself, without sexuality being involved? Where there is reproduction, there is sex."[1] It would therefore be important to inspect the relations that sexuality might entertain with politics in Africa. The importance of this approach is that it lets us see the diverse sublimations and repressive desublimations in black Africa, beyond all the forms of denial.

Politics, sexuality, and desire—the focus of this research—touch on the general regime of belief.[2] And when we speak of belief, we do not mean this in the narrow sense of religious belief, but of the investment by which the imaginary is coupled to the law. To interrogate the sexual kernel of order also means reading the social hieroglyphs by which African (or other) political institutions use and produce credulity, homogeneity, and stability. The social hieroglyphs in question are the "mythemes" by which the process of "constructing belief" [*faire croire*] prospers. Beyond the problem of desire, the law, sexuality, and myth, this field covers the general problematic of language. Why the problematic of language? Because, precisely, the stakes lie in "speaking"—one does not dialogue with the law, one makes it speak by way of classification, annotation, interdiction, prescription, and repetition. Law is thus transcribed into the everyday and unconscious life of black African subjects, transforming them into sounding boards. Whether subjects are sites where the law is inscribed, or simply amplifiers of the law, one cannot skimp on discussion of language in general and of saying in particular if one wants to study the levels, limits, and assets of power in Africa.

From where does one speak? This is the question of the site of speech, where site is understood here as "the set of determinations which fix limits . . . circumscribe who and about what it . . . is possible to speak."[3] To whom does one speak? What mediations and representations get sketched out between the site of enunciation and the receiver? What is the nature of the connection uniting and/or the division separating the black African subject and the law, whether as proclamation (the advertising function of the law) or as text (expression of an opaque context)? This series of questions certainly does not exhaust the motley field of the political in Africa, but serves as a prelude to the orientation of our investigation, which will be centered on two axes.

The first axis will explore questions of method concerning contemporary approaches to the matter of African politics. There have been many approaches to the opening of African public space, but all (or most) reveal themselves to be functionalist approaches that, far from exploring state liturgies from the perspective of the imaginary, believe they have found in the functionalist analysis of constitutions and decrees the truth concerning the state's being, its appearance, and its permanence. It will therefore be a matter of evaluating, first, in what way the African teaching and language of law appear to be "positive" and, on the other hand, how treatises of political science in Africa only speak of politics in calculating terms. The second axis will involve the "pathetic" approach, appealing to the imaginary. This part will be titled "Sites of the Political Imaginary: The Blockage of Indicating and Constituting Practices." Here it is a question of analyzing the libidinal base of African politics through which the *potestas ligandi* [power to bind] is read. The problematic of language touches upon the distortion of communication in the public space, a problem closely studied by Jürgen Habermas and by Karl-Otto Apel. In the African case with which we are concerned, it will be a question of:

1. Problems of the speech contract involving multiple strategies of concealment (seduction/persuasion) and various inflections and translations between making people believe [*faire-croire*] and making them act [*devoir-faire*].

2. Holistic strategies that very quickly transform the discourse of the law into moral discourse and vice versa. This whole analysis will have a single goal: namely, to show how the absence of a theory for producing and critiquing representations has allowed the emergence of political theories that function as representations with a depoliticizing effect.

The Functionalist Approach versus the Imaginary Approach:
An Epistemological-Political Critique of African Politics

Idealist Traps for Law and Politics

How are law and politics captured in treatises and manuals of political science and law involving Africa? In a positivist manner! This positivism is really what bogs the search for politics and lawfulness or rightfulness down in the focus on simple facts. One discusses forms of government, constitutions, relations between customary and modern law, etc. This approach misses the dimension of the "political unconscious," according to Pierre Kaufmann's apt formula.[4] The unconscious dimension is obscured and overshadowed by the enunciation of facts (multipartyism/one-partyism, integrity/corruption, tradition/modernity, savings/waste, abundance/poverty, administrative slowness/effectiveness). All those who criticize African politics have suffered and continue to suffer from a type of journalism that describes the doings of power, the strategies of African leaders and the seats of resistance, etc.[5]

The search for a fundamental relationship binding subjects to authority (at the conscious and unconscious level) remains unexplored. Everything happens as if Étienne de la Boétie had never posed his question about voluntary servitude—namely, how the majority of subjects come to sign an implicit pact to the point of adoring and loving power. What is the relation between political illusion and desire in Africa? What are the modalities by which the juridical illusion and the problem of guilt are deployed? How, and in the name of what, do diverse displacements of guilt operate? Put otherwise, how do the African state and civil society exchange roles? Is one of them sometimes an executioner, and the other sometimes the victim, and then vice versa? How and why do *"sublimated social groups"* emerge?[6] Instead of posing these questions, much less answering them, political scientists prefer to make the facts and facts alone their fundamental line of inquiry. Let us take some representative samples.

One of the specialists of African politics and law, P. F. Gonidec, will serve as a sort of "ideal-type" for us, since this jurist's analyses and methodological teachings have long influenced researchers in Francophone African politics and law. In a work titled *Les Systèmes politiques africains*, Gonidec proposes to carry out a sort of autopsy of African politics.[7] In this project, it is a question of analyzing political forces, discourses, structures, and action. Regarding political forces, the author follows the good positivist principle of stopping once the typologies and generative factors of political forces have been established. What is hidden at this level (and/or not examined) is any consideration of the unconscious contents of these political forces.

In section 2 of chapter 2 of the first part, Gonidec ingeniously analyzes what he qualifies as manifest and latent political forces. In speaking of the latter, one would have expected to see an exposé of the various ways in which unconscious relations between desire, discourse, citizens' activity, and "constructed belief" are structured. What we get is an account of relations between African rulers, the CIA, and other special services. If we look at the part about political discourse, we find once again long descriptions of pan-Africanism, nationalism, nonalignment, Africanness, etc. The analysis of sleeping discursive strategies refining the production, interpretation, and diffusion of political discourse is carefully avoided. He does not analyze what happens in the African public space when an "I" and a "you" exchange political-normative slogans (regardless of the discourse, whether pan-Africanism, *Négritude*, nationalism, etc.).

In sum, Gonidec's analysis remains positivist, because apart from combinations of instituted discourses (constitutions, liberation ideologies, juridical codes, actors, and pressure groups), we are left knowing nothing about practices or the whole instituting dynamic (i.e., investments/disinvestments). Gonidec's later research does no better, stopping short with the analysis of constitutionality.[8] Moreover, how can notions of force, of discourse, of structure and action be articulated in a single historical constellation? When these notions are applied to historical black African formations, what is their value relative to their theoretical/practical pertinence?

The notion of force in African politics opens onto (and/or covers over) a very fertile field. It refers to investments that may indicate how the play of transferences between emotional contents and identifications takes place at the heart of the black African public space. When a political force mobilizes to claim and/or keep political power, how is its symbolic and affective capital organized? How are flows of energy produced (object fixations, displacement of emotional contents, sublimation or desublimation of goals)? Regarding political action, how could the dialectic between conscious investments in a representation and (passive or active) counterinvestments sometimes "explain" why political action is accelerated or arrested at a certain moment? Why does a certain group, not evidently oppressed, pass at a certain moment to violent action while the oppressed group does the inverse? What are the modalities by which groups arrive at a reactive formation—which, in Africa, means becoming invested in some object other than political power? As for political discourses that, in Africa as elsewhere, are heavy with implicit content,[9] we can better comprehend the modalities of action by surprising discourses as they emerge from the intersection of their cotextuality and their contextuality. Finally, this enterprise requires that political analysis integrate defense mechanisms like denial.

In the political arena and in all the administrative chiefdoms, acting subjects do not dare to affirm what is evident—namely, that they want to "enjoy" power. The truth behind this rigamarole of nominations, reversals of alliance, and attempts to overturn those in power is the "desire to enjoy." But in these spheres, everyone proclaims their selflessness. The discourse of oblativity and of sacrifice already introduces us into a mystical universe.

From the side of legal anthropology, nothing has been done in Africa to integrate the dimension of the political unconscious into juridico-political analysis. A conference at the University of Paris I proves the extent to which the analysis of law is contemptuous of the instituting imaginary.[10] In a presentation by the president of the Supreme Court of Senegal, we see "in act" how the African analysis of law avoids posing the problem of the instituting imaginary and above all, how law can be used to wall off the black essence in the mythology of the sacred (if one can speak of essence in the case of human beings who are freedom, project, and surging-forth). The president of the Supreme Court postulates that religiosity is consubstantial with being black ("In the black African tradition, essentially spiritualist,"[11]) and continues without raising an eyebrow to declare that "African law does not present itself as a set of rules autonomous from custom, morality, or religion. Religious or metaphysical rules and juridical rules mix and a clear priority is given to normative principles to which . . . all members of the community submit and whose conservation is entrusted to the wisdom of elders and of 'public personalities.'"[12]

This declaration is a perfect example of ideological occultation. First, there is a firm will to not secularize the exercise of African law (though is European law truly secularized in its tactics, its reflexes, its nomenclature, and its methodology? We are only posing a question, but Pierre Legendre, for one, doubts it!). Second, subterfuge: this law is not associated with economic production; it is an autonomous superstructure. Finally, no place is given to the juridical unconscious. Why does a bond, code, etc. exist? These questions are not broached, and what is presented is the incurable religiosity of black notions of lawfulness or rightfulness, as well as the shadow this religiosity casts over diverse aspects of jurisprudence.

The idealist drift of African law and politics culminates in Jean-François Bayart's publication on *The State in Africa: The Politics of the Belly*.[13] This book has one advantage, which is that it grasps political problems starting from the grassroots: the author leaves aside problems of constitutionality in order to decipher the present situation of the postcolonial African state, with much help from historical references. One finds a bit of Balandier (the anthropological turn) mixed with a dash of Foucault (Africanist and African political scientists never stop talking about "governmentality" in Africa these days![14]) and a sprinkling of Gramsci (the notion of hegemony). But although Bayart's method may be contestable, as Jean Copans demonstrates,[15] he should be credited for breaking with the Africanist discourse of *Négritude* and the grand discourses about constitutionality. However, Bayart remains in the same vein as those who, in Africa, have never wanted to acknowledge the "political unconscious." With his subtitle "politics of the belly," Bayart could have investigated how and above all why politics is associated with the belly at the unconscious level of the popular Cameroonian imaginary.

In the symbolic economy of desire, what does the belly represent? A hole? Something too full? And since in one direction the belly refers to a hole (orality) and later on we find another hole (anality), why are politics, orality, and anality associated at a certain moment in history? Given that anality and orality are stages with a particular meaning in the subject's development, why associate them with an African society that claims to be emancipating itself? Is this how the popular imaginary indicates phenomena of regression, counter investments of the political sphere that turn into overinvestments in the private sphere? If one really wants to do "politics from below," why can one not pose questions related to the *arcana imperii* when interrogating the desire behind the constellation in which *libido imperandi* and *libido manducandi* are linked?[16] Rather than remaining content to identify facts about power, the "coups" of those who "act from below" and so-called "indocilities," perhaps it might be necessary to interrogate something even further down—the place where a subject is most profoundly bound to the registers of the imaginary and the symbolic—in short, *desire*.

It seems to us that politics "from below" would consist less in examining the ways that the oppressed patch things together on the explicit/factual level, than in examining the true background for their actions, which is the dangerous and improbable region of the unconscious. To observe or "do politics from below" would then mean analyzing not only alliances between parties, sovereign national conferences, state/civil society relations, but also the multiple styles of union between these powers and desire. By invoking "puppeteer politics," the problem must be placed at the level of this whole by which social action is sometimes structured. How does the African political space articulate these diverse modalities of desire: *conatus* (productive desire of African peoples to persevere in their struggle to be free), *cupiditas* (desire to seize everything under one's command), and *libido* (desire to enjoy everything including power)?

The theme of "politics from below" used in Bayart's edited collection *Le Politique par le bas* (Paris, 1992) is borrowed from Foucault (see *History of Sexuality*, vol. 1, Paris, 1976). In integrating this Foucauldian approach, Bayart and his team fail to answer two questions. How can Foucault's theory of anonymous power be inserted into an African history marked by the massive presence of state power? How can this Foucauldian analysis be recuperated without removing the obstacle on which his political theory is based? According to Foucault, every will to know is a will to power; every truth claim is a ruse of power. Now, his political theory tries to expose unexpected links between micropowers through genealogy. His project claims to know how power is produced and, like every will to knowledge, it wants to be powerful in its own right. How can Foucault be used, if not superficially, while this obstacle remains in place?

Let us give a detailed summation of the scorn expressed by legal scholars and political scientists who deal with Africa.

The aforementioned political appropriations of African reality suffer from many defects, both on the methodological and on the political plane. At the methodological level, although they are involved with research on African history, a scorn for history is evident, to the extent that these discourses inadvertently help to mask the fantasmatic dimension of desire. These are discourses in which logicalness and orderliness claim the normative high ground but that, in fact, remain visible ciphers of a self-referential, autotelic, and consequently legitimating discourse. The divisions between forms of constitution and forms of government are abstractions that do not get down to what is most profound about subjects. Whether or not the context is African socialism, whether or not a new capitalism is being constituted in the great pillage of economic investment, whether or not we have multipartyism, the problem of the subject's relation to juridical symbols and montages of these symbols remains undisturbed. For the moment, what remains is the *damnatio memoriae*.

The first great example of contempt is the absence of any sexual analysis of the state. All critics are silent on the sexual nature of order. Failing to interrogate the African state from the sexual standpoint is part and parcel of a very ideological reasoning style, since avoiding this question suggests that the state is neutral. If the state has neither sex, nor tribe, nor nature (and still less any real justification), it would inevitably follow (from this suggestion of neutrality) that the state is above all suspicion of partiality. Why ask that the African political order be analyzed from the sexual standpoint? Simply because at the level of investments, the state is the one that proclaims love for its subjects, and also because these subjects rarely protest or criticize unless they feel this love is inadequate. In their critique of the state, black Africans have never foreseen its pure and simple disappearance; what they criticize is its bad functioning, the state's lack of love for them. In many respects, their criticisms are much like symptoms of the abandonment neurosis that a child feels when he or she realizes that more attention is given to a younger sibling. It is therefore a matter and a question of love and of claims to love; in a word, an affair of pathos.

Where love is concerned, one can interrogate African politics from the sexual point of view—and this has not been done. We do not propose to ask about the sex of political actors, for this is evident to all, but to ask about the sexual identity of African states. Are they masculine or feminine? The question would be banal if it did not allow us to read beneath, beyond, and within the state's folds (the state also articulates itself in folds) the diverse ways that state and patriarchal tribal systems copulate with each other. How does the very patriarchal (and consequently repressive!) concept of the Fatherland, a concept naively taken up by African constitutional legal systems, allow trust to be cultivated in the minds of citizens? Why does one not say Motherland, why *Pater* and not *Mater*? What is the profound meaning of the contradiction that consists in giving the Fatherland a feminine connotation: the "mother Fatherland" (*la mère patrie*)? Would such a state be androgynous? If it were androgynous, then how can this bipolarity be reconciled with its massively patriarchal character? And if it is feminine, by what mediations is the feminine twisted into the masculine?

Beyond this question of sexual identity appears another extremely political problem, that of genealogy. This problem of genealogy—not in the sense studied by ethnographers, historians, and other social scientists—is more properly the general question of the social bond. How is the notion of the bond conceived, lived, and fantasized in the black African imaginary? And how does this notion of the bond—mediated by tribal genealogy and modern juridical montages—try to achieve concreteness? What does it ask from the subject (who lives out a double status as subject of the bond and as the object of attachment)? Finally, what are the determinations, or better yet the categories, that structure this notion of the bond? This fundamental question of the bond (as much an ethical question as a juridical one) is not broached at all by African and Africanist political scientists. But even beyond its importance for the subject and its categories, the question of the bond can also open up an evaluation of the problem of language, because, after all, bonds require signs. The social bond effected through language presupposes not only the examination of texts (jurists are already busy commenting on the legal canon as it is prescribed in people's hearts and presented as text), it also presupposes the web of constraints that structure the "speaking scene" and the "speaking ritual."

In other words, African and Africanist political scientists have not sufficiently theorized the way that the problem of communication is posed from the angle of deixis in African politics. Every political statement is realized in a situation defined by spatio-temporal coordinates. At the moment of enunciation, the subject (the African elite) refers its statement to communicative participants (other citizens) and to the site from which statement is made. But what really happens in African politics when an "I" addresses itself to a "you" in a "here" and in a "now"? What is emitted, transferred, obscured, or disclosed? How does the "incitement to believe" [*faire-croire*] call forth a compulsion to act [*devoir-faire*]? Beginning from this notion of deixis, we can work on the problem of the reproduction of the speaking scene in African politics. In short— how can a discourse produce the scene of its own enunciation by capturing and reusing other statements and, on the other hand, what are the explicit and implicit rules that structure this kind of reproduction?

A third kind of inquiry neglected by researchers in African politics concerns substantial reflection on the problem of representation. Why do we choose this theme? Because it serves, as in painting, as a liminal figure, in the sense that it is situated at the edge of the juridico-political field, on the outskirts of ideology, and at the interior of the philosophical arena.[17] We leave aside the very utilitarian meaning of representation as place-holder in order to think of it as a place through which the incitement to believe becomes effective. African political scientists and scholars of private and public law equally fail to theorize this fundamental notion of representation.[18]

While setting aside the utilitarian/instrumental use of the notion of representation in the analysis of African politics, because its character is too empirical, we do not anticipate a concept of representation that would only be an empty form, a pure *flatus vocis*. Such a conception is found, for example, among analysts of language. For them, formalization is essentially a representation, and formalization is a matter of language. This is because formalization most often bears on semantic relations (i.e., designation, meaning, truth) that play an essential role in the functioning of a language. The grand question from this point of view is to know how a system of expression can have the value of meaning; in other words, how are semantic relations possible? A further question appears: What are the criteria of formality? The formal is of the order of representation. Let us take an example.

In Wittgenstein (in the *Tractatus* and even in the *Philosophical Investigations*), it is a question of the possibility of language. In the *Tractatus*, the problem of form occupies a fundamental place, since it is at the very heart of his "picture theory" that constitutes the theory of meaning distinctive to that work. The *Philosophical Investigations* introduces the notion of "language game" and, to a lesser extent, that of "constitutive rule." But here, the question of form reappears, since a "language game" is like a "form of representation."[19] What is lacking among African political scientists is not this epistemological conception of representation. What they need is an adequate theoretical/practical reflection on the fundamental processes generating all the micro-consensuses that let the salesmen of spicy stories in Africa hold on to their market. And, as Umberto Eco emphasizes, "power lives thanks to a thousand forms of minute or molecular consensus";[20] thus, if it happens that the base of micro-consensus is destroyed, the ideology on which the system of imposition is founded quickly enters into crisis. Now, what is at the basis of the misrecognition of the system of imposition is indeed ignorance of its relations with the production of exteriority and the production of self. Representation seems to be one of the matrices by which becoming-slave propagates and self-generates.

The absence of a deep reflection on representation leads the critics of power in Africa to commit an error of perspective and of evaluation. All those who criticize power in Africa presuppose two things. First, that power has a heart, a kernel that need only be broken down for everything to improve. This organicist conception of power contends that power in Africa is uniquely an affair of government and that freedom could be produced in the public space if only the heart were changed (the government, whether through a coup d'état or through elections or some other path). When the state is criticized in Africa, this is generally a matter of state power. What is obscured in this approach is a rigorous criticism of all the micro-consensuses by which heteronomy becomes perennial.[21] But, at the same time that we criticize this theory behind treatments of the political in Africa, we must also demand that the organicist critique of the "state's heart" be displaced toward peripheral powers, if we are not to fall into the theory of faceless power that we find in Michel Foucault. The project is to employ a double strategy articulating the critique of the state with that of the micropowers whose enunciative scene is inseparable from the reduplication of discourse/practice.

Why have we associated psychoanalysis and politics? Was it to give in to fashion and play *nègres* who repeat their little hastily learned and badly mastered catechism in the latest theories and methodologies? How can we speak about possibility on the political plane in terms of the unconscious when we know that one side of political discourse is articulated in a predicative way and that the other, the unconscious, is a pre-predicative base from which the excess of expression detaches itself? If the unconscious that is the condition of all discourse is "nondiscourse," if it is absolute heterogeneity and the unrepresentable that one can only understand and not explain, how useful can it be in political analysis that, itself, draws on the domain of discourse? How can we use Freudian psychoanalysis to open the political field when it relies on historicism of a deterministic type (the past explains that which unfolds in the present)? Why speak of the possible in Africa by invoking such a deterministic psychoanalysis? Moreover, to speak of the unconscious can become a way of immobilizing it and making oneself its master! Why sketch the analysis of something temporal (politics) using the intemporal or the atemporal (the unconscious)?

Employing the notion of the unconscious in political analysis should drive from our heads notions of power and the morality of power (something that is not realizable in one generation nor even in two). We tend toward a society where everything must be controlled. In postulating the introduction of political analysis into Africa from the standpoint of the unconscious (as Wilhelm Reich, Herbert Marcuse, and Pierre Legendre have done in the West), we dispute an implicit belief haunting those who hold political power in Africa as well as their critics: in short, that power (but which one?) is the supreme Good/Evil. Political power wants to control civil society, and civil society wants to control political power (long live the ethic of control!). The domain of the unconscious whose existence was proposed by Freud calls the Western notions of control into question, since the unconscious—despite a certain psychoanalysis—cannot be controlled. One can learn to listen to it, perceive it, and become conscious of it, but by its very nature, it remains uncontrollable. The unconscious is defined by the absence of any principle of identity. In the unconscious, one desire can transfer part of its energy to another. A play is therefore effected that defies all identitarian logic. Psychoanalysis is taken here as a hypothesis and serves less to give a general explanation of the social than to clarify (or to obscure!) the political field by starting from something that can do without control.

Teaching

It is also very illuminating to see how law becomes hypostasized. Positive law on this continent (above all in black Francophone Africa) is reduced to the ideological patching up of bourgeois Western law.[22] To better bring out this conservative aspect of law in Africa, we must first take some precautions in specifying that law in Francophone African countries is only the appendix to French law. Thus, all the conservatism of French law is found again in so-called African law (which needs to be redone). The conservatism is rediscovered on several levels. First on the plane of nomenclature.[23] The overcoded language makes it possible to understand many voluntary omissions on the relationship between subjects and the ultimate reference in whose name the law is pronounced and promulgated.

Further, law in Africa maintains the pyramidal social structure in its teaching.[24] "Law schools are conceived in order to celebrate the cult of law thanks to which society can function. The cult is organized on the basis of a hierarchical initiatory cell."[25] More often than not, teachers who do not have lectureships have no autonomy or, more precisely, initiative. They are confined to an almost servile rehearsal of lecture courses that have mutated into unchangeable references (servile because, if one considers institutional cooptation with an eye to the *agrégation* of law faculties, the teaching assistants, who are future competitors, must try to please and be docile). As the authors of *Pour une critique de droit* justly remark: "The law curricula are immutable although universities have a certain autonomy in this domain. The methods of teaching have hardly varied since the nineteenth century. The lecture course remains the central pedagogical institution of ex-departments of law."[26]

Often the conception of law in such departments is quite idealist. This conception is also the one adopted by the state in Africa and sometimes in France. From this point of view, right [*droit*] is sometimes assimilated to law [*loi*] as a result of the general will, which is the very expression of reason. Right, law, general will, Reason: these four poles define the idealist enunciation of bourgeois justice and its tropical outgrowth. This trajectory is repressive to the extent that it suggests that law is the very expression of the universal language of a Reason (atemporal and disincarnate, let us add!) that suffers from no partiality. In addition to the pedagogical form, other basic problems arise, such as the autonomization or rather the atomization of law.

In their courses, French and African legal experts most often present the state as a "moral person" endowed with sovereignty. In one blow—as this teaching is presented to students—they evacuate the entire thickness of conflicts and social relations that subtend the state. In the eyes of students, the state becomes an abstract/formal unity concealing the real dimension of every state: the unity of diversity. Quite apart from the abstraction unity promoted by this notion, regarding the state as a "moral person" can legitimate authoritarian regimes to a certain extent, because obscure games are hatched on the plane of power beyond this abstract universality/unity.

The ideological teaching is really polished off with the fabrication of a caste of neocolonial elites whose role is to regulate the reproduction of *stare decisis*! The cult of law is organized like an initiatory sect (once schematized, is ideology not a sect that cuts individuals off from the social base of their representations, and that cuts up or atomizes the real to better control it?) in which relations of symbolic power exist and endure. In Francophone Africa, once again, the law departments function in a patriarchal way:

At the peak, the father-Colonel-dean. At the bottom, the son–second-class-student. Between the two, a complex hierarchy. In sum, the following categories: the undergraduate student [*premier cycle*], the masters student [*deuxième cycle*], the doctoral student, the teaching assistant, the course instructor . . . the assistant professor [*maître de conférences*], the professor, the dean. There remains only the student in the "legal assistant" track [*étudiant de capacité*], but he is not really part of the family-regiment. In some ways a lumpen-student, he only has right to some scraps of the juridical teaching. . . . The pedagogical relations are marked by this hierarchy.[27]

One thing to keep in mind—since we are dealing with hierarchical relations and symbolic violence—is that at a lower level, the functioning of a law school often mimics the form of the authoritarian state in its symbolic violence.[28]

Whether in its vocabulary or in its form of teaching, law, which in Africa is no longer "right" (*jus*) but takes on more of the sense of *lex*, is constituted as a factor for stabilizing and mummifying the imaginary. How does one recognize an idealist presentation of some reality? The idealist approach to a social institution cuts it off from its material base. This approach isolates and does not grasp reality as a knot of contradictory determinations between which many mediations are inserted. It is unaware of the standpoint of totality (Georg Lukács) and manifests a true indifference toward everything having to do with the links between a given institution and the production/reproduction of material life. How is this manifest at the moment of the teaching, or rather the display, of law? Does it bind legal education as an institution to the process of material production in Africa?

First, the presentation of law in Francophone Africa does not address material production/reproduction. To be sure, the civil code addresses the production/reproduction of life, but all this is completely hypostasized and subsumed under the concept of contract. In this notion, we see the problem of determination from the other side. Law is presented as priming and founding material relations and not the inverse; put otherwise, law and its canons become autonomous norms that legislate, prescribe, classify, and inform the social totality. What is occulted by giving primacy to law is the way an economic relation is transformed into a juridical relation, thus camouflaging the first by means of the second. Without saying so directly, this mystification claims to permit and to be the condition for the development of commercial relations (and power) in the logic of capital. Contrary to what the civil code recommends, "it is not individuals who are set free by free competition; it is, rather, capital which is set free."[29]

It is not just that the notion of contract hides the scent of idealism, but the notion of humanism so celebrated by civil Napoleonic law (endlessly trotted out in the tropics) is further revealed to be an avatar of this repressive conception of law. Historically, in the genesis of the civil code, law was presented as the expression of man's rational nature. But this presentation of law, which appears to exalt liberty and human will, hides a conception of law as autonomous system, the "active motivation" and voluntary creation of man. Conceiving law as an autonomous system conceals that "the civil code is a system of constraints that boils down to a very precise socio-economic context and to a philosophically fundamental political (or rather antipolitical) stance."[30] Historically, it is with the codification of law that this system seems to have taken on a certain autonomy vis-à-vis its economic foundations. Everything happens today as if it were law that unilaterally founded economic relations and circuits.[31] Thus Francophone African legal systems present themselves with the sophistication of a purified and idealized language that, although it handles empirical problems, occults the existence of real interests and tensions between individuals, relative to their class interests.

It becomes completely normal for the formulation of law emerging from this language to have an idealist nature.

We must be clear that at this level, our critique no longer bears solely on law as it is pronounced in Francophone black Africa, but also on law as a discursive genre that, by the production of a speech contract (between speakers and receivers) determines particular manifestations of speech within the public space:

> The discourse of law is the work of a communicating authority . . . who has power to legislate or . . . who is invested with this power. . . . In fact, this communicating subject is only a single abstract entity encompassing all subjects linked by the law. . . . Thus, the communicating authority is not represented by a particular subject . . . but by a collective subject whose figure may be, in a given case, society (by means of its civil and penal codes), the institution (which is defined by this or that juridical or administrative regulation), etc.[32]

It becomes quite evident that law as a discursive genre engages in hypostatization at this first level, to the extent that the communicating instance is often a sort of inclusive and legislating "one," encompassing the various protagonists (the *I*, the *you*, and the *he* of the speech act) in a dubious symbiosis that does not concern itself with levels of language. Everything is comprehended in the law or statute and "this" is everyone's business.

Perhaps one must return to the meaning of legislation to better understand the law's hypostatizing structure. To legislate is to speak, to pronounce, or interpret law. This supposes the institution of a narrative stage on which the role of actors is governed in a constraining way, because they are justified in and by the law and sanctioned if they find themselves outside the law. In the act of "pronouncing law," the speaker finds himself half-effaced, because the productive authority of this discourse is considered to be a collective subject. No specific mark identifies the intended receiver of this speech; it seems to include the whole world. (Most often, law appears to be spoken for all and the speaker of this law pretends [*faire croire*] that he is also its intended receiver, because if he happens to stray outside the law, he can suffer its sanctions—at least, this is what he persuades [*faire croire*] himself!)

From this discursive arrangement, we can extract an ideological attitude that consists of inscribing the speaker and the receiver in a *delocutive speech act*.[33] We know it operates as if the text spoke on its own, outside of all subjectification in a particular speaker. In this discourse of law, beyond the hems of jurists' robes and hoods, it is the statute that speaks, and nothing else, suggesting its neutral and asexual character to all those linked in the speech contract of the African public space. This delocutive speech act makes use of many assertive modalities (authorization, interdiction, obligation, possibility, appreciation, declaration) whose particularity is that they belong to other behaviors (allocutionary, for authorization and interdiction; elocutionary for the others). But at the same time certain injunctions are used as if they were delocutive, which is to say they assume the impersonal form that hides subjectivist interests (it is forbidden to . . .; it is possible that . . .; it is decided that . . .).

The discourse of the civil code in Francophone black Africa would therefore become one of the many ways instituting practices are smothered before their birth. In this discourse, germinating possibilities are regulated and framed before they even have the chance to take effect. Scholarly chatter on the democratization of African societies, the revolutionary polish of African intellocrats, the theoretical formulations of causes and mechanisms of African state regulation hide a reality—namely, that the discourse of juridical law in Africa is, first and foremost, a system for the communication of interests. In its interpretation/application, the civil code in Africa (and its byproducts: the penal code, the commercial code, etc.) would be the exemplary case of identificatory thinking. The civil code identifies beings at the heart of a public space, classifies them, marks/brands them, and then diminishes their value. It closes up what is *possible* in a categorization all the more repressive in Africa since the way it is lived is not defined as imprisonment.

The identificatory approach therefore hides everything on the side of the imaginary, investments, transferences, and finally denials. On the plane of method, political science and legal studies in Africa occupy themselves with nothing but the factual functioning while neglecting art, sexuality, in short the imaginary. This is what is proven by the manipulation/petrification of constituting practices.

Sites of the Political Imaginary: The Blockage of Indicating and Constituting Practices

We may conclude in part that discourses claiming to be critical of the status quo in Africa should be numbered among the multiple forms of identificatory or classificatory thinking; in a word "affirmative thought" (in the Marcusean sense). This is because one cannot criticize politics while obscuring everything that comes from pathos, which shows that one may only be able to seek a partial and provisional grid for clarifying the many strategies by which nonidentity (in Adorno's sense) is concealed in Africa from the deep side of the imaginary. If we only stick to observable facts, or reduce representations to empirical manifestations, we will be misled in politics, because the dimension of belief plays a huge role.[34]

The analysis of the imaginary in African politics could have treated it on several registers. For example, one could have looked at the visual and iconographic plane, the significance of armaments and flags that can elevate the state's importance by turning the subject into a statue. The question could have been formulated as follows: What is the status of emblems in the African republics? In other words, how does the symbolic function invade, animate, and invest the field of the black African public space? How can the emblem come to have a symbolic/real efficacy when it was once insignificant? And what is the function of the emblem in the state's underground efforts to scramble codes in communicative networks? But we are not occupied with the symbolico-political aspect of these emblems just now, for what interests us here is seeing how, beginning from the libidinal base, the possibility of thinking an alternate history can be eradicated.

The Libidinal Base (The Body)

How should the body be put into discourse, if not by proceeding according to certain metaphors: the body as site for inscription by the law, the body as text to decipher, the body as structure, etc.? And when dealing with metaphors of the body, is this still the body?

Scattered in the flux of time and stabilized in space, today the body has become that by which, with which, and against which the "colonization of the lifeworld" mentioned by Habermas is inscribed in temporality. Black African philosophical investigation has largely forgotten to address the way in which bodies relate to power on this continent. It would have been interesting to see, from a less anthropological perspective, how the subjects whose psychological lives are split between the paradigms of an ancestral mode of production and the effects of a quickly advancing modernity represent the body to themselves. How is the body presented and represented for the interiority of a subject who fantasizes but is cut in two? Anthropologists have occupied themselves with the mystical-aesthetic dimension,[35] but this perspective does not go to the bottom of connections *hic et nunc* uniting corporeality, temporality, praxis, and the *arcana imperii*. The failure of black African philosophers where reflection on the body is concerned leaves the path open to "pathological" phenomena—recuperated by a psychiatry that sometimes serves as a legitimating guarantee for the interests of capital.

Shamelessly, psychiatry in Africa accepts the authoritarian internment of the "mad" as it is practiced in the West—although in local usage and customs the "madman" or "madwoman" remains with his or her own people. One does not impose separation/sequestration on such people, nor "status as insane." They live in the "normal" world; at the extreme, they "are normal" since they remain in a world without sequestration. Given the present economic crisis in Africa, phenomena of body image alteration and dysmorphophobias proliferate. Many deliria can be grouped together (estrangement: certain people think that their body has been "stolen" by someone else; possession: others believe in a distant influence over their body; and dysmorphophobia: one develops an anxious fixation on a part of one's body that one detests, etc.). These deliria are recuperated by religions, which thereby build up their clientele. African philosophers could have posed the problem of how the body occupies one's own and the other's gaze. If there is dysmorphophobia, this is because I *see* my body and it is *seen* by others.

In other words, African philosophers have not explored this dimension of the *visible* with respect to the *body* in their culture: How do the "intertwinings," the "chiasms" and in a word the problematic of the *implexe* described by Merleau-Ponty take place?[36] If "my body as a visible thing is contained within the full spectacle" and if "my seeing body subtends this visible body, and all the visibles with it. There is reciprocal insertion and intertwining of one in the other"[37] then how, in the body-visibility relationship, does an obscure domination inscribe its strategies? From the problem of "possessions and rituals," a problem referring to anthropology and psychology, we pass to a general formulation of the problem of the body and of vision, and of the other person's body.

Before proceeding to a political interrogation of the body in black Africa, it is important to situate our questioning and above all to identify the manner in which it will be carried out. For this, we will employ a semiological method, leading to a political evaluation. We begin from a fundamental postulate: namely, that the body is ill and, insofar as it is a sick institution, one must learn how to make the body speak. This comes down to determining symptoms and signs through a careful, attentive look, because the sick body speaks through symptoms and signs that must be detected. How, by means of the body, can one conjugate and read most of the social hieroglyphs by which the body is submitted to instrumental rationality and to the productive principle? The body is inscribed, gets marked/branded, and marks are the first level on which the relations between the body and power in Africa must be studied.

When it is pronounced, the law must be inscribed in a space and become a text. Marking can mean the style of inscription. To mark a body is first to constitute it as a text by separating it from other bodies and above all from its initial condition, in order to make it enter into the regime of the signifier. To mark a body is thus to "mark" it in the sense that a player marks an adversary in soccer—namely, to keep an eye on him or her. The marks of the body throw back significations. Sometimes marking/branding was an affair of slaves (for example, slavery in the Americas), but it was also the means by which the body accedes to dignity and beauty (for example, aesthetic scarifications in certain groups in Africa; including the Beti from southern Cameroon). But the problem that we want to raise concerns the intrusion of functionalist reason (*ratio*) into the African economy of the body. We leave aside the genealogical problem of the juridico-historical constitution of institutions reifying the body, a Foucauldian study that could have been useful.[38] Nor will we take time to observe the transference of guilt by means of the body: Foucault has already studied the phenomena of "confession" through the production of *homo docilis* in the body's political administration.[39] Finally, we are not going to do a socio-political study of the various metaphors that the body may inspire as visible object and as object/subject of writing.[40]

To see how the body is instrumentalized in Africa, we must take note that the discourse on (or of) the body is often claimed to be impossible, because its evidence is so elusive; at times I have a body, at times I am a body; between this "I am" and "I have," a tension is often installed in which "this something" that would actually grasp the body is lodged. It is this very ambiguity of the body that is translated in its "self-showing." Sometimes it is shameful and one hides it with clothing, as much to forget it as to increase its value. It can fascinate and then one searches for an absent meaning that would have explained its pull. Because it is alive, the body is also contemporary with its own dying and this expresses its enigmatic and paradoxical character.

However, in this enigma, it is necessary to discern how the practice of mastery is carried out in Africa. The mastery of the body can mean two things. First, the power to control something or someone. Mastery as power is referred to a space, to a territory of control, and to an object being controlled, henceforth considered as a machine (this term gathers notions of machinery and above all of "machination" or plot). From there a trap is deployed in which the eye cleans space by sweeping through it—this is the panopticon of Bentham so remarkably analyzed by Michel Foucault;[41] and, altogether, it is the enterprise of organization. Secondly, mastery can also mean a progressive appropriation of quality and of experience, as in maturation, development, integration. This mastery is referred to time and to personal interiorization.

Now in Africa, one must focus on the first of these forms of mastery when the body is involved. On this continent, the body is transformed first of all into a sign, into a symbolic form that one consumes. Advertising and modeling agencies have made exoticism an aesthetic/commercial value in our day, and since it is indeed necessary to put clothes on the fashion market, mannequins "of color" are used. An appeal is therefore made throughout African capitals to acquire young women whose morphology conforms to commercial canons previously defined according to the laws of the Western commercial imaginary. "I will have your skin": this imperative of capital has reached its goal when the black woman's body type has been reduced in this way to a stereotyped morphology, defined on paper somewhere else. Her body becomes formless, or rather it must have a form governed and modeled according to commercial imperatives—reification of the body's form and expropriation of the body itself, because it must coincide with the dress size.

To be sure, reification attains its pinnacle when (in order to make consumer goods more appealing to blacks) one uses the image of the black body to advertise certain brands. When the smoothness of a breast, the suppleness of a waist, the spirit of a smile are only offered to the gaze to promote some brand's effectiveness, when long spread limbs are covered in equivocal lace (in hot countries), or a purpled mouth or buttocks open and seem to propose literally as well as figuratively that something will be born from them, this is the annexation of libido by *logos economicus*. At this level, the body becomes doubly alienated. If the black body of a young woman advertises a brand of potato chips (in countries that do not eat potatoes as a primary food), these potato chips are tools and the body becomes the tool of a tool. Thus "tool-ification" [*outilisation*] poses a classic problem of Marxist philosophy—namely, that of fetishism.

The body becomes structured like a fetish. Having become a representation in the market process, the body functions like a decoy inasmuch as the very principle of all fetishes is to pretend to be what they are not. But beyond a decoy, the stereotyped body ceases to be a place of thought at whose convergence the deepening of our spatiality and our temporality comes to light, and it becomes the place of an exchange principle of competitiveness and performance (exchange between our desire and all manufactured needs, barter between our credulity and the greed of capital, and finally exchange between our investments and the ruses of capital). A place, finally, which makes us forget the symbolic violence structuring capitalist processes of accumulation in the Third World. All the while it secretes this forgetfulness, this place effects a negation; the body negates itself as erotic power to serve capital.

We have not broached many points concerning the body and its submission in Africa—for example, the frenetic trend toward cosmetic products,[42] the inculcation of culpability with respect to desire, and the state branding of sports activities. Meanwhile, this reification of the individual body is transmuted into reification of the social body. Diverse manipulations that martyr the body lead black Africans to elaborate a sort of ethic of suffering where, like the characters in Théodore Géricault's *Raft of the Medusa*, the tension between suffering and hope, shipwreck and rescue can be read across the body. All this could be conveyed by the question: How to get rid of the front [*face*] and find a face [*visage*]?[43] Why a face? Because this is the only part of the body endowed with sight but impossible to see, constraining the subject to commit him or herself repeatedly to mediation! Put otherwise, how in the black African public space can one envisage and stare face to face at the other? Everything there is so deceitful and so troubling!

It would be very interesting to indicate briefly the exact place of the face in the symbolic economy of the human body. The face enjoys a luminosity shared by no other part of the body's surface. After being separated from the maternal breast, the newborn immediately perceives faces as signs of the other and as pledges of his or her future identification. In this specific case, the face becomes fascinating and meaningful, because it authorizes the relation to the other through which all humanization must pass. And besides, the face is the only spot on the human body to have many orifices.[44] More than other parts of the body, the face is the place of exchange and of reversibility: mouth to open onto the other, speech made for hearing and reply, smile mocking or inviting, gaze returned by which each expresses the little of him or herself that might be exchangeable and the ambiguous regret at not having been able to say more or at having said too much. . . . Masked for ritual, crowned for power, or hidden behind a veil of chastity, the face plays and is played with from all these sides, and consequently remains the place of power. In politics, the face is disguised to distract from what is not being expressed, and the faces of political protagonists swim in ambiguity inasmuch as they cannot be envisaged or stared down, for they are never themselves.

The instrumental logic facilitated by Africa's accession to modernity is certainly not the only foundation for the reification of libido, since one must also consider several anthropological parameters.

Genealogy, Myth: The State and Filiation

THE MYTHOLOGICAL REGISTER

The state often claims to be ontogenetic; i.e., it makes Being surge forth, but it needs an affective and historical foundation to make itself credible. This foundation will, certainly, have to be solid, but also and above all, must be based on the falsification of history and the atemporality of founding myths. Myth first: How does myth serve to mobilize affects in favor of the inscription of state law?[45] Rwanda gives us an example (we choose Rwanda because of the interethnic massacres that bloodied this country several years ago). The task of myth is to explain the existing order in terms of historical discourse and to justify it by reference to a moral or metaphysical base.[46] All means by which the dominant group can justify its hegemony are acceptable. Thus a Rwandan myth legitimates Tutsi hegemony over the two other principle ethnic groups of Rwanda—namely, the Hutu and Twa.

One day during the first ages of the world, *Imaana* (God) wished to impose a test on a Tutsi, a Hutu, and a Twa in order to know whom he should give power over the others. He gave each of them a jar of milk and charged them to keep it carefully throughout the night. The glutton Twa did not know how to contain his thirst; the Hutu fell asleep and knocked over his milk; and only the Tutsi was able to present his milk to *Imaana* the next morning. From then on, the Tutsi were able to command the Hutu and Twa. Taken to heart by Belgian colonization, this myth authorized the colonial power to "fabricate" a Tutsi bourgeoisie, which, consequently, led several years later to hatred and tribal massacres during which both communities hoped the state would be their savior and moderator.[47]

With respect to political change, a movement in two sequences can be observed: (a) the movement going from mythical-religious contestation to political revolt; and (b) the movement going from political revolt to a mythico-religious waiting game. A quick study of these two sequences shows more precisely how, by means of salvation myths, a political attitude of wait-and-see destined to depoliticize populations has spread throughout Africa. Instead of seeing in their ongoing history the latent factors and tendencies that will make the *novum* come about, these populations commit themselves to the teleologism of a history directed externally by the advent of a *soter* that, in fact, is one of the modalities of *fatum*.[48]

MYTHICO-RELIGIOUS CONTESTATION AND POLITICAL REVOLT

The negotiation of the colonial order has taken on many forms, but the mythical-religious form is surely the most preeminent. Mobilizing this required ideologies of salvation. Several great movements are worth mentioning: Ethiopism, Zionism, the Mau-Mau, and the Kimbanguists.

Ethiopism, remarkable for its eschatological type of activism,[49] must be counted among the salvation movements (myths) that developed in southern Africa toward the end of the nineteenth century. Ethiopism is founded on the exaltation of traditional aristocratic African values with special reference to the Old Testament. Influenced by the Coptic Church of Abyssinia (in which the name of Ethiopia simply designates Africa), this church adopted the myth of "God's elect black people," a status that permitted struggle against whites. The Zionist churches, on the other hand, hark back to the American church: the Christian Apostolic Mission in Zion City (Illinois), and to Mount Zion taken as an emblem of liberation. The dominant cultic element is a black Christ who, invested with divine power, celebrates initiation rituals. The struggle to expel foreigners assumes as much importance as the struggle against witchcraft.[50] During the same epoch, the Mau Mau emerged in Kenya: a mythical-religious movement whose salvation myth constituted a violent response to the British colonial order.[51]

The main thing to observe about these salvation myths is that they are transformed into an ideology of rupture because they put habits and human behaviors to work in contesting colonialism. But since the independences, salvation myths have been almost emptied of their subversive charge. This "disarming" process began shortly prior to the independences in such a way that the myth of salvation evolved toward political revolution and from there became a political attitude of studied patience.

FROM POLITICAL REVOLT TO RELIGIOUS AND MYTHICAL WAIT-AND-SEE

Parallel to the irruption of religious salvation movements on the political scene, messianic movements were formed that evolved from activism into adventism. Two examples are given to us: the Aladura movement in Nigeria and Matsouanism in the Congo. With respect to the Aladura movement, we must emphasize the fact that this movement was born in a very troubled era in the history of the Yoruba region: marked by flu (1918), the plague (1924–26), and the fall of cocoa production toward the 1930s. In 1920, the movement was founded by Moses Orimolade, who claimed to have been cured of his illness. Therefore the fraternity became a society of cherubim and seraphim and Moses Orimolade took the name Baba Aladura (the father of those who pray). This "religion," based on the myth of the regeneration of blacks, was very active during colonization, but has now fallen into simple adoration, into waiting for the coming of the "Kingdom."

The same paradigm shift is observed in Matsouanism, the mythical-religious current founded by André Matsoua.[52] Followers of this movement forge an apocalyptic cosmic vision in which the central theme is the imminent return of Matsoua, who will come to inaugurate a new world.[53] This messianism is a syncretism of Christianity, Judaism, and Gaullism! Matsouanist messianism has a Christian conception of the messiah as someone who has "already-come" and a Jewish conception of the same messiah as "still awaited." In Matsouanist worship, the two dimensions are inextricably linked: Matsoua/messiah has been (the dimension of the already-come) and will come again (the adventist dimension).[54] During his life, the movement founded by Matsoua—l'Amicale—was more syndicalist than religious. As a movement of rupture, Matsouanist messianism is situated on the plane of adventism (pure waiting). The dominant mythical aspect (Matsoua's return) refers, on the one hand, to the beatific contemplation of a beyond, and, on the other, to the futurist wait for the establishment of a paradisiacal era with Matsoua as savior.

The attitude of retreat from the world and escape toward the imaginary explains the Matsouanists' negation of temporal power. By means of these myths and messianisms, we have the exact types of depoliticization and apoliticization.[55] In these messianisms, myth does not incite people to action, but to wait with faith and hope for the kingdom that will be established.[56] These myths, which support the task of depoliticization and help to eradicate the sense of possibility, are tolerated by the single-party state in black Africa in the name of revalorizing national beliefs. But the state also uses genealogical affects.

The Problem of Genealogy

The black African imaginary never feels so much at ease as when entering into the meanderings of genealogies and filiations whose complexity is endlessly astonishing.

This tendency to accentuate problems of filiation has always sustained authoritarian practices under the pretext of conserving tradition. It has also given rise to a narrow nationalism, as exacting as it is willing to legitimize everything *ad defensionem natalis patriae*.[57] It is at this level that one must see how genealogy plays a capital role in the foundation of hegemony. Ethiopia gives us one case. The Amhara (Ethiopian ethnic group) claim to be inheritors of the glory of Tigrean civilizations (the Tigré is an Ethiopian region) and also to descend from the Queen of Sheba (this part appears to be false).[58]

The *négus*: Ras Tafari, alias Hailé Selassié, was crowned in 1930. His popularity came from his fight against Mussolini's Italy and above all from his alliance with the Allied forces. His international aura was justified by the fact that he had been one of the descendents of King Solomon and the Queen of Sheba.[59] To better systematize the legend around "King of Kings" Hailé Selassié, the Ethiopian crown emphasized the Abbé Tayé's classifications from the 1920s. According to this Ethiopian Coptic priest, Ethiopia was composed of four principal ethnic groups: Orit, Kam (or Ham and sometimes Kush), Shem (or Yoktan) and finally Israel. The sons of Orit descend from Adam and disappeared with the flood. The sons of Kush follow, whom Ethiopians call Kemant, Woyto, Skandella, etc.[60] Then the generation of Shem, Asians who crossed the Red Sea: Sabeans, Tigréans, and Agazians. One of these, Axoumis, will have the Queen of Sheba among his descendents. The sons of Israel will therefore mix with the daughters of Shem and from these unions will be born the Amharic descendents who are and "must" be the masters of Ethiopia.[61]

A certain number of conclusions must be drawn from the situation this created. (a) We are witnessing an a priori legitimation of authority in the name of genealogy.

The "in the name of" implies the relation to a reference (Legendre). (b) In the name of this reference, one governs by myth. On one side, this reference indicates special election; on the other side, a curse. The Amharics, sons of Shem and Israel, participate by way of filiation (one would say genetically) in the prerogatives of the "elect people" while the descendents of Kush are drowned, by their filiation, in the curse of a downfallen people.

Given that the categories of election and malediction are very authoritarian on the symbolic plane, the Coptic clergy tried, as much as possible, to emphasize its teaching on divine election and malediction. But what this objective alliance between secular political power, the myth of genealogy, and the clergy really shows is a manipulation of temporality by the state's official politics [*étatisation*] of memory. In this situation, the future (of peoples) is almost mechanically and ontogenetically determined by the past. The reactivation of this genealogy installs Ethiopian peoples in a necessitarist and hierarchically organized type of historical schema. The modalities by which thought about the possible could be expressed—namely, alternation (of political power) and altercation (in the historical continuum) are evacuated from this history. Legitimation through genealogy is one of the ways that the imaginary is imprisoned. What gets suffocated is the imagination as a contestatory project, a practice of disrupting compact totalities, and as excess in a world whose only measure is the reification of some and the enjoyment of others.

The authoritarian state in Africa definitely deals with the imaginary and aspires to be its "captor" according to the formula of François Fourquet.[62] It captures and assimilates the forces of the nation to mobilize and channel them. The messianic version of myth and the problem of genealogy constitute mediations, better yet *sites*, where the interrogation of the imaginary in African politics can take place. But to interrogate the political imaginary on this continent comes down to exploring, at the level of investments, the "spaces of capture" by which identificatory and state rationality find their future. Communication is doubtless one of the sites for these investments.

The Distortion of Communication in Africa: A Pragmatic Approach

To render the distortion of communication more intelligible, it would be methodologically fecund to use a model that lets us partially analyze *the confiscation of doing/saying*. We choose to focus on the pragmatic aspect that, without neglecting other aspects of communication, orients it toward the modification of behavior. To be more precise, this is the model adopted by Habermas, Karl-Otto Apel, and to a certain extent, Francis Jacques. It is specified as a *model of interlocution*. This model puts itself forward as an attempt to conceptualize the relation between discourse and the historical situation that surrounds its production. This model is born from reflection on a certain number of analyses elaborated by different authors including John Austin. The latter distinguishes the locutionary act: "simple production of a phrase endowed with meaning and reference,"[63] the illocutionary act, which accomplishes something in being spoken and which carries with it "a certain transformation of relations between interlocutors"[64] and finally, the perlocutionary act that produces an effect on the receiver outside of all convention or social ritual. Austin's thought is interesting because it gives us a conceptual frame through which we can grasp the relations of discourse and action.

But to be fair, we have to go back to Marx in order to think about the link between discourse and action, because he sees a bond between representations and practice. The concept of dominant ideology in Marx allows us to become conscious of an important problem: that of the circulation of statements at the heart of society.[65]

To interrogate the relationship between language and politics in Africa, we use a model of interlocution that considers the permutation of roles in a dialogical situation. If, indeed, the sender fashions his or her message to fit the receiver's expectations, this means that at one or another moment the receiver must have really sent him or her information enabling the aforementioned speaker to properly "size" his or her message. It is this very specific relation between senders and receivers, and this circulation of statements, that characterizes the space of interlocution. On its basis, there are many ways that the networks of the African public space can be jammed.[66]

On the Confiscation of Doing/Saying: The Denial of Interlocution

From the Confiscation of the Authority to Speak (*Instance Énonciative*) to the Creation of a Unique Referent

The performative value of discourse allows us to interpret African politics in the sense of a pragmatics of communication: in other words, as discourses accomplishing acts and deploying effects in a given historical situation. The first effect of political discourses in Francophone black Africa consists in the privation/confiscation of the space of discourse. By space of discourse, we understand the set of possible positions where the object of discourse can reside. It is certain that in a monopolistic situation, that space is actually reduced to a single position. This confiscation has as a corollary the creation of a referential figure, self-sufficient, and *causa sui*.

Given the (deliberately reduced) frame of this space, let us begin by emphasizing that all political discourse in black Africa is a call from governments to the governed and vice versa (whatever its genre: polemic, didactic, prophetic, etc.). Let us then pose a distinction, in the black African interenunciative space, between a speaking "I" and the communicating "I" (in politics, the one who speaks is not always the one who communicates), and between a receiving "you" and an interpreting "you."[67] How is the enunciative scene confiscated in African political space?[68]

The first way the enunciative scene can be confiscated in Africa is through the scrambling and the effacement of positions of enunciative authority. Confusion is imposed between the one who speaks and the one who communicates. The most striking example is when heads of state in military regimes and heads of single-parties say that their words are communicated from a position that they merely represent; in other words, in their pronouncements they separate the speaking "I" and the communicating "I." An example comes from Togo. "In the name of all the members of the national political office that you have just installed, I am eager to thank every one of you for the confidence you have placed in us."[69] Everything happens in this speech of Gnassingbé Eyadéma [president of Togo from 1967–2005] as if he were only an "I" who speaks/pronounces and the true "I" who communicates is the political office. What is scrambled/occulted is the coincidence and even the identity between the enunciator and the communicating "I." This communication is really that of an "I" (Eyadéma) who speaks and communicates his orders.

This confusion between the communicating position and the speaking position is part of the first way the enunciative scene is confiscated. But this is amplified with the strategy of effacement. Effacement is carried out in two ways: by masking and by simulation. By masking, the speaker (here the African politician or intellocrat) tries to efface from his discourse the marks that would allow it to be classified in a specific group, and to put his discourse under the sign of such or such an ideology. Mobutu incarnated this tactic enthusiastically: "The Congolese revolution has nothing to do with those of Peking, Moscow, or Cuba. It is not founded on ready-made theories, nor on borrowed doctrines."[70]

This concealment indicates a care for neutrality and independence—which are pure denials, since, contrary to Mobutu's affirmation that his revolution repudiates "capitalism as much as communism," Zaire has a market economy.[71] Masking the topos of discourse is often accompanied by a pernicious simulation tactic, in which one borrows the vocabulary of a group who is not one's own, and puts forward the discourse of one's own group as if it were someone else's. Mobutu again offers us an example of this. Addressing the Congolese people he says, "you have believed in the seductive and fallacious promises of politicians . . . see how you were rewarded! You were cruelly punished for having put your confidence in the wrong place."[72] This speech is one that might come from a simple, nonpolitician citizen reproaching others for having had faith in political sirens. Now Mobutu, a politician, pretends to hold a discourse against politicians while being part of the political class himself. He adopts the discourse of the group that opposes him, by using a discourse that he does not believe, but simulates.

The second way the position of enunciative authority is confiscated involves strategies of the speech contract. This is defined as the ensemble of constraints that codify socio-linguistic practices. These constraints result from the production and interpretation of speech acts. In fact it is a sort of "implicit code" that ensures that when one says to the *garçon* in a café: "Une bière, s'il vous plait!," he brings a drink (a beer) and not a coffin. Between the customer and the waiter there is an implicit speech contract. Now, in African politics, this socio-linguistic ritual of the speech act is determined by the one who has the highest social status in the hierarchy (military, clerk, intellectual, politician). The speech contract that has been installed in relations between the elite and other citizens is largely unfavorable to the latter. In the black African socio-institutional frame, legislators have the status of "knowledge-holders" and the simple citizen that of "nonknowledge holder." This imposed speech contract often produces Ubu-esque situations: the legislator will do everything to persuade the citizen that he does not know everything, but the speech contract (the contract of belief) that links him to the citizen can no longer permit him to be a "nonknowledge holder"; he is simply legitimated in advance.

Aside from this a priori legitimation, another submodality of the confiscation of the enunciative scene appears, consisting in the production of a type of perverse symbolic violence. It so happens that in the public space an "authority," or better yet an "excellence," is eclipsed, lets others express themselves and, after some time passes, reveals his status of authority (as doctor, colonel, reverend father, commissioner, etc.), imposing ipso facto a new speech contract that legitimates him a priori. Confiscation of the enunciative scene is accompanied by the production of a unique referent who is the supreme guarantor of all speaking and all acting.

In order for there to be a unique reference, the postcolonial state constitutes itself as a privileged sender, eliminating by this very fact competing senders. And when these resist, the state makes caricatures of them. How does the single-party state produce itself as privileged sender? Through two reductive operations. First the reduction of receivers. There can be three types of receivers on the horizon of political language. There are the nominal receivers, a category that includes people whom discourse designates explicitly as receivers in liminal positions of address, in general the high dignitaries and members of the bureaucracy (to M. le Consul, etc.). Second, the natural receivers are those who are not cited in a liminal way, in other words, the set of citizens toward whom the speech is directed. Finally there exists a group of receivers called "lateral," constituted by all those that the state does not name (the opposition parties, marginal pressure groups, etc.).

Beginning from this pluralist situation, where truth and lie haggle over the social order, the choice of receivers such as it appears in the liminal positions of address is an index of the bonds of interlocution determining the structure of the message's content. It is always the case that, in the parenetic discourse of the post/neocolonial state (a discourse exhorting to virtue), this choice reduces these three receivers to a single one. Speeches on patriotism, nationalism, or pan-Africanism try to win over these three positions whose divergence of interest one magnanimously overlooks. The reduction of receivers has for corollary a reduction in the senders. In many speeches, the state referred to its role as producer and sender of messages. The principal characteristic/prerogative was that of sending true and effective messages. Other senders were reduced to silence and then conflicts arose between messages (for example, the famous conflict between the Catholic Church and the Zairian government during the 1970s).

Besides these reductions in receivers and senders, this period also witnessed the constitution of the single reference through the misuse of citation. In the context of a discontinuous and paratactic writing, Adorno recommended the use of citation, or better yet a collection of citations, which would shake up continuist and repressive writing. But this mission of citation is completely inverted in black African political discourse. To better understand the ideological twisting of citation, and to better see how citation in certain cases contributes to creating a single referent, one must move on to a linguistic definition and to an enumeration of its functions.

Citation constitutes a class of distinct propositions thanks to the typographical trick of quotation marks. Roman Jakobson defines cited discourse (*oratio*) as "a statement at the interior of a statement, a message at the interior of a message."[73] This means the integration in one text of another text produced earlier. To insert a citation is to reproduce an existing text, to incorporate a past discourse in a present discourse, and also to incorporate some other speaker's discourse in the discourse containing the citation. Citation's first function in the case of political discourse is to attach something to the past, to what has already been written. In itself, this does not seem so bad. Attached to a sender other than the one who cites, citation confers the prestige and authority of its author on the information thereby circulated. Put differently, the function of attachment culminates in a reinforcement mechanism giving that information a surplus value of authority, since the message of the one who cites attaches him or herself to a speaker with uncontested authority in the communication community. The citing discourse indicates the referent, and the linguistic strategies at the heart of interlocutive space play out the production of meaning on the symbolic plane.

All discourse has a referent and, in this sense, citation has a laudable role. But the problem with the use of citation is when the gap that must separate the "already said" and a newly pronounced discourse is effaced. Jamming this gap constitutes and introduces the Absolute into the act of reference. Citation ceases to be the fecund gap between the "already said" and the "yet to say," and becomes the support of homophony. A support that gives being, consistency, orientation, and signification becomes "sublime." "One has never been able to govern a society . . . without relying on impressive constructions of the *in the name of*, enabling the system of organization to produce its legitimate effect, the juridical effect. Thus shines the Reference, under innumerable versions of the idol."[74] The reinforcement of this Reference has something centralizing and bureaucratic about it; if the Reference is rendered absolute, subjects enter immediately into that modality of language that is *silence*. Since the only discourse producing sense is the law, one does not dialogue with the Law at risk of producing non-sense— one respects it and one applies it. In the nonpluralistic state more generally, "not only do subjects lack the least possibility of either full or incomplete speech, but there is no speech at all, if communication (with whom?) has to pass through legalist ritualization, which is there to bring subjects under the control of jurists."[75]

Unquestionably, there is a veritable denial of interlocution in the black African public space to the extent that speaking and thus acting are captured in diverse ways, the number of senders reduced and an absolute Reference introduced. These diverse techniques result in confiscation of speech and, therefore, of action. But the desire for interlocution coexists with a dynamic for the production of reality, of a certain reality and consequently of fiction.

The New Captatio Benevolentiae: The Production of Fiction Effects and Effects of the Real

Wanting to be a *techne* at a certain moment, ancient rhetoric proceeded according to five well-known operations, which were: *inventio* (finding what to say), *dispositio* (putting what one found in order), *elocutio* (putting ornaments on the words), *actio* (performing one's speech like an actor), and finally *memoria* (appealing to memory). Among these operations, we choose to focus on *dispositio*, one of whose procedures is the exordium or introduction. Under this rubric, one finds the *captatio benevolentiae* to be an "enterprise of seduction with regard to the public."[76] Without always adopting the same techniques, the *captatio benevolentiae* has become a political tool by which language reinforces *asylum ignorantiae* in black Africa.

Political discourses in Africa generate a situation in which a certain being is missing. Becoming conscious of lack invites the subject to seek further, or better yet to become the agent of an activity (quest). This activity is a matter of trying to satisfy the lack (object of the quest) and to arrive at a certain result that is either a success or a failure. One gives the impression of believing that the lack is implicitly determined by the object of the quest. The most typical speech is the one that every regime makes about development. Political speech articulates/produces a discourse about *lack* of development. An awakening of consciousness regarding this lack is provoked among black Africans, who will then seek to satisfy it, on the fantasmatic plane as well as the real one. But in this tension between the lack thereby created and the black who desires to fill it, are inscribed multiple strategies of domination, to the extent that the subject invited to achieve satisfaction neither defines the lack nor the ways it can be satisfied.

A fiction is produced to facilitate acceptance of this discourse. For technocrats, this will always be a matter of triggering inductive reasoning. Their propositions are constructed in this way: if you want O (O represents the object of the quest), then D(L), (here D characterizes the discourse/proposition of legitimation; and L, the lack of the quest's object), since D(L)>O. This is how the persuasive act can be broken down in more detail:

1. You cannot possibly *not* want O, since the politician of the tropics must foresee the possible objection: "O does not interest me," in cases where the receiver does not feel concerned by the object of the quest. Let us replace O with independence or national unity: "The MPR proclaims that its goal is to liberate the Congolese from all forms of servitude and to assure their progress."[77] Playing on affects, the Congolese in

this specific case cannot fail to want independence. Thus, a lack and a desire for independence are created.

2. If one cannot fail to want O, we are guaranteed that only D(L) will allow us to obtain O. The possibility of conceiving any other means of attaining O must be banished from the receiver's mind, and incitements added to overvalue O. In this case, O would symbolize independence and D(L) the single party MPR (Zaire). The only way to have independence is by going through the party, because it alone can assure national cohesion, given the multiplicity of languages and ethnic groups (the grand argument!). Or: the *only* way to arrive at a democratic regime is by going through a "sovereign national conference."

Another modality of language—silence, and its assistant, the secret—is not forgotten by the *captatio benevolentiae* in Africa. In black Africa, one finds the very assiduous construction of silence since publicity is not the style in political matters. All the same, let us recall that politically the secret has something unhealthy about it: "'All actions affecting the rights of other human beings are wrong if their maxim is not compatible with their being made public.'"[78] The literature concerning Stéphane Mallarmé insisted on the poetics of silence, a silence that would be eloquent inasmuch as it constituted one of the modalities of speech, a sort of tendency and point of tension between the prior "said" and the future "still to say." But in the African public space, silence is sometimes retreat. In this space of confiscated enunciation, one encounters a heavy silence that is the desertification, exhaustion, and annihilation of language. The essential idea to take away would be that silence in Africa is a scission and internal separation of the self rather than a modality of speech (is not silence the way speech divides from itself?).

Ernst Kantorowicz may be the one who best characterizes the double bond between *silence* and *mystery* and between both of these and the *arcana imperii*.[79] Not to keep silence ("keep" in the strong sense of watching over, not letting escape) constitutes the principal *sacrilege*. And in the sphere of sacrilege we enter into the sacred: Is power in Africa anything other than the sacred? But this imposed silence functions phantasmatically to aid the cult of the *secret*. We know the mobilizing function of the secret and its secretion of an implicit content that animates and pushes the speaker as well as its multiple receivers to act. Think here of what Lacan said about the mobilizing function of the implicit content closed up in the secret (see the seminar on the "purloined letter"). In Africa, the construction of silence and the secret's weight in the public space have led to a sort of expression that has developed into an entire culture: rumor. Rumor is produced and secreted by those in power (lest one accuse us of having a restricted notion of power, note that it designates the state sphere but also the diverse pressure groups who can manipulate rumor).

The way this anticulture can be recuperated is through dissimulation of the site from which the statement's terms are enunciated and diffused (in the sense of "rendering diffuse"). The scenario is similar to the one described by Pascal in the first and second *Provincial Letters*.[80] In order to identify Monsieur Arnauld as worthy of public condemnation, and to make this censure acceptable to the doctors of the Sorbonne, the Jesuits mixed themselves secretly into the crowd. While in disguise, they proclaimed that Monsieur Arnauld was opposed to the [theory of] proximate power. But as to the definition of what proximate power might be, nothing was said, "in the design to ruin M. Arnauld, they have resolved to agree on this term proximate, which both parties might use indiscriminately, though they understand it diversely, that thus, by a similarity of language, and an apparent conformity, they may form a large body, and get up a majority to crush him with the greater certainty."[81] The people thus incited against him, the doctors could issue their condemnation with complete impunity. This tactic of confusing oneself with the crowd and creating rumor is heavily employed by elites in Africa. One simulates, while diffusing an imminent event in the interlocutive space, so as to render the production of silence and mystery natural.

Silence is certainly imposed, but to a certain extent, it might sometimes be much more useful than speech. And actors in the black African public space could truly signify their history, when they have recourse to the ante-predicative background constituted by silence. To do politics does not just mean knowing how to speak but also how to shut up. In its relation to politics and to the subject, silence would have three stakes here: onto-linguistic, poetic, and political. Maurice Merleau-Ponty wrote: "Our view of man will remain superficial so long as we fail . . . to find, beneath the chatter of words, the primordial silence."[82] By this thought, he meant to suggest that it is the silent background (in which words are thought before being spoken) that makes the word an opening, an advent, and an event. From this perspective, silence speaks inasmuch as it constitutes the ante-predicative ground from which speech detaches itself as excess. Every meaning (political, ethics, etc.) is inseparable from silence.[83]

Beyond this onto-linguistic aspect, silence is an "art of doing" that consists in quieting speech in order to let silence "speak." In the plane of action, there is a whole politics of silence, bringing together prudence and the art of seizing opportunity. Joseph Dinouart thinks that silence is an element of eloquence and deplores that "the furor of speaking and writing on religion and government are like an epidemic illness with which a great number of heads are struck . . . the ignorant along with the philosophers . . . one cannot pass for a fine mind or for a philosopher except when one speaks."[84] Against this "chatter," one can oppose a silence that is not desertion, abdication, or conspiracy, but circumspection: "The first degree of wisdom is knowing when to be quiet; the second . . . to speak little and to be moderate in discourse; the third is to know how to speak, without speaking badly and without saying too much."[85]

If one can resist a restrictive political order through speech, a certain silence may do it better than speech, as shown by the film of Jean-Pierre Melville on the period of Nazi occupation in France, *The Silence of the Sea*. At this level, silence has a poetico-dramatic function in the public space. It allows—as resistance and creation—the process of action (drama) to begin again in the *koine*. Politically, silence frustrates the instrumental rationality that seizes/instrumentalizes the African intellectual. The intellectual is often defined as the spokesman of his or her people. But, the functional ist mentality that would like to judge each being in light of his or her utility considers the intellectual a warehouse of certitudes and thoughts. For each situation, the intellectual is supposed to "churn out" a solution like an automatic cash machine. When there is a "crisis," the intellectuals who have integrated this functionalist *habitus* believe themselves obliged to "churn out" solutions. In considering themselves (and letting themselves be considered) as automatic tellers for certitudes and solutions, the spokesperson type of intellectual becomes a "speech whisperer" [*souffle-parole*] in the double sense of one who whispers what he is supposed to say to the people, and the one who stifles (in the sense of blowing out) the flame of the people's own speech.

Silence would therefore denounce this notion of the intellectual-icebox filled with a frozen and available language to be trotted out on every occasion. Silence as uncontrollable ground can be a modality of resistance to this instrumental logic. The status of the intellectual might thereby enter into the category of possibility: he will be the one who can be used for anything or nothing at all! The intellectual's silence will break instrumental logic, as well as the "soteriomania"[86] that makes intellectuals into the agents of a sort of messianic theology. The intellectual faced with crisis believes himself invested with an apostolic mission.

To pursue the nonidentical, to clear away all the veils by which subjects are repeatedly reduced to simple instruments of power, we are required to plunge into the two most unclear universes of the African public space: namely, the domain of the libido and that of communication. These sites that we have interrogated are not the only ones by which functionalism and domination efface any thought of the possible; other sites exist, but our task was to see how these *arcana dominationis* function. Meanwhile the problem of belief and investments in politics remains to be interrogated: "It happens that people hear official speeches as a conventional noise. From the balcony of his palace, the king produces sentences; his subjects, for their part, laugh below or sleep; the king sees this acutely and the grand vizier ... also notices it. The ceremony goes forward nonetheless with impeccable order and, at the moment of departure, all the people bow very low."[87] Question: Why do the vanquished always kneel down? Why, despite the many ways communication within the public space could be rendered clear, does the interlocutive space never end up containing transparent statements?

Translated from the French by Laura Hengehold.

African Cultural Diversity in the Media

Old Question, New Factors

The issue of cultural diversity in sub-Saharan Africa is an old problem that already concerned colonial administrations and postindependence African elites, the promoters of that common but extremely delicate commodity, democracy, and it still concerns today's promoters of cosmopolitanism.

The colonial administrations (both British and French) found themselves facing the issue of cultural diversity. How were they to bring under colonial law such differing peoples as those located in the same administrative region, who had been lumped together by the chance effects of colonial geographical divisions on a map? How were they to make the law, decipher signs of revolts, and set about recruiting collaborators in populations whose components did not speak the same language or conform to either the same ontological system or the same legal rationality, still less the same founding myths? In other words, how were they to understand that diversity of cultures, then bend it to the new colonial norm? How can obedience originating with the *one* (the civilizer) encompass diversity?

French colonialism came up with one answer to the question of diversity in the face of obedience: diversity must be assimilated—everyone had to deny themselves and become almost French. British colonialism came up with the opposite answer: everyone was to be equal but in servitude: *indirect rule.* The colonized peoples could keep their social structures, myths, and hierarchies provided they all, from smallest to greatest, served the greatness of the British crown.

African elites also faced the diversity problem at the moment when they had to shake off the colonial yoke. Having been united in the anticolonial struggle, how were they to manage the postindependence period? In other words, diversity here came up against the issue of the nations' constitutions. Colonization had left states but not nations. How were they to lump together ethnic groups that often had nothing in common and tell them to conjugate the same verbs in the same tenses in order to come up with the nation's founding narrative? How were they to manage living together? What would be the bond? Some African elites invented political philosophies based, for instance, on the *idea of family* as the bond; I could cite here former President Julius Nyerere of Tanzania's African socialism, Ujamaa. Others came up with an answer to the diversity question by promoting the extremely vague and quite essentialist notion of African Authenticity, which immediately makes us think of Marshal Mobutu Sese Seko of the former Zaire. Diversity is explained here by an unvarying essence that is African-ness.

With the disenchantment over independence in Africa, economic failure, the crimes of the elites from the independence years, the paralysis of symbolism, which was often accompanied by manifestations of the sacred—tailored to fit the official religions—and finally the states' loss of dynamism, the 1990s, assisted by the new order in international politics, ushered in a so-called phase of democratization. This was about rethinking citizenship and *the relationship to politics,* which was unfortunately reduced to the petty proportions of the state. There were international conferences, elites resigned from governments and, having resumed state titles and attributes, finally introduced multiparty systems, which were previously forbidden. This democratization was a response to the notion of diversity. With a multiparty system, ethnic logic would be silenced and a public sphere for discussion opened up. Sadly, the answer to the diversity issue fell far short of expectations. Multiparty systems designed to respond to the diversity question produced only *many versions of the same* by ignoring the fact that true diversity is less *the industrial-scale duplication of the same*—same parties, same newspapers unliberated from capitalist logic and the quest for sensation—than *the encroachment on the same of the strange,* the different, and the unexpected. In the meantime, there appeared the Chernobyl cloud—which passed over without worrying about border police—the Rwanda genocides, civil war and ethnic cleansing in Yugoslavia. Henceforth, with the creation of international penal courts to try those guilty of genocide—since this world is our *common habitat,* which is proved to us by sea pollution and climate change—the issue of cultural diversity has been included in cosmopolitanism. Henceforth nativism and nationalism are much too narrow for thinking about cultural diversity. This cosmopolitical issue with its many aspects has been formulated by Ulrich Beck and in Africa by Kwame Appiah.[1] But the question of cultural diversity is here seen holistically, without taking note of the emergence of the unique from within its structures.

My approach will bring in the copresence of the plurality of both media and cultures. I shall not give here the outline of a comparative study designed to evaluate how the media, in the specificity of their structures and the uniqueness of their context of enunciation, promote or not the peaceful coexistence of cultures. Such irenic coexistence, if it existed, would not account for the conflict necessarily implied in any human exchange. My approach, which is more modest and clumsy, will take an oblique route of asking through the media about notions of *bond* and *common world*. How do plurality of media and cultural diversity in Africa promote, tear apart, and knit together again *what constitutes the common world* for Africans? What kinds of *mediation make it possible for us to think* the common world? What is *the nature of the narratives* that this common world produces in the midst of diversity? What are the *illusions and failed attempts* that come with this common world created by the coexistence of cultures and the plurality of the media? What can cultural impasses and media diversity bring to the debate about living together that is one of the major problems around cultural diversity? And how does this cultural diversity behave in the kingdom of the *culture industry*? To get a better grasp of the issues around this diversity I shall start from a phenomenological approach that stresses facts (a) and from them I shall extract some problems. Then I shall explore the question of transparency and responsibility (b), which will be enriched by those of recognition (c) and orality (d). Finally I shall analyze the issue of diversity as regards the media at a time when terrorism (e) is becoming a major factor in international relations.

From Facts to Problems

1. *Fact:* In the 1960s a Bantu peasant from south Cameroon was frequently to be found working in his field of cocoa trees with a radio sitting on a bush and, at the same time as he followed news or music broadcast by the radio, he was able to interpret a drum (*nkou*) message coming from the next village, telling of a summons to an urgent meeting of the village. *Conclusion:* Here there is diversity of media. *Problems:* (a) In Africa there is starting to occur media competition between those belonging to traditional African cultures and those imported by technoscience; (b) In the same person there is already a cultural diversity that these two media remind us of. So the problem arises of *levels of understanding* when there is diversity of cultures.

2. *Fact:* Around the 1980s Radio Cameroun, a station from the center, broadcast programs in national languages (*Ewondo* by Antoine Bihina bi Manga and *Bassaa* by Tjeck Biyaga) to consolidate national unity after a disturbed independence period. Around the 1990s, Radio Mille Collines in Rwanda was encouraging part of the population to revolt against another part. *Conclusion:* From the situation of cultural and ethnic diversity, multiple uses can be found for the same medium of radio: unity for some, division for others. *Problems:* (a) What is the relationship between the media and consolidation or dislocation? (b) Media and conflict.

3. *Fact:* We are in an African city (Abidjan) on the street near a hotel in a working-class neighborhood (Marcory) at a newspaper stall, and we can see on sale side by side: (a) *Amina* (a women's magazine targeted at young African women and African

female elites), which is trying hard to show off a very slim woman called Ba who is supposed to be the symbol of African beauty; (b) *Elle* (a French women's magazine), which recounts the slimming efforts of Angelina Jolie, the Hollywood icon; and (c) *Ebony* (a women's magazine for the Afro-American elite), which show a laughing, almost comic doctor priding himself on taking part in cosmetic surgery on the nose of a certain singer called Jackson. *Conclusion:* Cultural diversity is here in the middle of Africa, a diversity that follows the route of a three-cornered trade. On this street corner in Marcory in the depths of Ivory Coast, we are living at one and the same time to the beat of Africa (*Amina*), France (*Elle*), and the United States (*Ebony*). *Problem:* How can we raise the question of cultural diversity at a time when there is a globalization of culture?

4. *Facts:* We are in an African capital or medium-sized town: a television set is on and images are flashing past, people round the set are chatting and gossiping about everything, glancing only sideways at the images. We are in a cybercafé still somewhere in Africa: net-surfers are browsing with their noses close to the screen; other people are all around just for a chat. *Conclusion:* We can see there are two categories of people: those with their eyes on the screen and those who are just there, for whom the medium is simply an opportunity to meet up. *Problem:* What spaces for sociability are being promoted by media diversity today, given these different audiences?

I could bring in other media, situations, and actors. It so happens that the pairing of *media* and *cultural diversity* raises at least three kinds of question. First, how does cultural diversity see its relationship with tradition and how has the replacement of traditional media by those from elsewhere come about? How has the problem of adapting or recycling those media been dealt with? Then, the relationship with violence, conflict, and peace is one of the future issues for the plurality of media and cultures. How do the same media serve the culture of peace and the summons to genocide? And how does globalization remodel both the relationship with our subjectivities and our conceptions of the other within postcolonial states? Finally, what is the relationship between cultural and media diversity and the production of new spaces for sociability and meeting in Africa?

Diversity, Transparency, and Responsibility

Media diversity and competition between messages in the public sphere raise an important problem. When the media are freed from state control, they are subject to economic constraint. This includes, among other imperatives, the requirement to produce ever more messages, which become clichés, or even slogans, as soon as they are uttered. Then begins the dictatorship of transparency. A demand for transparency from the audience on the one hand and a supply of transparency in industrial quantities from the media on the other. In this transparency market, the media no longer take sufficient time to investigate, question, and test, because citizens, who are reduced to consumers of news, see their speech, that opaque medium signaling their nearly failed meeting with others and the real, turned into chatter. What is missing here, in this dictatorship of the immediate and instantaneous, is the question of mediation. The matter of mediation raised by the media is one of the essential issues in cultural diversity. How are mediations to be produced between competing symbolisms? How is that in-between to be spoken and described that both divides and unites cultures in their diversities?

Where cultural diversity is concerned, the media situation indicates that it is urgent not only to take account of the mediations within cultures but also to reexamine the notion of responsibility. The great wish expressed by everyone in the social space is that the media should be responsible. By responsibility we often stop short at the legal sense alone. When it is given information, the media should respond by supplying both the sources and the means by which it can be verified. Only that responsibility, understood as a response to a call and as a legal accusation, sometimes lacks ethical depth. Thus Ricoeur, following Lévinas and many others, reminds us in his book on the *Juste II* that responsibility also means being responsible for the other—that is, answering for the weakest and the most fragile in the Latin sense of *sponsor.* How can we promote a responsibility today that takes account not only of the legal subject but of the other who is fragile, alien, strange, and weak? Cultural diversity already has problems of composition, and added to those, problems of trust. Our societies and African societies cannot escape them; they thought of the danger as coming from outside (the classical theory) but today the danger is internal. It is as if we were saying: children, watch your parents for when they are bathing you, they may make an inappropriate gesture. Parents, watch your children because they may take you to court. Wife, watch your husband who may abuse you. Husband, take legal precautions or else your savings will disappear, etc. So we are living in a suspicious world where intersubjective relations are potentially criminal. Therefore, how should we promote a notion of responsibility that takes account of the other, the weak person who is potentially a plaintiff?

The Fundamental Misunderstanding

The relationship between the media or between cultures is made up of misunderstandings. We can borrow Claude Lefort's definition of democracy: in his view, breaking with the *ancien régime* where the body of the king guarantees the social order, the law, and truth, "democracy is seen as the historical society par excellence, a society that in its form welcomes and preserves indeterminacy so that what is happening remains suspended."[2] That indeterminacy, which is in part the basis of dissension in society, is translated in communication terms by the indeterminacy peculiar to misunderstanding. Since democracy prevents people seizing power and since it is continually shaking up the democratic game, so will misunderstanding do the same in the space of cultural diversity. Misunderstanding is in fact a piece of luck and not an accident in understanding diversity. And as Jankélévitch says:

Blessed be poor hearing, the welcome mishearing that helps partners in dialogue tolerate each other by making themselves hardly deafer than they are, . . . Thanks to that lubricant of misunderstanding there will be less friction in interpersonal relations . . . it is an understatement to say misunderstanding has a social function, it is sociability itself. It stuffs the space between individuals with . . . the wadding of shock-absorbing lies.[3]

In diversity, misunderstanding is fundamental and structuring.

Recognition and the Issue of Contempt

In the context of cultural diversity there arises the problem of recognition. The public sphere, fraught with so much tension, often requires subjects in communicative situations to be able to engage in a process of recognition. This theme of recognition, as we have known since Fichte and Hegel, espouses the issue of struggle. It makes it possible to build bridges between a culture's various members and in particular between cultures—but, unlike Hegel and Habermas, Axel Honneth tells us that recognition is unlikely to succeed unless we take account of the forms of contempt and humiliation between individuals, cultures, generations, sexes, and peoples.[4] Honneth criticizes Habermas's theory of communicative action. For him, the play of argument that ends in consensus under the conditions defined by Habermas does not take account of the affective side of language. Prior to being argumentative, speech often has no intent to demonstrate, but in some cases its purpose is to humiliate. So then we must concern ourselves with the forms of contempt that prevent recognition from occurring. This recognition has three levels, which correspond to the relations with the self.

> 1. *The sphere of love*: Recognition gives the subject the *self-confidence* needed for good participation in public life.
> 2. *The politico-legal sphere*: It is because individuals are recognized as universal subjects with rights and duties that they can connect their acts with respect for their autonomy. Legal recognition gives the subject *self-respect.*
> 3. *The social sphere*: In order to establish an uninterrupted relationship with themselves, human beings have to enjoy a social consideration related to their particular qualities, which gives them *social esteem.*

These are the three stages through which healthy recognition must pass. The issue of the copresence of various cultures in the public sphere can be viable only if the question of contempt is raised by the media, which more often than not tend to become dispensaries of depression and consolation and thus promote only biased forms of expression.

Expression: Orality, Cultural Diversity, and "Telling Stories"

It is often thought that spreading rumors by word of mouth is one of the first media. Without looking at this belief from the conceptual point of view, we can instead see how that opinion might be relevant to Africa. We can accept that the idea would indicate that in Africa we cannot leave out orality when we are dealing with media diversity.

Always suspected of occupying a secondary and almost usurped position on the scale of knowledge—compared with what is thought to be its opposite: writing—orality emerges and slips into the ill-drawn furrows of the quest for meaning. Tracing both straight and broken lines, blurring the tracks and categories of thought of those who see it as the opposite of writing, it persists, indicating that it cannot be reduced solely to speech, since gesture and the whole bodily performance also contribute to orality. There is orality where there is *ex-pression* and not just communication or conceptualization. By *ex-pression* I mean that rising up that occurs with the meeting of speech, body, the subject in the world, action, and reaction. It is probably in Maurice Merleau-Ponty's work that this notion assumes its full weight when he calls *expression* an ontological structure in which speech, body, and the world attain a diacritical dimension of signification. Orality as *ex-pression* is thus a *figure of coming together,* which cannot be reduced either (a) *to a dualistic idea*—orality versus writing: science and precision being on the side of writing whereas tinkering and imprecision belong to orality—or (b) *to a monistic approach*—orality would be reduced to speech or rhythm—or even (c) *to a dialectical input* where orality would be simply a moment, a metaphor for writing or *"archi-écriture"* (Derrida), with these latter remaining its epistemological and ontological basis.

The German philosopher Walter Benjamin deplored what he called *"poverty of experience."* In Germany following the First World War, where attempts to establish a democracy in the short-lived Weimar Republic ended in failure, Benjamin diagnosed, among other ills, the fact that *people did not know how to tell stories any more.*

> Can people capable of telling a story still be found? Where do the dying still speak imperishable words that are passed on from generation to generation. . .? Who today can reach for the saying that will get him out of difficulty? . . . no, one thing is clear: the value of experience has slumped. . . . What has poured out in the flood of books . . . had nothing to do with any sort of experience, because experience is passed on by word of mouth.[5]

Orality as *ex-pression* has speech as a compass. Among the components of orality, speech *points the way* but is not the way, for the true mission of orality is to answer this question: How, while living in experience, can we create, not a *narrow space restricted* to our little conceptual and political habits, but a *place of passage* that moves boundaries and reformulates projects? *Speech transmitted,* which tells the story of subjects and their community *putting on stage* and *giving form to* the conditions of its formulation and appropriation; *speech assumed,* which liberates a subject or a group and allows them to articulate their sufferings and their joys; *the word (not) kept,* which, through promise or oath, *releases* and *binds* a before and an after; *diffuse speech,* which is held back and suffocates, expressing itself only in the process of its own extinction;

mimed speech, which gives the body the task of participating and controlling the life of the performance (of the self, the other, and institutions); *speech forgotten or directed*, which weaves together the components of memory; *ambiguous speech*, which, displacing meanings by playing with both implicit and explicit, inflames the imagination and mobilizes hermeneutic ingenuity—speech will be *that through which* the historical experience of orality will pass. After the colonial denigration of orality, from which it has never really recovered, how can orality be reevaluated as a basis for rethinking our epistemological categories and schemes for action? To answer that question, it is necessary to analyze how the different sites of orality operate.

At the present time, when new diseases bring new challenges to the issue of treatment, the narrative question reemerges: Is it possible to treat without taking account of the stories around disease? How should we update these relations between law, orality, and institutions in Africa? Creating a public sphere for discussion and deliberation is today one of the democratic requirements, but how does orality get involved in forming opinion, in rumor, and in debates and deliberations?

Media, Diversity, and Terrorist Violence

African (sub-Saharan) philosophical thinking did not really take account of the phenomenon of terrorism until the general mobilization by the Organization of African Unity (OAU) against the policy of apartheid, which was labeled terrorist by neighboring states (Mozambique and the two Rhodesias). This lack of interest in the terrorist phenomenon can be partly explained by the relationship the newly independent states had with the notion of violence. Up to the 1970s or thereabouts, the attention of African states was focused, on the one hand, on colonial violence—several countries, in particular Portuguese-speaking ones (Angola, Mozambique, Guinea-Bissau), were still struggling against Portuguese colonial "imperialism"—and on the other hand, on the category of the coup d'état.[6] African political vocabulary at that time—recycling both colonial administrations' terminology and Marxist rhetoric mixed with third-world jargon—only had these phrases: (a) subversive, (b) counterrevolutionary, (c) traitor to the nation, (d) *maquisard* (guerrilla), and (e) mercenary.[7] Terrorism, as the action of a person, group, or even nation-state whose "complexity is the source of difficulties around categorization," did not really appear in the African political lexicon until the African states' concerted struggle against apartheid.[8] The South Africa of that time, a "terrorist state," was not to have diplomatic relations with OAU members.

Gradually the term "terrorist" came to be widely used in Africa to refer to Islamist groups in Sudan, Somalia, Mauritania, Kenya, Tanzania, and the Comoros. Though in Africa the label "terrorism" tends to indicate any violent act of an unknown nature, terrorism already cohabits with longstanding concerns about coups d'états.[9] The terrorist issue encourages us not only to look at the *robustness of postcolonial states* with respect to their ability to contain, prevent, and circumscribe the phenomenon, but also to ask the question about victims. This area (state/victims) would itself be very restricted if we did not add questions of justification/legitimacy, group cohesion, survival, leadership, territory, and hope. Beyond this, it is necessary to examine how cultural and media diversity might help to better contain the social fact of terrorism.

At this point, the description of the current state of affairs mentions some significant dates of terrorist acts. The Horn of Africa has been a major site of terrorist activities, with the dislocation of the Somali state—Somalia has existed without a state structure for about fifteen years—and the liberation struggles in an Eritrea wishing to free itself from Ethiopian colonization and relatively close to Yemen. On 12 September 1969, two members of the Eritrean Liberation Front hijacked an Ethiopian Airlines plane; they were overcome and killed. On 8 December 1972, some others took over another Ethiopian Airlines plane. A bit further south in Sudan, when the civil war was at its height, a Palestinian commando took two Saudi diplomats hostage and executed them on 2 March 1973. In southern Africa Uganda was also the theatre for terrorist operations. On 27 June 1976 an Air France flight from Tel Aviv was diverted on to Ugandan soil, on 30 June non-Jewish hostages were released, on 3 July in the famous Thunderball operation, an Israeli commando freed the hostages. In neighboring Tanzania in February 1982, a commando from the Tanzanian Revolutionary Movement diverted an Air Tanzania plane; on 7 August 1998, the country also experienced an attack from an explosive-filled truck on the American embassy in which eleven died. In Kenya, another attack on the same day against the American embassy in Nairobi left 213 dead and 500 wounded. Other attacks—such as the explosion in mid-flight of a UTA DC10 on 19 September 1989 in the Ténéré desert in Niger—covered Africa with blood. But what interests us here is that, because of young states' "weakness," Africa today remains a favorable site for the proliferation of terrorist groups that could exploit the atmosphere of current conflicts:

- in Ivory Coast, with Liberia and Sierra Leone just emerging from civil wars;
- in Sudan, with Chad as a neighbor, which also has a bone to pick with pockets of former uprisings in the north from the 1970s;
- in Congo, with various interethnic massacres (Ituri) and in particular the Rwandan presence;
- in Rwanda, which is tending the wounds from the genocide with unstable Burundi alongside it
- in Burundi, which is not helped by either Rwanda, whose national unity is uncertain, or Uganda, worn down by the thorn of a fundamentalist rebellion.

These conflicts, which also cause conflicts of interest, involve values, collective identities, and religious elements as well. But in order to get to grips with the phenomenon of terrorism, it is also necessary to understand it without explaining it away.

Ressentiment

Why do people agree to band together against something? Several objective reasons may justify the fact that an individual or group gets involved in terrorist acts in Africa.

Ressentiment is one of those reasons. In the *Genealogy of Morality* (I, §10), Nietzsche defines it as the impression of being powerless in the face of evil, the feeling of always being taken advantage of, and especially internalized anger that one day explodes. Indeed, Nietzsche thinks *ressentiment* is a slave's morality: "The beginning of the slaves' revolt in morality occurs when *ressentiment* itself turns creative and gives birth to values; the *ressentiment* of those beings who, denied the proper response of action, compensate for it only with imaginary revenge."[10] Reality, for a subject who suffers from *ressentiment*, is binary (good/bad) and this binary character is fed by a kind of "falsification" (of reality) that reflects internalized hatred, the powerless person's vengeance when it lashes out at its adversary.

In Nietzsche, *ressentiment* is perhaps interpreted not only from the viewpoint of the weak wanting vengeance but as a ruse of the will to power. Freud adds that hatred itself enters into "impulses of self-preservation."[11] In the context of *ressentiment*, this preservation is itself accompanied by what Max Scheler calls "self-poisoning of the mind."[12] *Ressentiment* never develops alone, it needs precedents. The first is moral; a person feels unjustly treated. *The issue of the definition of the just* is certainly what is most fundamental in the question of *ressentiment* and precedes *the legal question*: "The desire for revenge . . . is always preceded by an attack or an injury."[13] Then *ressentiment* is a *stimulus to action*—which is not a simple reaction as Nietzsche thought—and *acts over the long term*. "The immediate reactive impulse, with the accompanying emotions of anger and rage, is temporarily or at least momentarily checked and restrained, and the response is consequently postponed to a later time and to a more suitable occasion."[14] Finally, *ressentiment* is subject to envy; there is no *ressentiment without desire*: "The nuances of [German] language are precise. There is a progression of feeling which starts with revenge and runs via rancor, envy, and impulse to detract all the way to spite...[but] [u]sually, revenge and envy still have specific objects."[15]

Several types of *ressentiment*, the seedbed of terrorism, can be found in Africa. We can start with *ressentiment* against the state. Since independence, the state has not found favor with civil society, which sees it as an instrument of injustice that covers up the deeds and misdeeds of minorities in power. Why do unpopular governments remain in power? The people—especially the young—find an answer: those governments are the work of *foreigners* and even if they wanted to change them, nothing would happen. Here we find the first stage of *ressentiment*, which is that *impression of powerlessness* and the *feeling of always being taken advantage of*. If the state is not only weak (becoming authoritarian simply because of that) but in addition does not play its regal part equitably, then informal responses emerge. Corruption, money-laundering, and hustling [*la débrouille*] are a veritable constellation on which terrorist activities can lean at both local and international level: "so a criminal with funds from corruption and well-placed contacts finds a favorable environment."[16] And so, as Beatrice Hibou sees it, money-laundering is an everyday operation in Africa because it is closely linked to the informal economy: income from money-laundering is paid into that economy. That *ressentiment* against the state also comes from rebel movements. Thus, when Charles Taylor was in revolt against the Liberian government, once the diamond mines under his control were exhausted, "he used the port of San Pedro in Ivory Coast to export the cannabis that grew in the areas occupied by his guerrilla forces."[17] It has also been noted that the MFDC (a Casamance rebellion in Senegal) grew *yamba* (a drug) to finance the rebellion.[18] The most significant and best known example is the trade in *qa'* (a herbal drug) in Somalia.

Ressentiment is a suppressed hatred, a feeling of powerlessness that awaits "its time" to express itself. Africa feels that powerlessness in various ways: (a) the price of raw materials is fixed by international economic factors; (b) countries' debt keeps on growing; (c) Africa has no permanent representation in the UN Security Council; (d) diseases constantly proliferate and above all the population, which is 60 percent young people, knows it has to beg for its future from other countries. The poor African nations live with the torture of economic and hence political domination. The aid that is given to them (and quickly diverted by their elites) is resented as a humiliation and an obstacle to creativity. What Georg Simmel says so pertinently about begging in the Middle Ages is applicable here: "The rise in begging in the Middle Ages, the crazy distribution of alms, the demoralization of the proletariat brought about by arbitrary donations . . . tended to undermine any creative work."[19] Those beggar nations also contain populations who are *ashamed*. In the context of black Africa, the particular relationships created between *shame, ressentiment*, and *terrorist acts* have not been sufficiently studied. Studies often focus on *hatred* but not on *shame* as the catalyst for some terrorist acts. The exclusion of Africa [from economic self-sufficiency] leads people to see terrorism as a means by which the movements and aspirations of populations will at last be attended to. Unable to join the game of great international decisions in economics and politics, terrorism—to put it bluntly—will force the movers and shakers to take an interest in Africa. That is how the issue of the drug trade in Africa has become important for all Western research into terrorism. And so Nigeria has assumed significance because it is both a hub for the drug trade and a hotbed of religious fundamentalism. The logic that supports these instances of *ressentiment* adds to a series of other very current problems like the humiliation—felt as such, at any rate—caused by massive expulsions of African immigrant populations from Western countries.

In the face of terrorism, the first solution is to *strengthen the rule of law in Africa*. Lack of guarantees for basic freedoms, impunity, and illicit enrichment weaken the state. Structurally incapable of fulfilling its true ruling functions in Africa, the state has left the door open to various fundamentalisms. The issue of relations between religions and states often concerns those who wish to understand the fundamentalist phenomenon, but in the case of sub-Saharan Africa we have to add in the ethnic factor, which may also play a crucial part. In the matter of the rule of law, setting up a *veritable public sphere for expression* and the issue of *social justice* are among the first priorities in Africa. In addition there is the challenge of *xenophobic nationalisms*—here I am thinking of ethno-nationalistic doctrines such as the famous *Ivoirité* in Ivory Coast, which is a half-cultural, half-biologizing symbol of exclusion—and the battles between religious law and essentially secular law (the example of Nigeria).

The role of the media is crucial here. They could give back to the public sphere the opportunity to bring a critical spirit to bear and not just *an ethos of consumption*. In particular, communication policies could think up a kind of control that is not censorship. In what conditions is it possible to control information without censoring it? That may perhaps be the challenge the terrorist phenomenon presents to communication in Africa.

As regards legal means, international arrangements for combating terrorism should perhaps look for the universal moment in each particular case. In other words, ensure that arrangements for combating terrorism are not seen as *colonization* or *repression*, but something relevant to the public good.

And finally, in the economic domain, it is necessary to take account of the informal economy, since all kinds of mafias are parasitical upon it. The informal economy gets more powerful when a state is economically weak; porous borders and gaps in administrative checks open a wide avenue to the parallel economy, which feeds terrorist sectarianism.[20]

Translated from the French by Jean Burrell.

Books between African Memory and Anticipation

THE BOOK SOWS; whether one likes it or not, the book always spreads seeds. The capital letter "L," one element of the symbol for Larousse dictionaries and encyclopedias in France (L is also the first letter of the word "book" in Romance languages), is there for a good reason: it "scatters in every direction." L (either for "livre" or for "Larousse," but let's choose "livre"!) strews to the winds: Would the L therefore be "drunk" [*ivre*]? If so, it would seem that this drunkenness of the book were being censored by all these proclamations concerning the "end of the book" being circulated these days by promoters of immediacy in the audio-visual industry, who promise readers of the early twenty-first century that they will have access to immediate visual, auditory, and iconographic knowledge. The temporal dimension of the detour is replaced by a temporality that is defined through instantaneity.

In their drunkenness, books deliver two paradoxical experiences to humanity. They only sow *unity* among people of the past, the present, and the future in order to better divide them when it comes to the use people make of their contents. That is because the rule [the common form] brings together, but usage and interpretation divide. Books offer knowledge—informative value—only to take it away from the majority: one only "enters" a book when initiated in the codes that cover the rules of spelling and grammar, the latter being the detectives in the police force of spoken and written expression.

Once introduced into African cultures said to be oral, books opened them up to the other cultures of the world—by reading the histories of other peoples, Africans opened up and integrated world history. But this opening immediately produced a closing. Because, just as books appeared in Africa, Africans only entered into world history to be locked into the category of the "Noble Savage." To truly affirm their alterity, Africans would have had to be the other of written civilization. The production and circumscription of books in African colonies—fostered by Islam long before European colonization—was contemporaneous with the acts of archiving, cataloguing, and classification by which geographers, linguists and ethnologists created a figure of the African as "the other."[1] Giving everything while taking back, opening while closing, books construct codes of reading, displace intentions and understandings, and obstinately sow doubts or expectations in an African history whose triumph over the instrument-book is no small achievement. Although they are instruments of knowledge, books cannot be reduced to a simple *Organon* because they are processes of fruition, sowing, and promise. Books are the seeds sown in Africa and they can bear both the fruits of knowledge (of oneself, of others, and of institutions) and the fruits of barbarism. The recording, publication, and dissemination of the ideological books of political dictatorships and religious fundamentalisms are eloquent in this sense. Books are therefore a rich soil of possibilities that, within each individual historic site, can promote the best, while being capable of the worst.

But is "Africa" a fertile site? One can only study the adventure of books, productive activity, and the product-book as a process. How do the symbolic products (books) in circulation in Africa speak, contradict, translate, betray, or cover up the contradictions woven between the places of production and the products? This seems to be the general question posed by the existence and enduring presence of books in Africa. Evaluating the space of the book (the place), as well as the actors involved in it, suggests that all analysis of the book's situation in a particular history should consider it not simply as a *product* but also as a *process*. Books as products are in turn *productive*. As an active link in a process, often in spite of itself, the book has produced a whole imaginary in Africa. Have books not been taken as something sacred there? Have they not been associated directly with scientific knowledge—as if all books were part of knowledge—as they are for the Beti of Cameroon, whose word for "book" is the same as that for "knowledge" (*kalara*)?[2] Process, product, producer: the book is also a symptom. The content of books, the frequency and quality of publications, the legal terms of literary and artistic property, the diligence, harshness, or laxity of censorship all put into perspective the manner in which a society plays around with its moments of creation, covers up the unbearable, and suffocates what can be said. Books in Africa thus become a mirror, displaying, creating doubles and simulacra, reflecting, deforming images, and capable of blinding.

To study books, we could orient our gaze toward at least three perspectives. First, the African collectors, the question here being to determine whether, outside of religious Muslim circles and before the arrival of the Europeans, there existed in Africa a tradition of collecting this tool, the book. What was collected? According to what criteria? Where? This orientation would probe the production circuits and centers of a certain type of knowledge in Africa. As useful as this approach might be, it would certainly miss the book's symbolico-material dimension. Second, one could propose an aesthetic approach, examining the conditions under which books are produced, along with their material form and their dissemination. The questions arising on this level touch upon the modifications that the ornamentation of books would have brought to African aesthetic perception. But this fertile approach would be incomplete if it did not consider the more general dimension of the symbolic. From whence, finally, our orientation here: to understand books by joining them to a social history that is in the process of being made in Africa.[3] The aim of this orientation would be to see how the book—this mirror, this medium, and this symptom—unveils the social categories of a determined history by articulating material production (books are firstly objects), intellectual production, economic accumulation, and symbolic appropriation. Object, knowledge, capital, and policy: books can only be assessed in Africa with respect to this constellation. Our enquiry will turn about four axes to determine how books, so closely tied to the imaginary as objects of mystery and censorship, give Africa access to the other by modifying its relationship with historical memory, on the one hand; and on the other, establishing a form of politics.

Books in the Imaginary: Attractions and Fears

Books and the Libido Imperandi

Books have been perceived by Africans as means of access to political power. Africans were conquered by the military, and they were convinced that the power of the white man came from his books. African novelists describe this quite well. Cheikh Hamidou Kane, Senegalese author of *L'Aventure ambiguë,* wrote of how the young Samba Diallo is torn between the Koranic instruction given by schoolmaster Thierno and the Western school.[4] This dilemma requires a referee, and it is La Grande Royale, an aunt of the young Samba Diallo, who decides in favor of the Western school. Why? "To learn to vanquish without being right." Books and school are therefore the signs of the power that must be won at all costs, a power that would wring the law's neck if necessary. The thirst for reading is here the thirst for power. In the same vein, the novelist Mongo Beti describes, in *The Poor Christ of Bomba,*[5] how newly converted African Christians, to the chagrin of the pious colonial priest, return to "fetishist" practices. The priest consults his cook, the African Zacharie, who answers him something like this: "The Africans followed you, you the Whites, so that you would teach them how to build planes, arms, etc. Instead of this, Father, you spoke to them of the Holy Spirit, of life after death, etc. Did you think they knew nothing of these notions? Well, now, they return to their fetishes." What is in question here is the status of the school and of books as the essence of knowledge and, therefore, of power. The Africans who embraced the school—sometimes under constraints—did not do so to find a substitute for mystical initiation, but to acquire political power, because the introduction of books itself was political.[6] Father Henneman, a German Pallotine priest, remarked that: "The conversion of the pagans of Cameroon began with school: books were the mysterious magnets . . . in the absence of compulsory education and often without their parents' permission, boys and young people hurried to learn the art of reading and writing."[7] There is political significance in the historical fact that the German teacher Christaller was "auctioned off" by the six kings of Douala (Cameroon) who were fighting over him. The teacher was to establish himself on the territory controlled by the highest bidder, which shows that books were perceived by these kings as a sign that would increase their power.[8]

Books as Sacred Objects: Taboos and Fears

In African Islam, the sacred book the Koran is the object of particular veneration. The personal protective talismans of certain marabouts contain pages of Koranic verses carefully enveloped by leather thongs. The page protects, and so does the inscription. This protection works even with a simple reproduction. If a student in a Koranic school, learning to read and write Arabic through the Koran, reproduces a verse on his slate, he will drink the water with which he washes it. This water is reputed to be purifying. Even a mere reproduction maintains the purifying value of what is written. With regard to the Bible, there are examples of conversions based on the "threat of the Bible or the breviary" of the Catholic priests. The Liberian preacher William Wade Harris—founder of the messianic movement that is Harrisism in Ivory Coast and Liberia—had a Bible and a stick with which, according to legend, he defied the power of the sorcerers. Books in general, the Bible in particular, have remained mysterious objects. The breviary, the prayer book of the Catholic priests, also had a mysterious connotation. Was it not, for the first generation of Cameroonian Catholic priests, an instrument of blackmail against the pagans? It is said that when someone refused to give up his or her fetishes to the priest, the latter would often put the breviary on the roof of the house of the fetishist, who trembled with fear before this mysterious object, the Book.

Agents of power, objects of fear, books have incessantly exercised this fundamental contradiction in the imaginary. Years later, the fear of the book would provoke a general distrust of those who "know books." This unconscious fear of books as devilish objects fuels the censorship coming from above.

Books and Prohibition: The Question of Censorship

Seeing and Knowing: The Forbidden

What is censorship? It is the prohibition on knowing the contents of a cultural model, a ban on the spread of images, and an interdiction against being informed of the contents of a book presumed able to have an illocutionary effect modifying a subject's behavior. Prohibition concerns not only the knowing but also the having. Censorship prohibits possession. Any object that is charged with negative motives and symbolically soiled—even if its content is not revealed—can seem dangerous from the censor's point of view, which is why having it is prohibited. Touching, appropriating, and merely approaching the forbidden object are equivalent to blasphemy. It is prohibition against knowing, having and, above all, prohibition against seeing. The dimension of the visible is also important in the contamination of the stain, because the visible excites attention, inflames the subject's imagination, and can lead to action—the censorship of films is illustrative of this point in Africa—hence the voraciousness of interdiction. To know, to see, to have: censorship forbids *homo loquax* to speak. Speech is uncontrollable, a wave that spreads, a fire that consumes and more: if well ornamented with rhetorical frills, it can captivate, enchant, and seduce—that is to say, it can lead one away from the righteous path. A regulation, or even an obliteration of this speech, is therefore useful to the censors. The best example is the impious words that are thought to entrench believers in their sinful state. Censorship is thus a refusal to transmit and communicate, setting up a logic of an identity that has difficulty allowing debate, difference, transition, and contradiction. Through censorship, things must stay the same.

Censorship is not only an interdiction, a negative activity of privation. Transformed, it has become today an example that guides, authorizes, and channels toward what is believed to be just, worthy, and good.

The Franco-German Battle of Books: An Aspect of Colonization

The intensity of Franco-British rivalries in Africa is well known. Historians remember the clashes between the British ambitions to spread their zone of influence from the Cape to the Nile, and those of the French, who also wanted control of the Great Sudan. But the way in which these European rivalries expressed themselves through a battle of books, not just diplomacy or military treatises, has not been sufficiently emphasized. Germany had just lost the war in 1918, and the Treaty of Versailles took away its colonial territories. Under the supervision of the League of Nations, Togo was given to France, South West Africa (Namibia) to South Africa, Rwanda-Urundi to Belgium, and Tanganyika (Tanzania) to Great Britain. As for *Kamerun* (Cameroon), the eastern part was given to France and the western part to England. In French Cameroon, as early as 1923, the French administration took affairs in hand by cleansing all school programs of any "*boche* elements."[9] Those who had attended German schools were "mentally reformed," with an interdiction on speaking or reading German. When it came to the Catholic clergy, this battle of books reached its apex. After the departure of the German Pallotine priests, the Vatican entrusted the direction of Cameroon to a certain François Xavier Vogt who, originally from the Alsace region, had been a German bishop in Tanzania (Alsace was still German before 1918). This bishop, who was German when he set off for Africa, changed his nationality there and practiced in Cameroon, from 1923, as a French bishop. In trouble with the French administration over the forced labor carried out by the indigenous people, he was accused of anti-French activity and especially of having, as an Alsatian, a "*boche* mentality." The best proof was that he dared to read books in "*boche*" and to write a few personal notes in German.[10] In 1928 the conflict between the bishop and the administration escalated and everything was done to remove the former from his episcopal seat. But the Vatican, instead, gave him an adjunct (a bishop's aide), in the person of Monseigneur Graffin, who being very French, would not read "*boche* books."

What was at stake in this battle of books was the very nineteenth-century notion, which had nourished colonial anthropology, that each race has an individual mindset or spirit transmitted by many vectors including books. In order that the "French spirit" might enter Cameroon, therefore, it was useful to forbid books in German.

The Protestant Reform and the Spirit of Trent in the Colonies: Books and Authority

The second form of censorship had to do with the Roman Catholic Church's plans for reading and the politics of books. After the reforms of Martin Luther, John Calvin, and Ulrich Zwingli, the Catholic Church regained control of the formulation of its doctrine—moving toward a more rigid stance. Dogmas were more forcefully redefined, liturgy opted for greater visibility, and information control guided a teaching that became more didactic. It was precisely this modified stance that made for greater control in the training of clerics. The Council of Trent revoked recommendations on seminary reform and the young seminarian involved in theological studies would first learn *to censor himself*—by not reading just any book—and then *to censor others*—in his preaching he would warn Christians against the devilish ruses that insinuated themselves into certain texts. Internal self-censorship meant that all books read by the cleric required the authorization of a bishop or of his parish priest, of the "Ordinariates," according to the formula in use in Canon Law, the well-known *nihil obstat* (no obstacle). The same went for books written by the ecclesiastics, who had to submit their manuscripts to the bishop or to his replacement in order to receive the authorization to publish: the famous imprimatur. The latter was not a mere editorial authorization, but acted as a symbolic witness. The bishop was a witness and guaranteed the purity of a book's content.

This instruction was strictly adhered to in African seminaries. Books published by the Protestants were regarded as heretical. Catholics, who used the catechism in their teachings, distrusted readings from the Bible as conducted by Protestants. The latter, in turn, mistrusted the Catholic catechism, which was not the Bible but a *pensum* of questions and practical answers. In the off-screen battle between the catechism and the Bible, Catholics leaned on the fact that a reading of the Bible without institutional mediators could only lead to misunderstanding and eventually heresy. It was therefore necessary, for them, to use the catechism, the ecclesiastical authorities' mediation par excellence. For Protestants, the catechism was simply a compendium that distorted the basis of the doctrine of faith contained in the Bible. This quarrel between the catechism and the Bible had as its backdrop the problem of authority. In a question of interpretation, who fixes the limits of authority, the ecclesiastical hierarchy or the "holder of truth" that is the biblical text itself? What is interesting is to see and note that in the bosom of the Christian faiths, African believers were exposed to a reciprocal censorship, one side (Protestants) censoring the other (Catholics) over the problem of transmission and instruction.

Censorship through Devalorization: Colonization and the Question of So-Called Vernacular Languages

European linguistic policy mistrusted local languages. I should stress that British colonization, with its system of indirect rule, left up to the "natives" the initiative to speak and even to teach their mother tongues in schools. German colonization was more ambivalent, at times accepting, tolerating, the use of local languages in education: "In the time of the German colonization of Cameroon, the first book used in Yaoundé was Father Nekes's (Fibel) primer or ABC book in Ewondo (a native language). . . . In 1913, the translation of this work into Douala completely abandons gothic writing. . . . We have the schoolmaster's book for the two years of the bilingual (German-local languages) schools, set up, as the preface indicates, in order to respond to government stipulations."[11] Consequently, the book policy that developed did not inhibit local languages. With the ideology of promoting the understanding and assimilation of the religious message, it was useful to know the languages of the colonized, and only the latter have perfect knowledge of their own languages. That is why the first book translated into local languages was the Bible: "Religion was only taught in the mother tongue. Nothing touches hearts better and nothing enters the head more easily than one's own way of speaking."[12] The same policy for books was in effect in German Rwanda-Urundi. Thus, the "catechism itself was a strange mixture of degenerated Kirundi, Swahili, and Kinyarwanda."[13]

Up to a certain point, then, the promotion of local languages was not subject to real censorship or devalorization. Their censorship was mainly an outcome of the assimilation policies adopted by French colonialism. In 1885, Victor Duruy thus defined the role of the French language in school: "If the sword subdues the body, if the plough enriches the peoples, it is the book which conquers souls. Behind each regiment, there must be a teacher. . . . When the natives learn our language, it is our ideas of justice which little by little enter into their spirits: markets open for our industry; it is civilization which arrives and transforms barbarism."[14] To do this, it is necessary to kill local languages. At first degraded to dialects, they were then submitted to infamy. It was forbidden in the colonial schools under French administration to speak in the "vernacular languages." To do so was to expose oneself to the shame of a symbolic punishment: the wearing of a symbol around the neck. This symbol was either a bunch of leaves or the shell of a tortoise or snail. The student who was thus marked for having spoken an African language had to catch another of his comrades speaking the forbidden language in order to be rid of the symbol.

The censorship exercised by the colonizers finds its aides among these young Africans, who learnt in this way to despise themselves [*Selbsthass*]. In these conditions, censorship is not applied to books but to the precondition of books—that is, to language.

State Censorship and Domestic Censorship

Because the state always aspired to be all-powerful in the colonies, its pretensions have often gone beyond its real means: these are *teleological* pretensions (the state defines social goals) and *axiological* pretensions (it participates in the definition of what has worth alongside the other entities of morals and religion). From a terminological point of view, these pretensions are clothed in a legislative artifice called "functions of rule." First of all, the state must protect its citizens from themselves. This is why the undemocratic state dictates how and when to speak. It is up to the state—or so it believes—to outline what it is possible to say, to publish, and to read.

European ministries discreetly control publications in Africa, and in the past books and newspapers there were carefully surveyed. Books were known to be forbidden in France and in the African ex-colonies alike. The case of the book by the novelist Mongo Beti of Cameroon is a good example. In 1972 the essay *Main basse sur le Cameroun* was published by Éditions Maspero in Paris. This described Franco-Cameroonian relations from a polemic angle. It was barely published when it was banned in France by the minister of the interior at the time, Raymond Marcellin, as well as in Cameroon. Other cases probably exist in English-speaking Africa—especially during the apartheid era in South Africa. State censorship can also be passive. Its methods are well known: the book is simply ignored, or made the brunt of an orchestrated "university assassination," ranging from little barbs to ambiguous critical reviews in which the arguments are invariably ad hominem.

Domestic censorship was often practiced within families, notably with regard to comic books and "photo novels," which were purely and simply banned by parents in certain African families, who saw them as the seeds of "banditry." This is how the heroes of these publications (Zembla, Akim, Bleck, Zagor, Miki the Ranger, Spirou, etc.) simultaneously became forbidden objects and role models for young school and college students.

The adventure of books in Africa is inseparable from the notion of prohibition. With censorship—an ancient practice that exists everywhere—one can reflect on its new forms, and on the ambiguous relationships between *creation* and *prohibition*.[15] It is clear that prohibition obstructs creation, but paradoxically it can also be a precondition for it, in the sense that cunning [*métis*], the art of detour, added to the enjoyment of transgressing forbidden territories, produces an oblique form of writing (the famous *logica equina* evoked by Leo Strauss in *Persecution and the Art of Writing*). Individuals are never more creative than when they are forbidden to create.

Books and African Memory: Reviewing the Link

Books and Their Aporias: Horizon, Signs, and Meanings

With the introduction of books, Africa rethinks its relationship to memory, which must be defined in terms of the multiplicity of its entrance points. A collective memory asserts itself over time only by producing detours, spaces, and liaisons.[16] This double role of linking, while at the same time separating, is taken on by books. In this way, books open a *horizon*, because in their writing and in their materiality, they seem to present the exigency of a meeting with the real, while taking upon themselves the asymmetrical character of this meeting. In wanting to reduce the real through the written, books condense the signs while dispersing the meanings. It is this coming and going between the finitude of a book's signs (which can today be counted) and the infinity of meanings that makes books into objects of dissatisfaction, of hunger. All books "hunger to exist" and, when they want to be the reflection of historical reality, they are only received as the opposite. If they want to be only a counterpoint to reality, complicities of tone and expression will quickly be found for them within the reality they set out to critique.

Books are therefore in a tenuous position where all that is left to them is to admit their indigence, which is also their wealth. This object-book is a pile of statements—polished or crude—that opens onto a horizon represented by the process of saying, of enunciation. This historical object, the book, introduces a significant change into African historical memory. First it indicates that this memory must see itself in an aporetic manner. African memory, like the book, is a hunger for being. Afterwards, its own endeavor, on the margins of the accumulation of experiences, remains the permanent negotiation between the finitude of the signs of sociohistoric experience and the infinity of their meanings. How does a historical memory produce its horizon of meaning in the middle ground between signs and their significance?

Memory and Narrative Community

How does a historical memory combine the *closed* nature of its statements (always local, nationalistic, and dated) with *openness* through its enunciation process (which is a constant call toward the possible)? Books beckon the African memory to pay attention to the notion of narrative community. A book is always a composition enriched by the work of imagination. The latter situates and inserts a book into the tragi-comedy of existence. The imagination, and not just the market, makes the book a wandering object that, albeit limited in its diction and circulation within university, commercial, or media circles, finds the drive to move elsewhere, so as to tell the readers, who would shut it into its own little particular story, that it is a wanderer and belongs to everyone, to humanity. It can only justifiably belong to humanity if it is, however, anchored in a narrative community that a group has adopted. Every book expresses the narratives elaborated by a community. Hence the African historical memory, taking its inspiration from the experience of books, will have to operate this change of perspective; to be not only evocation, or invocation of the past, but also convocation of the *not-yet* present. And for this not-yet to come into being, memory must "cobble together" its relationships with the multiple ways in which it is "put into narrative." Memory narrates its self-constitution—as well as that of the book—as a putting into narrative.

All this coexists in a process where, as in the case of a history book, one articulates "that which really happened," both narrated and conveyed through speech and practices, and "that which did not really happen" but is nevertheless conveyed through speech and practices. In the book-transmission process, one can set apart the books that reveal what has happened,[17] thus denoting a kind of authenticity, as well as the apocryphal stories that are also conveyed, but play varying roles of confusing or illuminating the discreet charms of authenticity. The process of establishing apocryphal stories in the transmission of books connotes one thing: all transmission is the construction of a fiction. In relation to the African memory, the question arising from this experience of books is that of reintegrating, within the fragmentation and transmission of collective memories, no longer the truth of past facts, but the inauthenticity of fiction. How can African historical memories, today trapped in a depressive attitude that reflects a feeling of permanent victimization, make a self-critical turnabout that can discern the apocryphal dimension in the constitution of discourse?

Not everything that a book reports is true, even if it is valid from an argumentative point of view; likewise, not everything that Africans say about themselves and African history is true, even if it is valid. This leads to another problem that books raise in Africa: in a historical experience, should one favor the truth of the reported facts or the validity of the discourses? And can there be a fact without the discourse that organizes it, gives it its logic, and reports it? What is a fact without the fiction that shapes it and organizes its presentation? In other words, what is a *truth* without the process of demonstration that *validates* it? In the truths transmitted by collective African memories, what is the dimension of the discourse of fiction and how are the "apocryphal stories" of oral transmission organized?

Between the Oral and the Written: Books, Distances, and Imprints

Some historians, like Le Goff, think that writing effects a historical transformation in the collective memory of oral civilizations. Moreover, it has almost become a habit in university circles to talk of oral societies only in the framework of the distinction between the oral and the written. On the one hand, we find those who, like Jack Goody, believe that the appearance of writing is an advancement that implies modifications of the psyche because mnemonic processes that allow for "word for word" memorization are linked with writing.[18] On the other hand are those who hypostasize orality, finding in its plasticity the catalyst par excellence of historical memory. What has not been said and done about the phrase of the colonial official and Malian writer Amadou Hampâté Bâ: "An old man who dies in Africa is a library that burns"?[19]

I would rather go beyond the written/oral distinction to emphasize, as Paul Zumthor did, that every written text carries "oral clues" [*indices d'oralité*] that writing cannot purely and simply liquidate.[20] Far from choosing between the written and the oral, what is important is to scrutinize how the oral and the written are interwoven in the constitution or destruction of social memory. This interweaving finds its significance in the notion of the *trace*. The trace obeys time, and tries to struggle, both against the rubbing out of its former marks and the untraced territory awaiting marks. From this moment on, the trace "commemorates" its support: the written is always a memorial that, somewhere, signs the death warrant of the object it designates, while speech (which traces and is also a trace in its own way) perpetually replays its future to escape dissipation. In this dialectic between a trace turned over in memory as a monument, and one that traces its furrow in the very terms that imply its disappearance, the book since its arrival in Africa has helped African memory to rethink the notion of trace in a critical period. What does it mean to leave a trace in a time of crisis? Can one reduce everything to the scriptural trace? Events such as the genocide in Rwanda, beyond the question of justice, were not seeking the effacement of traces; and that was the reason for urging African intellectuals to write about the genocide during a training course in a Kigali hotel (under the surveillance of the local government), to trace on paper an experience that no words can adequately describe. Can these genocides, these wounds that will always remain open before the African consciousness, be "condensed," summarized by a few carefully distilled and controlled formulae? Books remain an appeal to the other.

"Structures of Appeal" and "Horizons of Waiting"

Studies on reading distinguish, in every reception of a book, structures of appeal and horizons of expectation. It is the famous literary school of Constance (Hans Robert Jauss and Wolfgang Iser)[21] that has put forward these two notions. Every book is produced and received through the angle of fulfilled or still-open social expectations, which pull it beyond the boundaries of its little community like vacuum sweepers [*aspirateurs*]. Society's expectations are usually in contradiction. And as books are pulled between the time of expectation and the time of appeal, how is the concordance of time created in the heart of a society? How can one think temporality through books in the very terms of their *discordance,* given that expectations are always disappointed by appeals? Books are a means of instituting the social because, through them, we are at the center of the games that are played with time by the anticipations of imagination and the relations of the subject with otherness. Books are thus "memory" and "promise."[22] As promise, they are our "link with the future." And when they become "critical," they deliver the future.

The Politics of Books: What Is Their Future?

Colonial Ideologies: What Educative Politics for Books?

When books—excepting the Koran—were introduced in the colonial period, they served several purposes, the first of which was economic. The governor of French West Africa, Mr. Brevié, affirmed that "colonial duty and political and economic necessities impose a dual task on our work: it is to train native managers who are destined to become our auxiliaries in all fields. . . . From an economic point of view . . . it is to prepare the producers and consumers of tomorrow."[23] Brevié also declared, on 10 May 1924, a decree that reorganized education, of which Article 64 stipulates that: "French will be the only language in schools. Teachers are forbidden to use local idioms."[24] The second purpose of books was political. Books served to give a dependent mentality and an inferiority complex to Africans. Regarding teaching programs, Ernest Nestor Roume, another governor-general of French West Africa, affirmed: "Through well-conducted instruction, the native must be led to a suitable perception of his race. . . . It is an excellent means of subduing the vanity with which he is reproached, to render him modest. . . . All teaching of history and geography must tend to show that France is a rich, powerful nation capable of making itself respected."[25] The final purpose was pedagogical. Books also contributed, during this period, to a better knowledge of others, because after all, whatever their intentions, the best grammars, dictionaries, and judicial compendiums of African languages and civilizations resulted from the patient work of missionaries and colonial administrators. How has this legacy of books been taken up after independence?

INDEPENDENCE AND CONTRADICTION: BOOKS "BREAK DOWN"

African independence was culturally supported by the various nationalist movements and by *Négritude*,[26] the aim of which was to give back to Africans their "souls." Literature was written in national languages, and the means for the diffusion of African thought were created (publishing houses, collections by specialized publishers in France). The need for books made itself felt in domain of literacy education and governments formulated audacious strategies. But with the economic crisis of the years 1970–90, the politics of books suffered a great setback. Here are some obstacles that prevent African books from fully playing their role today:

- Authoritarian regimes (single-party and Marxist), through censorship, have not encouraged free publishing.
- Editorial initiatives are often constrained by subsidies from the French government, from Muslim or Christian ideologies, and from NGOs, all of whose priorities dictate what is and is not publishable.
- The bankruptcy of libraries, which depend either solely on the French government's Francophonie program, with its strategic goals, or on state sources, with the demands implied by this.

- Notions of profitability and timeliness that show less confidence in the university than in the army and the market.
- The lack of faith in thought that universities and intellectual elites display as they invest in financial and political networks.
- The absence of a tradition of reading, which worsens the ideological subproducts diffused by the audiovisual media.
- The fact that African intellectual production (not counting sculpture and music) is considered to be a fringe production at the international level.

To Conclude, Perhaps: Books and the Fiduciary Relationship

The problem of books in Africa is not only logistical. What is needed is neither just libraries, nor computerization—which heralds a little too soon the end of books in favor of the Internet—but a *relationship of trust*. In Africa, there is less and less faith in knowledge. Faith is invested in religiosity, money, and power. One therefore needs to search on a symbolic level for the founding prohibitions structuring our relationship with a faith that is not religious. What does it mean to have confidence within the public sphere? One should perhaps reconsider the *symbolic wounds* on whose basis something can be said among Africans. It would not be without interest to review the subject's attitudes in relation to what the *promise* means, how to assure critical vigilance, and the "maintaining of oneself in the promise."[27] Books are promise, and the important thing is not the content of the promise (which can be harmful or dishonest) but its momentum. Through books, we sound out what makes the link and who institutes the social. "*Lier et lire* [link and read], they are the same letters, pay attention to this," Lacan says.[28] Books link us to history and make us "inhabit time" through the power of this liaison. They will bear fruit in Africa only if a trusting relationship with knowledge is reestablished. "The history of the representation of books . . . is like that of the mirror: symbol of knowledge and vanity, of life and death. A double search—for oneself and for others—books are a mirror; to read is to look in the mirror."[29] The mirror reflects, deforms, produces the double. But watch out—it must be handled carefully: it is fragile!

Translated from the French by Lesley Kemp.

The Internet and the
African Academic World

Any practice, technology, or form of expertise needs an account that can explain its basis and organization as well as its objectives. Whether the Internet is understood as a practice, or as a journey through a space that knows no borders, or whether one curses it as the latest example of human excess (*hybris*), its reality nevertheless raises questions about our experience of the world (*experimentum mundi*). By means of the Internet, we test the world's consistency and go beyond our assumptions to arrive at an exact measure of the relationship between humans and machines. With this in mind, a multicultural, multidisciplinary study was set up in the United States through the publication of *Academy and the Internet,* jointly edited by Helen Nissenbaum and Monroe Price.[1] The book sets out to examine the relations between the Internet and economic issues, as well as the Internet and social problems of equality, politics (the question of public space), and the communicative relationship in a virtual world. Interculturally speaking, only the Chinese contribution gives the debate—which is almost tribal since it is American to the core—an off-center tone. A debate makes statements and analyses, but it also may omit and skate over other perspectives. Africa, which is absent from this debate, almost forces its way in via this paper. What is the relationship between the Internet and present-day African experience? Hardly coping as it is with the consequences of the recent introduction of writing, how is Africa experiencing this Internet adventure, in which the status of images, words, and time seems to be called into question? This brief presentation will look first at the status of technoscience—under which heading the Internet is subsumed in Africa—and then at the challenges the Internet throws up in the region. Our method will be to examine Internet capacities from the viewpoint of oral cultures that are dominated economically.

The Internet in Africa: The Problem of Technological Rationality

On Messianic Expectations

African society's relationship to the Internet should be viewed solely within the general context of the encounter between Africa and techno-scientific rationality. Until the end of the nineteenth century—the period that coincides with the effective colonization of the African continent—it was understood in Europe that science and technology were uniquely European possessions. Given their low intellectual level, Africans should be content merely with a smattering of science. In this connection, a quotation from Georges Hardy, who was involved in colonial education in Senegal in the early twentieth century, is instructive. Hardy quotes Maynard, an apostolic official who eventually became a bishop in the colonies, as saying "we must give a people a moral code before teaching them humanistic knowledge: for pride does not inculcate virtues whereas morality inspires people with the love of work, virtue and science. . . . Such people do not need sciences, they need religious principles, a pure, strict moral code."[2]

In any case, the science that was offered was science as conceived by a kind of nineteenth-century positivism. It was a deterministic science that believed in the idea of progress—a progress that, in the case of the colonized peoples, was destined to take them from a lower to a higher stage. The model of rationality that this science gave colonized people was that of the understanding (*Verstand*)—a rationality that opts for an instrumental apprehension of relations between subjects as well as between subjects and objects.[3] Instrumental rationality had an economic implication in the colonies. Nature and the colonized peoples were to be treated as mere instruments of economic output. Along with progress and instrumental rationality, the techno-science that was presented in the colonies was to cast off myth insofar as myth is an arrangement of narratives that cannot be judged by the criteria of scientific experimentation.

It was in the name of this positivist science that the colonial enterprise constructed a whole hierarchy of civilizations, putting Africans at the bottom of the scale. In order to criticize colonization, black African writers took that technological superiority as their starting point, either to set Africa on the road to progress or to reflect ironically on the unscientific nature of African civilization. At the second black writers and artists' conference, held in Rome from 26 March to 1 April 1959, Alioune Diop, the publisher and founder of the Présence Africaine publishing house in Paris, stated that, "the worst thing we suffer from is our fragility. It has been given different names: inferiority, colonizability, dependency complex, etc. But it has more to do with the fact that the development of technology in the West has got such a big lead that the gulf between our two ways of life has become dangerously hard to bridge."[4] Aimé Césaire, for his part, was sarcastic about Africans' supposed savagery and took aim at the achievements of Western techno-science: "People who did not invent gunpowder or the compass. People who have never managed to conquer either steam or electricity. People who have not explored the seas or the heavens, but know every last inch of the land of suffering. People whose only journeys have been displacements, who have been domesticated and Christianized."[5]

If we wish to assess the relationship between the Internet and African societies, we must not forget that in Africa technology and science are emerging from a feeling of failure on the historical plane. The issue of power has therefore become crucial; the power of whites to discover and domesticate, and from the side of colonized peoples, the power to conquer in order to get free.

In the novel *L'Aventure ambiguë* by the Senegalese writer Cheikh Hamidou Kane, there is some discussion about sending young Samba Diallo to the Western school after instruction in the Koran. But the family is afraid the boy will forget his own culture and put it behind him in favor of Western education and culture. While the family was still debating this issue, young Samba's aunt, La Grande Royale, made the decision: Samba must go to the Western school. Why? Because he needed to acquire the power of science and to learn, in particular, how to use science to conquer as the colonizers did—"to conquer without being right." Marcien Towa, the Cameroonian philosopher, is also one of those who think technology and science would be liberating. "Africa will develop a great modern philosophy only if she becomes or moves towards becoming a great modern power that can affirm her responsibility for the fate of the world without raising a smile. . . . [I]nternational capitalism has imposed itself on our societies because of its superior physical power, which it draws from the scientific knowledge of natural elements and processes and the application of this knowledge to military and productive activities."[6]

What Towa and La Grande Royale do not know is that the model of science offered in Africa is a triumphalist science that no longer exposes its errors and uncertainties but only its increasing ascendancy. What those two thinkers forget is that this model of science entails the famous concept of *development* with its corollaries of *underdevelopment* and *developing*. Thus science becomes the messiah that will save Africa. This messianic conception of the role of science in Africa is realized in the well-known technology transfer. Technologies are transferred to a place whose inhabitants do not know the conditions of production under which these technologies emerged. The Internet arrived in Africa amid this messianic euphoria and is surrounded by this climate of messianic expectation. But what in fact can the Internet do in Africa?

The Issue of Public Space and Equality

The Internet is supposed to promote a new space for citizens. The question of political sovereignty can be considered with reference to the community of citizens. That community is associated with the law and the issue of the social bond. Previously, as Émile Durkheim defines it, religion used to be the basis for social order and hierarchies, but nowadays, with the world's disenchantment (Max Weber), the nation state is attempting to continue the churches' role, with formal citizenship and equality promoting the reign of the autonomous individual. Thus, nations have arisen with political modernity, in which king and priest no longer hold sway, only to be replaced by a vague grouping of individuals called "the people." Not only does the Internet weaken priestly power, but it allows the voices of the smallest to be heard. Therefore, with the Internet we are supposed to witness the creation of forums for public discussion. Each individual at home counts as part of a discussion network. For once the individual's place is clear for all to see.

But in fact, the Internet raises more questions for democracy than it solves. Nowadays the twin phenomena of economic globalization and worldwide standardization of cultures are proof of the weakening of the nation state, so "what today is the vital source of a lasting social bond?"[7] For there to be a public space for discussion, "publicity" alone (in the Kantian sense) is not enough; there must be a genuine education of citizens beforehand. This is not the case with the Internet. The burning question remains: "Is it possible that the Internet phenomenon as a new public space may be moving in the opposite direction, following the tendency to reduce the political space to the level of my agenda?"[8]

First of all, the personalization of forms of discussion—someone writes and someone replies—ends up confirming inequality of access to information,[9] and it has been observed in the context of the United States, that the disparity between men's and women's access to verbal expression is notable.[10]

In Africa, the Internet allows sites of social contact to be created. The cybercafé, regardless of the computers, which may or may not be working, is a place for people to socialize. They come, not to go off into the virtual space of the Web, but to meet friends or strangers and recreate in the communal space of the cybercafé the village baobab or the old folks' veranda: a place to discuss, learn, find out about themselves and others. In Africa, the knowledge acquired from the Internet is not in itself what creates a spirit of citizenship, but the space housing the computer performs that role; people do not come to it to escape from reality into the virtual; they come to meet other people with their respective experiences.

Challenges and Questions from the Internet to the African Experience

Memory: The Panopticon Returns?

The Internet allows my human memory to acquire a stock of information in a short time. Forgetting, whether accidental or deliberate, is one of the great threats to memory. Here, the question of memory affects the different ways Africa tells its story: with its vast memory, for example, the computer could quite easily solve complicated problems of genealogy. Often kinships, alliances, and organization of lineage peter out in the gaps in stories. The anthropological result is confusion in these genealogical narratives between what is *historical* and what simply falls into the category of *cosmogonic* myth. Having a more or less reliable memory, the computer could quite easily help to reconstitute the history of African peoples by making a sharp distinction between *historical narrative, mythological narrative, the gap between these two types of narrative,* and in particular, by showing when and how *history turned into myth* and vice versa. This "infallible" memory would contribute to social peace in Africa. Indeed, a number of conflicts in traditional Africa were fed by the confusion between several types of oral narrative concerning the identity of the first occupiers of a certain space. Resulting problems over land ownership would be quickly solved if there was an instant memory—such as the computer gives us—that could in record time provide us with information on kinships, generations, and succession.

But we could turn this apology for a reliable memory on its head, and consider Ricoeur's "excessive memory" as an argument in favor of memory lapses and forgetfulness. With the computer and the Internet we live in the shadow of generalized surveillance. Michel Foucault, in his preface to Jeremy Bentham's *Panopticon,* reminded us that the eye of power, whose disciplinary strategies tended not only to fragment into a multitude of micropowers but also produced political technologies, was particularly concerned to capture and record all our movements. An all-seeing, all-controlling eye, the desire for blanket control—which is not far removed from a totalitarian will and a *hybris* that pays no attention to finitude—forgets that a good memory is in fact one that to a certain extent allows for a redemptive oblivion. When it is not organized ideologically, forgetting is a sign of the human condition's vulnerability. The Internet no longer allows individuals to feel that vulnerability in their nature; they live with the illusion of omnipotence that an infallible memory reinforces. Referring to "Luis Borges's fable about *el Memorioso,*" Paul Ricoeur reaffirms that: "Forgetting may not therefore be the enemy of memory in every respect, and memory may have to negotiate with forgetting, groping to find the right measure in its balance with forgetting. . . . Could a memory lacking forgetfulness be the ultimate phantasm, the ultimate figure of this total reflection that we have been combating in every register of the hermeneutics of the historical condition?"[11]

The Issue of Speech: Between What Is Said and What Remains to Be Said

The Internet liberates *what is said*; it *gives a platform* to groups who, in that very act, affirm their identity and diversity. What is said does not exhaust the "saying," which is nourished by speech. Once arrived in Africa, the Internet might harm speech, if we do not take care. At the grassroots in Africa, speech is the site of *transposition*; it is not just a means of communication. Through the Internet we communicate, but the issue of *transposition* is often not raised. In Africa, a word issuing from a complaint formulated by a sick person is transposed from the level of the individual sickness to the more political one of the social conflicts of the group to which the sick person belongs.

In the 1960s, Victor Turner, an anthropologist, gave a description of a shamanistic cure among the Ndembu in Zambia, and in that cure ceremony the transposition of the spoken word occurred. A sick person who came to a shaman for his back problems complained about the people living in his village. After a short investigation, the shaman brought the whole village together so that everyone could have a say. While the villagers were speaking, the shaman was pretending to pull out the sick man's tooth. At the high point of the ritual, the sick man was cured. It was an opportunity to explore what was going wrong in the village. The role of speech here was to effect the transition and transposition from the simple situation of the sickness to recreating order in the group by bringing to the surface the contradictions and conflicts that were undermining it. Speech opens a space for transposition moving from *sickness* (an organic problem) via *mysticism* (the shaman invoking the spirits) to end up in *politics* (recreating order by reassessing social conflicts).

The *what is said* involved in Internet communication, however, does not allow these various transpositions—or rather, might do so only slightly—and, in particular, there is no room to raise the serious question that inspires and concerns oral cultures: What happens to speech? The question is not so much "how fast can we communicate?" or "who are we communicating with?" or even "what kind of technical efficiency are we dealing with when we communicate?"—questions that would be relevant to the issue of the Internet's unlimited scope. Speech takes us to the heart of the problematic of *gift* and *debt*.

In African societies the gift of the word is always accompanied by the affirmation of an ethos. The gift of the word is not received or given unless it is enriched by an ethical depth that gives the person who receives or gives it extra meaning, which a simple arrangement of well-chosen words cannot give. The spoken word is associated with a presentation of the self—in other words, the self is always dependent on several narratives that render it a historical being, a being that tells stories.[12] The gift calls for welcome, hospitality, and transmission. It is in this direction that an authentic speech structures individuals' daily lives in Africa. With the Internet, communication brackets the fact that speech is a "gift" and places a duty on giver and receiver to transmit according to strict rules. Here we find the close bond between speech and obligation. You speak only by binding yourself and others.

The Internet, however, does not really create any obligation. On the contrary, it gives those who surf across borders—with no obligation to receive and give speech—the illusion of having words that are not bound by any obligation except that of technical efficiency. But all speech binds: that is the basis of what is specifically human; we say "I give you my word," he "does not keep his word," "I have only one word"; we do not say "I give you my communication," "he does not keep his communication," "he has only one communication." The fact that the word often stands for someone's *honor*, to the extent that it is the guarantor in the *trust relationship* (believe me, I give you my word) encourages us to place it prior to and following any communication. In some African cultures, such as the Dogon, the world emerged from and is supported by spoken words.

African cultures that emphasize speech—ontogenetic speech that makes something come into effect, the curative speech of the traditional healer, an ancestor's speech blessing or cursing—seem to make us aware of this mania for communication, which, if it does not make a space for speech, eventually runs the risk of turning humans into mere beings trained up for banal exchange. Valère Novarina, the drama theorist, tells us there is a difference between speech and communication:

> We shall one day end up dumb if we communicate so much, we shall finally become like the animals, since they have never spoken but communicate very well. Only the mystery of speech separates us from them. In the end we shall become animals: trained by images, brutalized by exchanging everything, turning back into consumers of the world and into material for death. The end of history is speechless.[13]

More than communication, which promises us transparency, speech must have its fair share of mystery that is not related to belief but indicates a distance. Speech opens on to the unknown whereas we communicate only what is known: "Communicators say only what they know while speech possesses other powers. To be precise every word designates the unknown. Say what you do not know. Give what you do not have. What cannot be spoken of is what needs to be said."[14] Speech cultivates that paradox and that impossibility, which is nevertheless possible, and this is why, more than simple communication via the Internet, speech creates both distance and closeness. Distance is part of the very etymology of the word speech (*parole*):

> In French "*parole*" is a contraction of the word "*parabole*" (parable), which appeared around the 11th century. What is a parable? First it is an idea that cannot be expressed directly, a detour of language that has to be made, often using the resources of analogy. But a parable is above all speech with a purpose. It is not delivered merely for the pleasure of speaking or being listened to, or to convey banal information to an audience. A parable is speech that expects change. It is like a detour that can make it possible to reach someone . . . in order to suggest a change. A parable is an appeal.[15]

Conclusion

The Internet raises important questions about African received experience (*Erfahrung*) and lived experience (*Erlebnis*). Beyond the problem of speech, the Internet revises the conception of time in Africa. The Internet's instantaneous time challenges the cyclical nature of *time* in African cultures. What happens to the African Internet user's experience of time when the "instantaneous" encounters the "cyclical"? The second problem is one of *space*. The Internet knows no territorial boundaries and produces a virtual space. What happens when African space, which is generally two-dimensional (visible and invisible), comes up against the question of the virtual? What is a virtual space? By sweeping away the distance between the subject and time, by offering the subject a linear time (in which there are *receivers* and *senders*) with no thickness, Internet users might learn that in Africa time is always a matter of availability and opportunity (*kairos*). This propitious time and space (*kairos*) are an invitation to *action* (*handeln*) that is taunted by the simple doing (*machen*) of the Internet.

Translated from the French by Jean Burrell.

Notes

Preface to the English Edition

1. Theories of reception, such as those of Hans Robert Jauss, Wolfgang Iser, and Umberto Eco, indicate that a text has "structures of appeal" and a "horizon of expectations." The crisis of reading is always a matter of matching up the structures of appeal that a text generates and the historical horizon of expectations in place at the moment of the text's publication.

2. Gerard Genette's considerations in *Seuils* (Paris: Seuil, 1987) are instructive in this regard.

3. Peter Sloterdijk, *Rage and Time: A Psychopolitical Investigation,* trans. Mario Wenning (New York: Columbia University Press, 2010), 138.

4. Jean Godefroy Bidima, *Théorie critique et modernité négro-africaine: De l'école de Francfort à la "Docta Spes Africana"* (Paris: Publications de la Sorbonne, 1993).

5. The Franco-Romanian thinker Cioran confessed sarcastically that he had "been lucky enough to be able to turn his back on the university . . . if he had pursued a university career . . . [he would have] truly been obliged to adopt a serious tone, an impersonal thought. As he once told a French philosopher with a named chair, 'you are paid to be impersonal.'" Glossary, in Emile Cioran, *Oeuvres* (Paris: Gallimard, 2003), 1789.

6. Louisiana is the only state in the United States that employs the resources of the common law as well as the civil code. See Vernon Valentine Palmer: *The Louisiana Civilian Experience: Critiques of Codification in a Mixed Jurisdiction* (Durham: Carolina Academic Press, 2005).

7. Jean Carbonnier, *Flexible Droit*, 9th ed. (Paris: Librairie générale de droit et de jurisprudence, 1998), 24.

8. Manuel Atienza, "Juridicité," in *Dictionnaire encyclopédique de théorie et de sociologie du droit*, ed. André-Jean Arnaud (Paris: Librairie générale de droit et de jurisprudence-Story Scientia, 1998), 208.

9. Slavoj Žižek, *Did Somebody Say Totalitarianism? Five Interventions in the (Mis)use of a Notion* (London: Verso, 2001), 141.

10. Žižek, *Did Somebody Say Totalitarianism?*, 142.

11. Žižek, *Did Somebody Say Totalitarianism?*, 142.

12. Maurice Merleau-Ponty, *The Prose of the World*, trans. J. O'Neill (Evanston, IL: Northwestern University Press, 1973), 68.

13. Gershom Scholem, *Fidélité et utopie, essai sur le judaïsme contemporain* (Paris: Calmann-Lévy, 1994), 84.

14. See Ernst Bloch, *The Principle of Hope*, vol. 1., trans. Neville Plaice, Stephen Plaice, and Paul Knight (Cambridge, MA: MIT Press, 1986).

15. Oskar Negt, *L'espace public oppositionnel* (Paris: Payot, 2007); Laura Hengehold, *The Body Problematic: Political Imagination in Kant and Foucault* (University Park: Pennsylvania State University Press, 2007), 243.

16. Axel Honneth, *La Société du mépris: Vers une nouvelle théorie critique* (Paris: La Découverte, 2006), 191.

17. Nick Nesbitt, *Universal Emancipation, the Haitian Revolution and the Radical Enlightenment* (Charlottesville: University of Virginia Press, 2008), 66.

18. Seneca, *De Ira*; Seneca, "de la colère" I, XVIII, 1, in *Entretiens. Lettres à Lucilius* (Paris: Robert Laffont Bouquins, 1993), 123.

19. Sloterdijk, *Rage and Time*, 69, 111.

20. Sloterdijk, *Rage and Time*, 183.

21. Sloterdijk, *Rage and Time*, 121.

22. Emil Cioran, *Précis de décomposition*, in *Oeuvres* (Paris: Gallimard, 1995), 707.

23. Champagne Thiénot, *Rapport sur les études historiques* (Paris: Imprimerie Impérial, 1868), 356.

24. Herbert Marcuse, *Hegel's Ontology and the Theory of Historicity*, trans. Seyla Benhabib (Cambridge, MA: MIT Press, 1987), 1.

25. Alain Touraine, *Pour la sociologie* (Paris: Seuil, 1974), 94–97.

26. François Hartog, *Les régimes d'historicité* (Paris: Seuil, 2012), 38.

27. Reinhart Koselleck, *Futures Past: On the Semantics of Historical Time*, trans. Keith Tribe (Cambridge, MA: MIT Press, 1985), 275.

28. Hannah Arendt, *Crises of the Republic* (New York: Harcourt, Brace and Co., 1972), 142–43.

29. Arendt, *Crises of the Republic*, 143.

30. Paul Ricoeur, *Oneself as Another*, trans. Kathleen Blamey (Chicago: University of Chicago Press, 1992), 220.

31. Translator's note: The concept of a founding Reference, which is mentioned several times in this book, can be found in Pierre Legendre, *Leçons III: Dieu au miroir. Étude sur l'institution des images* (Paris: Fayard, 1994).

32. Antoine Garapon, "Présentation." In *Pour une démocratie active* (Paris: Odile Jacob, 2007), 18.

33. Stephen Breyer, *Active Liberty* (Oxford: Oxford University Press, 2008), 10.

34. Max Horkheimer, *Notes Critiques (1949–1969)* (Paris: Petite Bibliothèque Payot, 2009), 52.

35. I have already posed this set of questions in an unpublished document, which will constitute a major independent project led by law professor Vernon Palmer and myself.

36. France, which claims to uphold the secular [*laic*] character of its state form since the law separating church and state in 1905, has given francophone legal scholars and philosophers who follow its model the illusion of the state's secularism. Two facts bring out the problematic nature of the French state's secularism:

1. Mgr. Roncalli, the future Pope John XXIII—whom Hannah Arendt, in *Men in Dark Times* (New York: Harvest, 1970, 57), called a Christian on St. Peter's chair—was named apostolic nuncio in France to 1944 and charged with carrying out the purge of French bishops who had collaborated with the Vichy government. Roncalli became cardinal while in office in Paris and "January 15, 1953, President Vincent Auriol, taking advantage of a special privilege traditionally reserved for French heads of state . . . gave him the red biretta. He then awarded Roncalli with the Legion of Honor and made a speech" (in Peter Hebblethwaite, *Jean XXIII, Le pape du Concile* [Paris: Le Centurion, 1988], 261). What Hebblethwaite does not mention but can be seen in the visual archives is that the future pope is kneeling before the president of the very secular French Republic and its government to receive the emblems of his title as cardinal of the Roman Catholic Church. The year 1953 (the date of the ceremony on which the future Pope John XXIII received the cardinal's biretta) is forty-eight years from 1905 (date of the Combes law on the separation of church and state in France).

2. Nicolas Sarkozy, ex-president of France, received the Honorary Canon of St. John Lateran in Rome (a title reserved for heads of the very secular French state). The question of the state's secularism in France, at least, is a huge matter of denial, which is why it is so important to reopen *palabre* during crises such as those of the Islamic veil in the French public school.

The United States at least assumes this contradiction calmly: the president takes his oath on the Bible and the Constitution begins by invoking the people: "We the people."

37. Michel Foucault, *The Birth of Biopolitics, Lectures at the Collège de France 1978–1979*. Ed. Michel Senellart, trans. Graham Burchell (New York: Picador, 2008), 249.

38. Foucault, *The Birth of Biopolitics*, 254.

39. Gérard Courtois, "La vengeance, du désir aux institutions" in *La vengeance*, vol. 4, *La vengeance dans la pensée occidentale* (Paris: Éditions Cujas, 1985).

40. Véronique Nahoum-Grappe, *Du rêve de vengeance à la haine politique* (Paris: Buchet-Chastel, 2003), 21.

41. Lawrence M. Friedman and Jean Guy Belley, "Juridicisation," in *Dictionnaire encyclopédique de théorie et de sociologie du droit*, ed. André-Jean Arnaud (Paris: Librairie générale de droit et de jurisprudence-Story Scientia, 1998), 204.

42. François Ost, *Dire le droit faire justice* (Brussels: Éditions Bruylant, 2007), 34.

43. Ost, *Dire le droit faire justice*, 40.

44. Ost, *Dire le droit faire justice*, 52.

45. Certainly Germany was a great military power in the twentieth century. The tribunals of Nuremberg, Yugoslavia, and Rwanda each had specific concerns. However, we have never seen international trials on French "activities" in Indochina and Algeria, on the Chinese authorities' response to the revolution of Tien An Men, and on the spread of Russian "security" in Chechnya and Georgia, not to mention Abu Ghraib.

46. See Statute of the International Military Tribunal of Nuremberg, article 19, in Jean-Paul Bazelaire and Thierry Cretin, *La justice pénale internationale* (Paris: Presses Universitaires de France, 2000), 129.

47. Robert Cario is professor of criminology at the Université de Pau in France. See Howard Zehr, *The Little Book of Restorative Justice* (Intercourse, PA: Good Books, 2002). We have been told that the book has already been translated into Spanish and German. See Robert Cario, "Preface," in Howard Zehr, *La Justice restaurative. Pour sortir des impasses de la logique punitive* (Geneva: Éditions Labor et Fides, 2012).

48. Zehr, *The Little Book of Restorative Justice*, 21.

49. Zehr, *The Little Book of Restorative Justice*, 21.

50. Paul Ricoeur, *Reflections on the Just*, trans. David Pellauer (Chicago: University of Chicago Press, 2007), 62.

51. Cheikh Hamidou Kane's novel *L'aventure ambiguë* emphasizes this point of view by means of La Grande Royale's opinions. The school and the book aid in the acquisition of a power to conquer.

52. Michel de Certeau, *Histoire et psychanalyse entre science et fiction* (Paris: Gallimard, 1987), 72.

53. Bernard Stiegler, *Taking Care of Youth and the Generations*, trans. Stephen Barker (Stanford, CA: Stanford University Press, 2010), 175.

54. Stiegler, *Taking Care of Youth*, 131–32.

55. Two Internet subscribers in the same room logged on to two different servers seem to share the virtual space even though it is apparently fragmented. Everything happens as if each Internet provider had privatized space with a key, which is nothing other than the access code.

56. Henri Musso, *Critique des réseaux* (Paris: Presses Universitaires de France, 2003), 326.

57. To have a network, to manage a network, is often supposed to mean: to be in contact with a set of people who do not know one another and who will not meet one another, but who must serve each of us to the extent of their competences and at the pleasure of circumstances. The only way to enrich this network—Facebook, Badoo, etc.—is by extension, because it misses the symbolic dimension of the encounter with the other.

58. Antoine Garapon, *Le gardien des promesses: Justice et démocratie* (Paris: Éditions Odile Jacob, 1996), 74.

59. Pierre Legendre, *Dominium Mundi* (Paris: Mille et Une Nuits, 2007), 32–33.

60. Here we are thinking of the French title of a book on Nietzsche by Sloterdijk: *La compétition des bonnes nouvelles: Nietzsche évangéliste* (Paris: Mille et Une Nuits, 2002).

61. Read on this topic the illuminating analyses of Dany-Robert Dufour, *L'Individu qui vient . . . après le libéralisme* (Paris: Denoël, 2011), 113–14.

62. Jean-Pierre Vernant, *The Origins of Greek Thought* (Ithaca, NY: Cornell University Press, 1982), 49–50.

63. The Hellenist Nicole Loraux tells us that the ancient Greek term for designating reconciliation is close to the term for expressing division: "*Dialuō*: I untie; *dialuō*: I reconcile. I separate/I weave again what has come undone." In *The Divided City*, trans. Corinne Pache with Jeff Fort (Cambridge: Zone Books, 2002), 95.

64. Cynthia Fleury, *Les Pathologies de la démocratie* (Paris: Fayard, 2005), 125.

65. Étienne Leroy, *Le jeu des lois: une anthropologie "dynamique" du droit* (Paris: LGDJ, 1999), 139.

66. Chantal Delsol, *L'âge du renoncement* (Paris: Éditions du Cerf, 2011), 195–97; Denis Salas, *La volonté de punir: Essai sur le populisme pénal* (Paris: Hachette, 2005), 251.

67. Pierre Rosanvallon, *Democratic Legitimacy: Impartiality, Reflexivity, Proximity*, trans. Arthur Goldhammer (Princeton, NJ: Princeton University Press, 2011), 29.

68. Mylène Botbol-Baum, ed., *Bioéthique dans les pays du sud* (Paris: L'Harmattan, 2005).

69. Bénézet Bujo, *Foundations of an African Ethic: Beyond the Universal Claims of Western Morality*, trans. Brian McNeil (New York: Crossroad Publishing, 2001). Bujo was professor of moral theology at the University of Freiburg in Switzerland.

70. Madeleine Rivière, *Lettre de la psychiatrie française*, no. 90/99 (2000): 23.

71. Emmanuele Danblon, "Rhétorique, universalité et ritualité: Réflexions à propos de la palabre." In *Les Cahiers de la MSHE Ledoux*, 2009, 195–207. Emmanuelle Danblon is a specialist in rhetoric and teaches at the Université Libre de Bruxelles.

72. Klute, Georg, Birgit Embaló, Idrissa Embaló, "Local Strategies of Conflict Resolution in Guinea-Bissau. A Project Proposal in Legal Anthropology." In *Recht in Afrika* 2, 2006: 253–72.

73. Jacques T. Godbout. *Ce qui circule entre nous: Donner, recevoir, rendre* (Paris: Seuil, 2007), 370.

74. See Robert Campana, "De l'intervention punitive ou de l'extension du droit pénal aux relations internationales," in *Studia philosophica* 64, 2005, 233; and Daniel Lopes, "Médiations politiques africaines "par le haut;" Analyse empirique et essai de théorisation," In *Perspectives Internationales* 3, Janvier/Juin 2013, 58.

75. Sévérine Kodjo-Grandvaux, *Constructions et déconstructions de l'idée de "philosophie africaine": Étude comparative des œuvres de Jean-Godefroy Bidima, Souleymane Bachir Diagne, Henry Odera Oruka et Kwasi Wiredu* (Université de Rouen, 2006). This thesis will be published under the title *Philosophie africaines* (Paris: Présence Africaine, 2013).

76. Francis Abiola Irele; "Bidima Jean-Godefroy," in *Africana: The Encyclopedia of the African and African American Experience*, ed. Kwame Anthony Appiah and Henry Louis Gates, Jr. (New York: Oxford University Press, 2005).

77. The encyclopedic dictionary *Quillet* (Paris: Larousse, 1970) defines *palabre* as "a gift that merchants made to small kings along the coast of Africa; interminable discussion in the course of which these gifts were made; by extension, long and unnecessary discourse . . . to "palabrer" . . . to converse at length with indigenous authorities; by extension, long and unnecessary discourse," 4853. One could cite numerous examples of this way of conceiving *palabre*.

Introduction: "Speech, Belief, and Power"

1. Tsenay Serequeberhan, *The Hermeneutics of African Philosophy: Horizon and Discourse* (New York: Routledge, 1994).

2. Two examples might be Mohammed 'Abed al-Jabri, *Arab-Islamic Philosophy: A Contemporary Critique*, trans. by Aziz Abbassi (Austin: University of Texas Center for Middle Eastern Studies, 1999) and Olúfémi Táíwò, *How Colonialism Preempted Modernity in Africa* (Bloomington: Indiana University Press, 2010).

3. Marcien Towa, *Essai sur la problématique philosophique dans l'Afrique actuelle* (Yaoundé, Cameroon: Éditions Clé, 1971).

4. Jean Godefroy Bidima, *Théorie critique et modernité négro-africaine: De l'école de Francfort à la "Docta Spes Africana"* (Paris: Publications de la Sorbonne, 1993).

5. Bidima, *Théorie critique*, 24–25, 282–83.

6. Frantz Fanon, *Black Skin, White Masks*, trans. Charles Lam Markman (New York: Grove Press, 1967).

7. See section 2 of *La Palabre*, "A Political Paradigm."

8. Hannah Arendt, *On Revolution* (New York: Viking Press, 1963).

9. Hannah Arendt, *Lectures on Kant's Political Philosophy*, ed. Ron Beiner (Chicago: University of Chicago Press, 1982).

10. Hannah Arendt, *Between Past and Future: Eight Exercises in Political Thought* (New York: Penguin, 1993), 223.

11. Immanuel Kant, "Perpetual Peace: A Philosophical Sketch," in *Political Writings*, ed. Hans Reiss, trans. H. B. Nisbet (Cambridge: Cambridge University Press, 1970), 130.

12. Arendt, *On Revolution*.

13. Paul Ricoeur, *From Text To Action*, vol. 2, trans. Kathleen Blamey and John B. Thompson (Evanston, IL: Northwestern University Press, 1991), 320, 324.

14. O. Oko Elechi summarizes some of these concerns in *Doing Justice without the State: The Afikpo (Ehugbo) Nigeria Model* (New York: Routledge, 2006), 42–43.

15. Ricoeur, *From Text to Action*, 335.

16. See section 2 of *La Palabre*, "A Political Paradigm," The public sphere is a political notion often associated with Jürgen Habermas, whose groundbreaking historical study of the eighteenth-century European public sphere laid the basis for his account of the public sphere's role as representative of the "communicative rationality" of the lifeworld in modern deliberative democracies over thirty years later. See *Between Facts and Norms: Contributions to a Discourse Theory of Law and Democracy* (Cambridge, MA: MIT Press, 1991).

17. See section 2 of *La Palabre*, "A Political Paradigm."

18. Bidima, *Théorie critique*, 94–95.

19. Jean-François Lyotard, *The Différend: Phrases in Dispute*, trans. Georges Van Den Abeele (Minneapolis: University of Minnesota Press, 1988).

20. Nancy Fraser, "Rethinking the Public Sphere: A Contribution to the Critique of Actually Existing Democracy," in *Habermas and the Public Sphere*, ed. Craig Calhoun (Cambridge, MA: MIT Press, 1992), 109–42.

21. See section 3 of *La Palabre*, "Convergent Suspicions"; Bidima, *Théorie critique*, 151–53.

22. Bidima, *Théorie critique*, 143–44, 208; see section 3 of *La Palabre*, "Convergent Suspicions"; also, Nkiru Uwechia Nzegwu, *Family Matters: Feminist Concepts in African Philosophy of Culture* (Albany: State University of New York Press, 2006).

23. See section 3 of *La Palabre*, "Convergent suspicions."

24. See also Elechi, *Doing Justice without the State*.

25. Florence Bernault, ed. *A History of Prison and Confinement in Africa,* trans. Janet Roitman (Portsmouth, New Hampshire: Heinemann, 2003); see also section 1 of *La Palabre,* "The Public Space of *Palabre.*"

26. Michel Foucault, "The Eye of Power," in Jeremy Bentham, *Le Panoptique* (Paris: Pierre Belfond, 1977).

27. Achille Mbembe, *On the Postcolony.* Berkeley: University of California Press, 2001.

28. See section 1 of *La Palabre,* "The Public Space of *Palabre.*"

29. Angela Davis, *Are Prisons Obsolete?* (New York: Seven Stories Press, 2003); Hermann Bianchi, *Justice as Sanctuary: Toward a New System of Crime Control* (Bloomington: Indiana University Press, 1994); Ruth Morris, *Penal Abolition: The Practical Choice* (Canadian Scholars Press, 1998).

30. Táíwò, *How Colonialism Preempted Modernity.*

31. See in this volume "Strategies for 'Constructing Belief' in the African Public Sphere."

32. See section 4 of *La Palabre,* "A Difficult Place in Political Thought."

33. Nzegwu, *Family Matters*; Marc Epprecht, *Heterosexual Africa? The History of an Idea from the Age of Exploration to the Age of AIDS* (Columbus: Ohio University Press/University of KwaZulu-Natal Press, 2008)

34. Bidima, *Théorie critique,* 194–95; see also Jean Godefroy Bidima, "Croire: Interrogations Philosophiques sur les Réligions en Afrique: Représentations, Institutions et Médiations," in *Philosophy of Religion,* vol. 10, *Contemporary Philosophy,* ed. Guttorm Fløistad (Dordrecht: Springer, 2010), 275–302.

35. Bidima *Théorie critique,* 16, 135.

36. Bidima, *Théorie critique,* 18.

37. Bidima, *Théorie critique,* 121–23.

38. See section 2 of *La Palabre,* "A Political Paradigm."

39. See section 4 of *La Palabre,* "A Difficult Place in Political Thought."

40. Bidima, *Théorie critique,* 166.

41. Bidima, *Théorie critique,* 182.

42. Bidima, *Théorie critique,* 190–92.

43. Bidima, *Théorie critique,* 164–66.

44. See "The Internet and the African Academic World" in this volume.

45. Táíwò, *How Colonialism Preempted Modernity.*

46. See Conclusion to *La Palabre.*

47. Bidima, *Théorie critique,* 229.

48. Wole Soyinka, *The Burden of Memory, the Muse of Forgiveness* (Oxford: Oxford University Press, 1998); Richard A. Wilson, *The Politics of Truth and Reconciliation in South Africa: Legitimizing the Post-Apartheid State* (Cambridge: Cambridge University Press, 1999).

49. *Gacaca* is a traditional conflict resolution procedure used in Rwanda. See Philip Clark, *The Gacaca Courts, Post-Genocide Justice and Reconciliation in Rwanda: Justice without Lawyers* (Cambridge: Cambridge University Press, 2010). *Ubuntu* is a term in some South African languages that philosophers and theologians have developed into a principle linking ontological human interdependency to collective moral obligation. See Mogobe B. Ramose, "The Philosophy of *Ubuntu* and *Ubuntu* as a Philosophy," in *The African Philosophy Reader, Second edition,* ed. Pieter H. Coetzee and Abraham P. J. Roux (London: Routledge, 2003), 230–38.

50. Paul Ricoeur, "Entretien," in *Éthique et responsabilité: Paul Ricoeur,* ed. Jean-Christophe Aeschlimann (Neuchâtel: Éditions à la Baconnière, 1994), 26.

51. Jacques Derrida, *On Cosmopolitanism and Forgiveness.* Trans. Mark Dooley and Michael Hughes. Preface by Simon Critchley and Richard Kearney (London and New York: Routledge, 1997).

52. See in this volume "African Cultural Diversity in the Media."

La Palabre: Introduction / 1. The Public Space of *Palabre*

1. Japanese businesses use the practice of *ringesei*. This is a sort of permanent *palabre* consisting in negotiated, temporary interactions that stage a provisional cooperative consensus within the enterprise.

2. With respect to the *irénè* and the *agôn*, we are borrowing the classification in Francis Jacques, *Espace logique d'interlocution* (Paris: PUF, 1985).

3. Translator's note: The concept of a *différend* is employed by Jean-François Lyotard to indicate a conflict that cannot be resolved for lack of a common language or frame of reference. Jean-François Lyotard, *The Différend: Phrases in Dispute*, trans. Georges Van Den Abbeele. Theory and History of Literature, vol. 46 (Minneapolis: University of Minnesota Press, 1988).

4. Benoît Atangana, "Actualité de la palabre?" *Études* 324 (1966): 461. All quoted material translated by Laura Hengehold and David Stute unless a specific English-language edition is cited.

5. Translator's note: *Entretien* means discussion, but also a way of maintaining.

6. A. J. Greimas, "Pour une sémiotique topologique," in *Sémiotique de l'espace* (Paris: Denoël-Gonthier, 1979), 12.

7. Jean Carbonnier, *Flexible droit* (Paris: Librairie générale de droit et de jurisprudence, 1975), 279.

8. Translator's note: The term was employed by anthropologist Edward T. Hall.

9. Having no experience of a centralized type of government, the societies called "acephalic" (e.g., the Beti of Cameroon) have a weaker attachment to the procedure of *palabre*, while state societies (e.g., the Buganda of Uganda) had a very rigorous approach to this procedure.

10. Translator's note: *Juridiction* is a complex term meaning simultaneously legal authority, those over whom legal authority is exercised, and the space linking them. Jurisdiction can also mean "court" or "tribunal" and I have translated in this sense sometimes to show the interplay between both meanings.

11. Gérard Balanda, "L'organisation judiciaire chez les Basakata, les Badja et les Boma" in *L'organisation judiciaire en Afrique*, ed. John Gilissen (Brussels: Éditions de l'Institut de Sociologie, Université libre de Bruxelles, 1969).

12. We will come back to this distinction *brevitatis causa* that, to be sure, has no exact equivalent in African tradition.

13. Translator's note: With the author's agreement, the singular "he" in French has been rendered "he or she" where appropriate.

14. Katik Diong Bakomba, "La palabre africaine," in *Les imaginaires* (Paris: Union Générale d'Éditions, 1976).

15. These oracles are also found among the Banda of Central African Republic. See Maryse Raynal, *Justice traditionelle, justice moderne* (Paris: L'Harmattan, 1995), 220 ff.

16. Raynal, *Justice traditionelle*, 236. The Ngbaka, for example, seek the intervention of the deceased in the search for truth with the help of a calabash placed on the tomb. As it releases fluid, the calabash will fill and, depending on the angle of seepage, a diagnosis will be pronounced.

17. Raynal, *Justice traditionelle*, 241.

18. Raynal, *Justice traditionelle*, 242.

19. Raynal, *Justice traditionalle*, 248.

20. A standard practice among the Ngbaka and Nzakara of Central African Republic.

21. Translator's note: In the French judicial system, *cours d'assises* are responsible for serious crimes that can lead to significant prison terms. It is the only court whose jurisdiction is restricted to criminal cases and in which trials are conducted before a jury in addition to the usual panel of professional judges.

22. Bakomba, "La palabre africaine," 190. The citation is taken from André Jolles, *Formes simples* (Paris: Seuil, 1972)

23. Bakomba, "La palabre africaine," 185.

24. Raymond Mel Meledje, "Emokr: Systèmes de gestion des conflits chez les Odjukru" (PhD diss., École des Hautes Études en Sciences Sociales, 1994), 102. www.theses.fr.

25. See the unfolding of *palabre* among the Beti in Philippe Laburthe-Tolra, *Les Seigneurs de la forêt* (Paris: Publications de la Sorbonne, 1981), 347.

26. Marc Augé, *Théorie des pouvoirs et idéologie* (Paris: Hermann, 1974), 61.

27. Balanda, "L'organisation judiciaire," 113–14.

28. Atangana, "Actualité de la palabre?," 462.

29. There exist in Ivory Coast tribes who established a system of perpetual peace. This was "signed" on the occasion of a human sacrifice. Between the Dida and the Odjukru, for example, a prohibition was placed on resorting to war and, in return, both were obliged to aid each other. See H. Memel Foté, "De la paix perpétuelle dans la philosophie pratique des Africains," *Présence africaine* 55 (1965): 21–22.

30. Atangana, "Actualité de la palabre?," 462.

31. Meledje, "Emokr: Systèmes de gestion," 125.

32. Among the Pkellé of Liberia, to save honor, one blames both the winner and the loser of the trial. James L. Gibbs, "The Kpelle Moot: A Therapeutic Model for the Informal Settlement of Disputes," *Africa* 33, no. 1 (1963): 5.

33. Meledje, "Emokr: Systèmes de gestion," 109.

34. Translator's note: The concept of a "language game" is used by Wittgenstein to indicate the collective *practice* making meaning possible.

35. Erving Goffman, "The Interaction Order: American Sociological Association, 1982 Presidential Address," *American Sociological Review* 48, no. 1 (1983): 1–17.

36. Hans Georg Gadamer, *Truth and Method,* 2nd revised edition, trans. Joel Weinsheimer and Donald G. Marshall (London: Continuum, 2004), 446.

37. Catherine Kerbrat Orecchioni, *Les interactions verbales,* vol. 1 (Paris: Armand Colin, 1990).

38. Orecchioni, *Les interactions verbales,* 164.

39. Orecchioni, *Les interactions verbales,* 171–73. See also Pierre Bange, *Analyse conversationnelle et théorie de l'action* (Paris: Hatier/Didier, 1992), 35.

40. Guy Menga, *La Palabre sterile* (Yaoundé, Cameroon: Éditions Clé, 1970), 94.

41. Translator's note: While both *droit* and *loi* can be translated as "law," *droit* conveys the ideal, abstract sense of law as "lawfulness" or "justice" as well the body of legal writings and practice taken as an object of study, while *loi* refers more to specific statutes and decisions.

42. This principle is formulated in the following way: "Given the topic of your comments and what you hope to achieve, let your contribution to the conversation conform to what is required by the commonly accepted framework." François Flahault, "Le Fonctionnement de la parole," *Communication* 30 (1979): 73. During this "cooperation," we find the symbolization of the interlocutor and a demand for mutual recognition.

43. Orecchioni, *Les interactions verbales,* 92.

44. This is an interrogative figure used by the speaker in order to trap the one spoken about [*énonciataire*]. It gives the latter an opportunity to justify him or herself.

45. Cataplexis is a threat, a figure intended to clarify the sentence of a criminal judged guilty. It uses hyperbole to show the accused the gravity of the acts he or she is accused of committing. It brings psychological pressure to bear on the accused.

46. Gérard Cornu, *Linguistique juridique* (Paris: Montchrestien, 1990), 217.

47. Cornu, *Linguistique juridique,* 217. Translator's note: Loosely: the application or petition, the object of the claim, the allegation, the supporting evidence, and the legal justification for a decision. From D. C. Van Hoof, D. Verbruggen, and C. H. Stoll, eds., *Elsevier's Legal Dictionary: In English, German, French, Dutch and Spanish.* (Amsterdam: Elsevier, 2001).

48. Cornu, *Linguistique juridique,* 244.

49. "A discourse can be juridical even if it uses no legal terms. . . . A juridical discourse can be composed of nothing but everyday words" (Cornu, *Linguistique juridique*, 213).

50. See Pathé Diagne, "Accès à la justice dans les quartiers urbains pauvres: Dakar, Abidjan, Niamey, Ouagadougou," in *Pauvreté urbaine et accès à la justice en Afrique*, ed. Alioune Badiane et al. (Paris: L'Harmattan, 1995), 60.

51. See *La justice dans les pays francophones* (Paris: ACCT, 1995) (results of the conference of francophone ministers of justice, October–November 1995), 3–5.

52. See the analysis of diverse meanings of the judiciary robe given by Antoine Garapon in *L'Âne portant des reliques: Essai sur le rituel judiciaire* (Paris: Le Centurion, 1985), 65–80 (reedited under the title *Bien juger, essai sur le rituel judiciaire* [Paris: Odile Jacob, 1997]).

53. Garapon, *Âne portant des reliques*, 100.

54. Garapon, *Âne portant des reliques*, 101.

55. Menga, *La Palabre sterile*, 94.

56. See Diagne, "Accès à la justice," 59–69.

57. Translator's note: "Justice of proximity" was an effort to integrate mediation and community-based justice into French legal theory and practice during the 1980s and 1990s, partly in response to an increase in the criminal justice caseload and its potential for politicization. For an overview, see Adam Crawford, "Justice de proximité—The Growth of Houses of Justice and Victim/Offender Mediation in France: A Very UnFrench Legal Response?," *Social and Legal Studies* 9, no. 1 (2000).

58. Here one could also cite the *san* custom in Burkina Faso during which there is a reciprocal offering of presents. On this subject see J. Yado Toe, "Les modes informels de régulation des délits et des conflits dans les quartiers pauvres de Ouagadougou," in *Pauvreté urbaine et accès à la justice en Afrique*, ed. Alioune Badiane et al. (Paris: L'Harmattan, 1995), 333.

59. D. Main, "L'acte de juger," *Pouvoirs* 55 (1990): 108.

60. Diagne, "Accès à la justice," 63.

61. George Hérault, "Modes informels de résolution des conflits dans les quartiers pauvres d'Ibadan," in *Pauvreté urbaine et accès à la justice en Afrique*, ed. Alioune Badiane et al. (Paris, L'Harmattan, 1995).

62. In the first group we must mention Mali, Madagascar, Guinea, Ivory Coast, Benin, Rwanda, and Burundi. In the second group, consider Central African Republic, Cameroon, Niger, Togo, and Chad. From *La justice dans les pays francophones*, 19–27.

63. Michèle Guillaume Hofnung, *La médiation.* "Que Sais-Je?" (Paris: Presses Universitaires de France, 2000), 113–14.

64. Jean-Pierre Bonafé-Schmitt, *La médiation: une justice douce* (Paris: Syros, 1992), 257–58.

65. Jean Carbonnier, *Flexible droit* (Paris: Librairie générale de droit et de jurisprudence, 1979), 45.

66. Antoine Garapon, *Le gardien des promesses* (Paris: Odile Jacob, 1996), 119–31.

67. Garapon, *Le gardien des promesses*, 95.

68. Garapon, *Le gardien des promesses*, 82 ff.

69. Garapon, *Le gardien des promesses*, 222.

70. Title of a book by Martin Heidegger, *On the Way to Language*, trans. Peter D. Hertz (New York: HarperCollins, 1971).

2. A Political Paradigm

1. Translator's note: In these texts, the "symbolic" dimension should usually be understood in the Lacanian structuralist sense of discourses, laws, identities, and institutions that situate the speaking subject and represent him or her in cognition and deliberation.

2. Atangana, "Actualité de la palabre?."

3. Atangana, "Actualité de la palabre?," 462.

4. Translator's note: The reference is to the poem "La Beauté." Charles Baudelaire, *Les Fleurs du Mal*, trans. Richard Howard (Boston: David R. Godine, 1982), 202.

5. Translator's note: The distinction between "hot" societies organized around a sense of linear time and "cold" societies dominated by awareness of cyclical patterns in time comes from Claude Lévi-Strauss, *Structural Anthropology*, vol. 2, trans. Monique Layton (New York: Basic Books, 1976), 29.

6. Georges Balandier, *Anthropo-logiques* (Paris: Le Livre de poche, 1985), 250. Balandier criticizes exactly this point of view.

7. Atangana, "Actualité de la palabre?," 461.

8. Georges Bataille, *Inner Experience*, trans. Leslie Anne Boldt (Albany: State University of New York Press, 1988), 45.

9. Translator's note: Latin for "self."

10. Georges Bataille, in *Écrits posthumes: Oeuvres complètes*, vol. 2 (Paris: Gallimard, 1970), 370.

11. Translator's note: "Learned ignorance" is a concept employed by the late medieval philosopher Nicholas of Cusa.

12. Raphaël Draï, *Le pouvoir et la parole* (Paris: Payot, 1981), 150.

13. See Hannah Arendt, *Men in Dark Times* (New York: Harvest, 1970), 79.

14. Arendt, *Men in Dark Times,* 30.

15. Immanuel Kant, "Perpetual Peace: A Philosophical Sketch," in *Kant: Political Writings*, 2nd edition, ed. Hans Reiss, trans. H. B. Nisbet. (Cambridge: Cambridge University Press, 1970), 126.

16. Claude Lefort, *Democracy and Political Theory*, trans. David Macey (Minneapolis: University of Minnesota Press, 1988), 218–19.

17. See Emmanuel Lévinas, *Le temps et l'autre* (Paris, Artaud, 1948), 64. Translator's note: *À-venir* means "to come"; *l'avenir* means "future."

3. Convergent Suspicions

1. Pierre Macaire, *L'héritage makhuwa au Mozambique* (Paris: L'Harmattan, 1996), 100.

2. Macaire, *L'héritage makhuwa*, 103.

3. On this topic, read Augé, *Théorie des pouvoirs*, 60–65.

4. See M. E. Guernais, "Aînés, aînées; cadets et cadettes," in *Âge, pouvoir et société en Afrique noire*, ed. Marc Abélès and Chantal Collard (Paris: Karthala, 1985), 322.

5. "For rich countries, the colonies are an one of the most profitable ways to invest assets, . . . given the crisis which is making its way through all European industries, the foundation of a colony is the creation of a market/outlet [*débouché*]." Jules Ferry, *Discours sur la politique extérieure et colonial* (Paris: Armand Colin, 1897), 194–96.

6. "Must one leave as wasteland, or abandon to the brambles of ignorance or incapacity, these vast uncultivated spaces where foodstuffs could spring up?" Albert Sarraut, *Grandeur et servitude colonials* (Paris: Éditions du Sagittaire, 1931), 111.

7. Ernest Renan, *La réforme intellectuelle et morale* (Paris: Lévy, 1871), 141.

8. Victor Hugo, "Discours sur l'Afrique, 18 mai 1879," in *La France colonisatrice*, ed. Paul Arène et al. (Paris: Liana Lévy, S. Messinger, 1983), 110.

9. "This Africa has only two aspects: populated, it's barbarism; deserted, it's savagery." Hugo, "Discours sur l'Afrique," 110.

10. Hugo, "Discours sur l'Afrique," 111.

11. This prejudice about child-peoples is shared in a pernicious manner by Lévi-Strauss, who elsewhere stands aside from the presuppositions of colonial ethnology. For him, every society is adult even if certain members have not taken stock of their childhood and adolescence—in other words,

have not consigned their history to writing. The critical study of facts can be lacking in a society but not the facts themselves. See Claude Lévi-Strauss, *Race et histoire* (Paris: Denoël, 1967).

12. This is the standpoint of F. Passy; see his speech of 22 December 1885 to the Chamber of Deputies. Cited by Charles-Robert Ageron, *L'anticolonialisme en France de 1871 à 1914* (Paris: Presses Universitaires de France, 1973), 49–51.

13. Georges Clemenceau, speech to the Chamber of Deputies, 30 July 1885.

14. Jean Grave, *La colonisation* (Paris: Publications des Temps Nouveaux, 1912), 5–6.

15. Read *L'Afrique sous la domination coloniale 1880–1935. Histoire générale de l'Afrique*, vol. 7, ed. Comité scientifique international pour la rédaction d'une histoire générale de l'Afrique (Unesco) (Paris: Présence Africaine Édicef/Unesco, 1989).

16. In Ghana, for example, the king of the Ashanti preserved his group's prerogatives in the matter of customary law (problems of education, hygiene, tax collecting, etc). In northern Nigeria, the kings had a treasury at their disposal (native treasuries), a police force, servants. and jurisdictions managed by different dignitaries (*malam, al Kali*).

17. The "chefs de cercle" were charged by the French administration with collecting the tax, with providing colonial companies with labor power, and with repression. As with the case of the British colonial administration, their action was controlled by the colonial authority (the head of the subdivision and the head of the region).

18. Dominique Manaï, in *Dictionnaire encyclopédique de théorie et de sociologie du droit*, ed. André-Jean Arnaud (Paris: Librairie générale de droit et de jurisprudence, 1988), 146; Aristotle, *Grand Éthique*, book 2, 114–15, cited by Manaï on 145.

19. Manaï, in *Dictionnaire encyclopédique*, 146.

20. Aimé Césaire, *Discourse on Colonialism*, trans. Joan Pinkham (New York: Monthly Review Press, 1972), 21. Italics added.

21. F. Youlou (first president of the independent Republic of Congo), cited by Jean Michel Wagret in *Histoire et sociologie politiques de la république du Congo (Brazzaville)* (Paris: Librairie générale de droit et de jurisprudence, 1963), 107.

22. One must read the penetrating analyses of Lanciné Sylla, *Tribalisme et parti unique en Afrique noire* (Paris: Presses de la Fondation nationale des sciences politiques, 1977), 257–80.

23. Sylla, *Tribalisme et parti unique*, 260.

24. Cited by Ahmed Mahiou, *L'avènement du parti unique en Afrique noire* (Paris: Librarie générale de droit et de jurisprudence, 1969), 200.

25. Nyerere, cited by Albert Meister, *L'Afrique peut-elle partir?* (Paris: Seuil, 1966), 326.

26. There was a change in Cameroon from the Mbida cabinet to that of Ahidjo; in Mauritania from the Ould Banana cabinet to that of Ould Dadah; in Dahomey from the Apithy cabinet to that of Maga. The most characteristic case was that of Chad, which went through four governments in four months in 1959—namely, the cabinets of Lisette, Sahoulba, Koulamallah, and Tombalbaye.

27. Maurice Duverger, *Les partis politiques* (Paris: Armand Colin, 1952), 312.

28. See Mahiou, *L'avènement du parti unique*.

29. This situation strongly resembles the one described by Wilhelm Reich in *Psychologie de masse du fascisme* (Paris: Payot, 1972), 34.

30. Theodor W. Adorno, *Critical Models: Interventions and Catchwords*, trans. Henry W. Pickford (New York: Columbia University Press, 2005), 195.

31. This is a behavior that appears to be political but is magical at bottom, because in this case being inscribed in political space implies a totemic type of project.

32. In Benin, Mgr. de Souza was put at the head of the conference; in Republic of Congo, Mgr. Kombo; in Gabon, Mgr. Basile Mvé; in Zaire, Mgr. Monsengwo; in Togo, Mgr. Kpozro.

33. Lawyer Kafureeka, "Multiparty Movement in Africa," in *Democracy and Democratization in Africa,* Final Report (The Hague: Institute of Social Studies and Global Coalition for Africa, 1993): 92–93.

34. This is the view of Samuel Decalo, "The Process, Prospects and Constraints of Democratization in Africa," *African Affairs* 91 (1992): 7.

35. Acronym for the International Monetary Fund, an organization controlled by American bankers whose function is to allocate loans to developing countries.

36. Maxwell Owusu, "Democracy and Africa—A View from the Village," *The Journal of Modern Studies* 30, no. 3 (1992): 369.

37. Basil Davidson and Barry Munslow, "The Crisis of the Nation State in Africa," *Review of African Political Economy* 49 (1990): 9–21.

38. Jean Copans, "No Shortcuts to Democracy: The Long March towards Modernity," *Review of African Political Economy* 50 (1991), 92–101.

39. Andre Gunder Frank, "No Escape From the Laws of World Economics," *Review of African Political Economy* 50 (1991), 21–32.

40. Reich, *Psychologie de masse,* 183.

41. The object of Heidegger's critique in *Being and Time.* See Martin Heidegger, *Being and Time,* trans. John MacQuarrie and Edward Robinson (New York: Harper & Brothers, 1962).

42. Hannah Arendt, "What is Authority?" in *Between Past and Future: Eight Exercises in Political Thought* (New York: Penguin Books, 1993), 120–23.

43. Marcel Gauchet, "La dette de sens et les racines de l'État," *Libre, Politique—anthropologie—philosophie* 77, no. 2 (1977): 29; and "La dette de sens consubstantielle à la vie sociale," in *La condition politique* (Paris, TEL/Gallimard, 2005), 45–90.

44. On this subject, read Fabien Eboussi-Boulaga, *Les conférences nationales en Afrique noire* (Paris: Karthala, 1993) and Jean-François Bayart, *L'état en Afrique, la politique du ventre* (Paris: Fayard, 1991). These authors have only discussed African societies with respect to the state. What interests them is the critique of state power and not the redefinition of modalities of collective life. African society is only an ancillary thought within a general reflection on state power—but should one not follow the model of *la palabre* and reunite in a single reflection the problems of power and those of authority? The perspective will change at once, no longer being a reflection on African society contained within reflection on the state; rather, the latter will enter into the greater context of reflection on African society. Why? Because the state is a part of society and not the reverse. Political reflection on democratization is very focused on the critique of the "postcolonial" state, and this demonstrates a reductionist conception of political reflection.

45. It would be interesting to ask why it is so fashionable to critique the "postcolonial" state. Would it be a disappointed and sublimated love of the splendor of the state's attributes? Why not criticize the false transparency of the supposedly "independent" media in Africa?

46. Politics is not just a matter of constitutions but above all of passions. An analysis of political affectivity will perhaps explain the rather curious phenomenon taking place in Africa today: the return of old rulers. Benin, the first Francophone African country to have instituted a national conference while organizing elections lost by the former dictator, General Kérékou, brought him back five years later. The same scenario has just come about in Madagascar where the expresident, Admiral Ratsiraka, returned to power by the ballot box.

47. See books 2 and 3 of Montesquieu, *The Spirit of the Laws,* trans. and ed. Anne M. Cohler, Basia C. Miller and Harold S. Stone (Cambridge: Cambridge University Press, 1989).

48. Karl Marx, *Le 18 Brumaire de Louis Bonaparte* (Paris: Éditions Sociales, 1969), 19, 46.

49. Following the title of Georges Balandier, *Le Pouvoir sur scènes* (Paris: Balland, 1980).

50. Jean-François Bayart, Achille Mbembe, Comi Toulabor, *Le Politique par le bas en Afrique noire* (Paris: Karthala, 1992).

51. Translator's note: *héxis* is a concept found in Aristotle's ethics, meaning a disposition to act in a certain way based on repeated practice or habit.

52. Bayart, *L'état en Afrique*. Bayart's point of view is rather curious. The African, if one follows him right, only enters the political domain and political activity for the sake of the digestive tract. If Bayart, instead of explaining African multipartyism using the Foucauldian theme of politics from below—derived from the famous microphysics of power—and using the Gramscian theme of hegemony—had lingered on the aesthetics of power, he would have been able to discover that in the African problematic of the body, politics sometimes enters into thematics having nothing to do with the belly. Important normative stakes are also at work.

53. Ernst Bloch, *L'héritage de ce temps* (Paris: Payot, 1978), 37–146.

54. We critiqued this point of view in our work, *Théorie critique et modernité négro-africaine* (Paris: Publications de la Sorbonne, 1993). See in this volume "Strategies for 'Constructing Belief' in the African Public Sphere."

55. Denis Constant Martin, "La Politique en Afrique noire: Pouvoir, compétition, invention," *Études* 5 (1989).

56. This is one of the arguments given by certain heads of state for naming former bureaucrats of the World Bank or the IMF as heads of governments: André Milongo in Congo, Alassane Ouatarra in Ivory Coast, and Nicéphore Soglo in Benin.

57. Regardless of the rules of international law, Western ambassadors involve themselves directly in local elections.

58. The analysts of the national conferences such as Eboussi-Boulaga (*Les conférences nationales en Afrique noire*) say nothing about the omnipresence of the Catholic Church's power during these conferences. Curiously, it is sometimes the bishops themselves who demand (in Burundi, for example) that the state be secular.

59. The *Daily Nation* (Nairobi, Kenya) of 13 May 1990 cites the case of D. Kuguru and Kiambu, brothers-in-law of the Kenyan expresident, who invoke invisible forces of the Kikiyu ethnicity in order to found their legitimacy on ancestral memory and get themselves elected.

4. A Difficult Place in Political Thought / Conclusion

1. Read Melchior Mbonimpa, *Idéologies de l'indépendance africaine* (Paris: L'Harmattan, 1986); Adekunle Ajala, *Pan-Africanism* (London: A. Deutsch, 1973).

2. Founder of the Imperial League of African Communities, du Bois did not accept the return of American blacks to Africa; for him, that was a disguised form of colonization of blacks by other blacks. His "Pan-Africanism" consisted of helping Africans and even Asians to get rid of colonialism. Mbonimpa, *Idéologies*, 217.

3. Nkrumah had the renunciation of national sovereignty as a principle written into the constitution of Ghana. He believed Ghana was called to disappear in a great African grouping. Nkrumah wanted to build the United States of Africa.

4. See Kwame Nkrumah, *Africa Must Unite* (London: Heineman, 1962), 218ff.

5. Nkrumah, *Africa Must Unite*, 55.

6. See the provisions of the OAU concerning mediation during conflicts.

7. Those who emphasize the inefficacy of the OAU always limit themselves to deploring the lack of legal tools (the controls and guarantees offered by treaties and resolutions) and materials (an army that either does not exist, or is ineffective and heterogenous when it does exist). What they do not do is critique the evacuation of the symbolic dimension and the great anthropological references from the statutes of the OAU. Can one speak of the law with respect to Africa without invoking collective fears, myths, conceptions of happiness, relations to the absolute, to space and to time, and to the difference between the sexes? Why not privilege informal negotiation rather than large hearings when managing crises? In African traditions, informal consultations are often more important than a large

palabre. The latter is often only a façade; for example, among the Ochollo of Ethiopia, the essential things play out before the *palabre* (*dulata*) takes place; see Marc Abélès, "Aînesse et generations à Ochollo," in *Âge, pouvoir, et société en Afrique noire*, ed. Marc Abélès and Chantal Collard (Paris: Karthala, 1985), 128.

8. Kwame Nkrumah, *Consciencism: Philosophy and Ideology for De-colonization* (New York: Monthly Review Press, 1970), 79.

9. Nkrumah, *Consciencism*, 100–101. Nkrumah was criticized on this point by Paulin Hountonji, in *Sur la philosophie africaine* (Paris: Maspéro, 1977).

10. "I . . . son of . . . grand-son of . . . having killed the brave So-and-So in the course of a duel which lasted . . ., having married so many women . . . I say to you . . ." J. Freedman, "Je suis Nyakagarura . . ." in Abélès and Collard, *Âge, pouvoir, et société*, 270–72.

11. May Mandelbaum Edel, "Property among the Ciga in Uganda," *Africa* 11, no. 3, (1938): 325–41.

12. Among the Lugbara of Uganda, they are called "masters of the lance." John Middleton and David Tait, eds., *Tribes without Rulers* (London: Routledge, 1958), 97–203.

13. Nkrumah states that "to improve effectively and quickly the serious damage done to Africa . . . the emergent African states need strong, unitary states capable of exercising a central authority." See *Africa Must Unite*, 214.

14. [The latter] is the case among the Nyakyusa of Tanzania.

15. For example, adultery led to a death penalty among the Ngbaka (Central African Republic) while the Beti required only that the plaintiff be compensated.

16. See Mamadou Dia, *Nations africaines et solidarité mondiale* (Paris: Presses Universitaires de France, 1960).

17. Julius Nyerere, *Freedom and Socialism/Uhuru na Ujamaa: A Selection from Writings and Speeches, 1965–1967* (Oxford: Oxford University Press, 1968).

18. He employs the concept of "self-reliance" (self-confidence).

19. Julius Nyerere, "Ujamaa: The Basis of African Socialism," in *Freedom and Unity/Uhuru na Umoja: A Selection from Writings and Speeches, 1952–65* (London: Oxford University Press, 1967), 162.

20. Nyerere, "Ujamaa," in *Freedom and Unity*, 164.

21. Nyerere, "Socialism and Rural Development," in *Freedom and Socialism*, 337.

22. Julius Nyerere, "The African and Democracy," in *Freedom and Unity*, 104.

23. Nyerere, "Ujamaa," in *Freedom and Unity*, 170.

24. Julius Nyerere and Pierre Buis, *La déclaration d'Arusha, dix ans après* (Paris, L'Harmattan, 1978), 49.

25. The TANU (single-party in Tanzania at the time of Nyerere).

26. On this topic, see Louis-Vincent Thomas, *Le socialisme et l'Afrique* (Paris: Le Livre Africain, 1969), 2 vols; and Pene Elungu A. Elungu, *L'éveil philosophique africain* (Paris: L'Harmattan, 1985).

27. Léopold Sédar Senghor, in *L'homme de couleur* (Paris: Plon, 1939). Reissued in Léopold Sédar Senghor, *Liberté I: Négritude et humanisme* (Paris: Seuil, 1964), 258.

28. Senghor, *Liberté I*, 258.

29. Senghor, *Liberté I*, 258–59.

30. Senghor, *Liberté I*, 254.

31. Léopold Sédar Senghor, *Liberté II: Nation et voie africaine du socialisme* (Paris: Seuil, 1971), 54.

32. Senghor, *Liberté II*, 107, 108, 190.

33. Senghor, *Liberté II*, 255.

34. Senghor, *Liberté II*, 264.

35. Césaire's words illustrate the suffering of blacks in *Cahier d'un retour au pays natal*, (Paris: Présence Africaine, 1956), 25. In the same tone, Senghor deplores "the contempt for blacks . . . that whites display" in *Anthologie de la nouvelle poésie nègre et malgache de langue française* (Paris: PUF, 1969), 13.

36. "Haïti où la négritude se mit debout pour la première fois." Césaire, *Cahier*, 46.

37. Senghor, *Liberté I*, 255.

38. Césaire, *Cahier*, 89.

39. Senghor, *Liberté I*, 167.

40. Senghor, *Liberté I*, 362. Senghor adds that it is a language incapable of seizing the "African soul."

41. Senghor, *Liberté I*, 360.

42. Senghor, *Liberté I*, 142–43.

43. See Césaire, *Cahier*, 55.

44. Thomas Melone, *De la négritude dans la littérature négro-africaine* (Paris: Présence Africaine, 1962), 116.

45. Mongo Beti, *Mission terminée* (Paris: Buchet-Chastel, 1957), 141–61.

46. Ferdinand Oyono, *Chemin d'Europe* (Paris: Union Générale d'Éditions, 1962), 105.

47. David Rubadiri, "Why African Literature?" in *Transition* 4, no. 15 (1964): 41.

48. Gerald Moore, *Seven African Writers* (London: Oxford University Press, 1962), 4.

49. Jean-Paul Sartre, *Orphée Noir. Black Orpheus*, trans. S. W. Allen (Paris: Présence Africaine, 1976), 59.

50. Stanislas Spero Adotevi, *Négritude et négrologues* (Paris: Union Générale d'Éditions, 1972), 115.

51. According to Georges Ngal's expression when speaking of Césaire, in *Aimé Césaire: Un Homme à la recherche d'une patrie* (Paris: Présence Africaine, 1994), 108.

52. See the declaration of the evangelical Société des Missions de Paris (2 Dec 1822) in Jean Comby, *Deux mille ans d'évangélization* (Paris: Desclée de Brouwer, 1992), 208. Among Catholics, many pontifical texts reaffirm the necessity of "winning everyone for Christ"; this is the meaning of the teaching of the "Propaganda Fide" of 23 Dec 1845 titled *Neminem profecto*.

53. History remembers the famous papal bull (4 May 1493) of Pope Alexander VI in which the latter blesses the kings of Portugal and Spain in making them a gift of the lands discovered by Christopher Columbus. From this perspective, evangelization would also be a universal empire governed by the Pope. See the Portugese ambassador's declaration of obedience to Pope Leo X in March 1514 (on which, see Johan Specker, "Motivations . . ." in *Studia Instituti Missiologici* Soc. Verbi divini, no. 13 [1974]).

54. One thinks here of the reaction of Belgian Catholics in the Congo against the implantation of Protestantism.

55. The proposals of the Methodist pastor André Roux for Ivory Coast are illuminating here: Andre Roux, *L'évangile dans la forêt* (Paris: Cerf, 1971).

56. One must refer back to the teachings *Quae a presulibus* (1883) and *Cum postremis* (1893).

57. One must note here the Tembu (1884) and Ethiopian (1854) churches in South Africa; the Province Industrial Mission (1914) in Malawi; Kitawalism (1908) in Zambia; Kimbanguism (1921) in Zaire; the Christian Army in Uganda; the Church of the Holy Spirit in Kenya (1927); the Church of the White Bird in Zimbabwe; the Apostolowa Fe in Ghana; Harrisme in Ivory Coast and in Liberia; and finally the Musama Disco Cristo Church in Ghana.

58. The teaching stipulates: "Do not put any zeal . . . to convince these peoples to change their rites, their customs . . . unless they are contrary to religion and to morality . . . do not introduce our countries into theirs, but faith, this faith which neither pushes away nor hurts the rites of any people."

59. For views before Vatican II, see the collective work, A. Abbele et al, *Des Prêtres noirs s'interrogent* (Paris: Cerf, 1956); for those after, we are thinking of the Conferences on Inculturation of Accra (1979) and Abidjan (1975).

60. Julien Efoué Pénoukou, *Églises d'Afrique: Propositions pour l'avenir* (Paris: Karthala, 1984), 52.

61. This concept indicates the passage between the cited text (the Bible) and the commentary on a historical situation it suggests. Here the fundamental text plays the role of anecdote.

62. The notion of the church-family was defended by Mgr. A. T. Sanon (Burkina Faso) before the Roman synod of 1985, in Maurice Cheza, Henri Deroitte, and René Luneau, *Les Évêques d'Afrique parlent, 1969–1991*. Documents pour le synode africaine (Paris: Centurion, 1992), 96.

63. Cardinal Zoungrana of Burkina Faso insists that liturgies should "create increased . . . respect for speech" [*liturgies fassent croître . . . le respect de la parole*], in Cheza, Deroitte and Luneau, *Les évêques d'Afrique parlent*.

64. Besides, one invokes the argument: "Jesus did not write, he spoke."

65. The titles "Monseigneur" and "Eminence" are still being used.

66. The prayer of the consecration during the French mass reads: "Watch over your servant the Pope . . . our bishop," but in Ewondo this becomes: "Watch over our great-grandfather . . . our grandfather." Elsewhere, the same titles are designated by terms derived from German—the influence of German colonization is visible there—the priest will be *fara* (*Pfarer*), the bishop *bisob* (*Bischof*), and the Pope *pabs* (*Pabst*). The Zairean priest Kabasele elaborates an African Christology in which Christ is by turns chief, ancestor, or proto-ancestor. See François Kabasele-Lumbala, *Le Christianisme et l'Afrique, une chance réciproque* (Paris: Karthala, 1993), 100.

67. This is the position of Mgr. Kombo (Republic of Congo); see his declaration of March 1988, cited in Cheza, Deroitte, and Luneau, *Les Évêques d'Afrique parlent*.

68. See the authorization of the Vatican office of the Congregation of Holy Worship to Zairean bishops to conduct their "*palabre*-mass" in *Decret Zairensium* of 30 April 1980.

69. The words of Mgr. Monsengwo, archbishop of Kisangani, in Gode Iwélé, *Mgr. Monsengwo, témoin et acteur de l'histoire* (Brussels: Duclot, 1995), 93.

70. Iwélé, *Mgr. Monsengwo*, 94.

71. Iwélé, *Mgr. Monsengwo*, 95.

72. This is the meaning of the theory of reconciliation (of *palabre*) held by Mgr. Kourouma, bishop of Nzérékoré (Guinea) during the Roman synod of October 1983.

73. Priests make themselves into healers and compete with other priests (*vaudou* in Benin or *bouiti* in Cameroon and Gabon).

74. René Luneau reports that the refusal of interactive dialogue is emphasized by Jean Zoa (archbishop of Yaoundé). Luneau, *Laisse aller mon peuple! Églises africaines au-delà des modèles?* (Paris: Karthala, 1987), 83–84, 89.

75. Luneau, *Laisse aller mon peuple!*, 83–84.

76. This is the meaning of the declaration of Mgr. I. De Souza, archbishop of Cotonou (Benin). See *Documentation catholique*, 13 (1984), 689.

77. See his exhortation to the bishops of Kenya, *Documentation catholique*, 1 June 1980.

78. Responding to journalists in Ivory Coast, Pope John Paul II said of the Christianity of the African churches that "they are young, they are equally young in faith, in their Christianity. Our Christian traditions are thousands of years old, by contrast, in Ghana or Zaire, the Church is 100 years old, in other countries even less. They are young, they have therefore the maturity of a youth." *Osservatore romano*, 13 May 1980, 1. This response of the Pope raises a question about inculturation: Can one found theological research uniquely on a single claim? What does one expect to follow theologically from the act of making this claim? What comes after the crisis of adolescence?

79. The Cameroonian Hegba responded preemptively to this papal discourse on the right of elders: "Personnalité de l'église particulière," *Telema*, January (1979), 19.

80. Christophe Wondji, "De la Bouche de l'ancien," in *Courrier de l'UNESCO*, April (1996), 12.

81. Claude Lefort, *Les formes de l'histoire. Essais d'anthropologie politique* (Paris: Gallimard, 1978), 32.

82. Throughout book 5 of the *Politics*, Aristotle analyses conflicts, and, observing that societies live in an unstable equilibrium (*stasis*), recommends prudence (*phronésis*) as the political virtue par excellence.

83. According to Ricoeur, the first task is to show how, although ethics may be more fundamental than morality, the latter, with its norms and obligations, remains the necessary path because of violence. The second question bears on the transition from one to the other: "Why is it not possible to dwell in the sphere of ethics . . . must one absolutely pass to the plane of morality?" Paul Ricoeur, "Entretien," in *Éthique et responsabilité*, ed. Jean-Christophe Aeschlimann (Neuchâtel: À la Baconnière, 1994), 16.

84. Paul Ricoeur, "Ethics and Politics," in *From Text to Action: Essays in Hermeneutics, II*, trans. Kathleen Blamey and John B. Thompson (Evanston, IL: Northwestern University Press, 1991), 335.

85. Ricoeur borrows this notion from Wilhelm Schapp. See Ricoeur, *Éthique et responsabilité*, 20.

86. Translator's note: The reference is to Walter Benjamin. Paul Ricoeur, *Oneself as Another*, trans. Kathleen Blamey (Chicago: University of Chicago Press, 1992), 164.

Rationalities and Legal Processes in Africa

1. Here "retention" does not have the meaning Husserl gives it when he defines it as that time that is not yet of the order of the past but has just been the present. He distinguishes it from *protension*, which designates what is immediately to come, whose presence is already on the horizon.

2. Jürgen Habermas, *La pensée postmétaphysique: Essais philosophiques* (Paris: Armand Colin, 1993), 184. All quoted material translated by Jean Burrell unless a specific English-language edition is cited.

3. Alasdair MacIntyre, *Whose Justice? Which Rationality?* (Notre Dame, IN: University of Notre Dame Press, 1988), 7.

4. Pierre Legendre, *L'empire de la vérité* (Paris: Fayard, 1983), 104.

5. Gérard Timsit, *Les noms de la loi* (Paris: Presses Universitaires de France, 1991).

6. Catherine Kerbrat Orecchioni, *Les interactions verbales*, vol. 1 (Paris: Armand Colin, 1990), 17.

7. Gérard Timsit. "Théorie des faces et analyse conversationnelle," dans *Le frais parler d'Erwin Goffmann*. (Paris: Minuit, 1989), 156.

8. Roland Barthes, "The Old Rhetoric, an aide-mémoire," In *The Semiotic Challenge*, trans. Richard Howard (New York: Hill and Wang, 1988), 74.

9. See book 1, chapter 1 of Aristotle's *Rhetoric*, 1356a13, in *The Basic Works of Aristotle*, ed. Richard McKeon (New York: Random House, 1941), 1329.

10. See book 11, chapter 6 of Montesquieu, *The Spirit of the Laws*, trans. and ed. Anne M. Cohler, Basia C. Miller and Harold S. Stone (Cambridge: Cambridge University Press, 1989).

11. Olivier Jouanjan, "Nommer; Normer," in *99 Sciences et humanités. La denomination*, no. 1 (1999): 105.

12. Jouanjan, "Nommer; Normer," 105.

13. Here see François Ost, *Du Sinaï au Champ de Mars. L'autre et le même au fondement du droit.* (Brussels: Éditions Lessius, 1999).

14. Pierre Legendre, *Paroles poétiques échappées du texte* (Paris: Seuil, 1982), 73.

15. Legendre, *Paroles poétiques*, 73.

16. Legendre, *Paroles poétiques*, 73.

17. John Glissen and Jacques Vanderlinden, "L'Organisation judiciaire en Afrique noire," in *L'Organisation judiciaire en Afrique noire* (Brussels: Editions de l'Institut de Sociologie, 1969), 38.

18. G. François and H. Marriol, *Législation coloniale* (Paris: Librarie Larose, 1929), 182.

19. Robert Pageard, *Le droit privé des Mossi: Tradition et évolution*, vol. 1, *Recherches voltaïques* 10/11 (Paris/Ouagadougou: CNRS-CVRS, 1969), 93.

20. Michel Jeol, *La réforme de la justice en Afrique noire* (Paris: Éditions A. Pedone, 1963), 105.

21. Claude Durand, *Les anciennes coutumes pénales du Tchad* (Paris: L'Harmattan, 2002), 100.

22. Durand, *Les anciennes coutumes*, 100.

23. Durand, *Les anciennes coutumes*, 101.

24. Durand, *Les anciennes coutumes*, 102.

25. Hans Kelsen, *Théorie pure du droit* (Paris: Dalloz, 1962), 2.

26. Paul Dubouchet, *Le modéle juridique, droit et herméneutique* (Paris: L'Harmattan, 2001), 28.

27. See Bidima, *La Palabre, une juridiction de la parole* (Paris: Michalon, 1997), in this volume.

28. Bruno Oppetit, "Sur le concept d'arbitrage," in *Études offertes à Bertold Goldmann*, "Le droit des relations économique internationales" (Paris: Libraries techniques, 1982), 237.

29. Aristotle, *Éthique à Nicomaque*, 1137b10-15, trans. J. Tricot (Paris: Vrin, 1994), 267.

30. Jean-Étienne-Marie Portalis, *Discours préliminaire sur le projet de code civil* (Paris: Editions Confluences, 1999), 18–19.

31. Oppetit, however, sees in "codification" the movement by which we can escape this legislative inflation; see Bruno Oppetit, *Essai sur la codification* (Paris: Presses Universitaires de France, 1998).

32. Eduardo Silva Romero, *Wittgenstein et la philosophie du droit* (Paris: Presses Universitaires de France, 2002), 48.

33. Paul Ricoeur, *The Just*, trans. David Pellauer (Chicago: University of Chicago Press, 2000), 131.

34. Ricoeur, *The Just*, 131.

35. Ricoeur, *The Just*, 131.

36. Michel Van de Kerchove and François Ost, *Le droit ou les paradoxes du jeu* (Paris: Presses Universitaires de France, 1992), 61.

37. Ost, *Le Temps du droit*, 29.

38. See Wilhelm Schapp, *Empêtrés dans des histoires: L'être de l'homme et de la chose* (Paris: Éditions de Cerf, 1992).

Strategies for "Constructing Belief" in the African Public Sphere

1. Pierre Legendre, *Jouir du pouvoir* (Paris: Éditions de Minuit, 1976), 120.

2. Translator's note: Here "belief" has the sense of trust or commitment as well as a cognitive content. See Bidima, "Croire," 2010.

3. Michel de Certeau, *La culture au pluriel* (Paris: Union Générale d'Éditions, 1974), 268.

4. Pierre Kaufmann, *L'inconscient du politique* (Paris: Librarie Philosophique J. Vrin, 1988).

5. Here we are thinking of Jean-François Bayart, *L'état en Afrique: La politique du ventre* (Paris: Fayard, 1989); *The State in Africa: The Politics of the Belly*, trans. Mary Harper, Christopher Harrison, and Elizabeth Harrison (New York: Longman, 1993).

6. See Kaufmann, *L'inconscient du politique*, iii.

7. Pierre F. Gonidec, *Les systèmes politiques africains*, 2nd ed. (Paris: Librairie générale de droit et de jurisprudence, 1978).

8. Pierre F. Gonidec, Alain Bockel, *L'état Africain*, 2nd ed. (Paris: Librarie générale de droit et de jurisprudence, 1985).

9. See the analysis of Catherine Kerbrat Orecchioni, *L'implicite* (Paris: Armand Colin, 1986).

10. Kéba M'baye, "Sacralité, croyances, pouvoir et droit en Afrique," in *Sacralité, pouvoir et droit en Afrique: Table ronde préparatoire du 4ème colloque du Centre d'Études Juridiques Comparatives organisée par le LAJP*, ed. Mamadou Wane (Paris: Editions du CNRS, 1979), 143–60. Translator's note: The concept of the instituting (radical) imaginary can be found in Cornelius Castoriadis, *The Imaginary Institution of Society*, trans. Kathleen Blamey (Cambridge, MA: MIT Press, 1987), esp. 369–73.

11. M'baye, "Sacralité, croyances, pouvoir et droit en Afrique," 152.

12. M'baye, "Sacralité, croyances, pouvoir et droit en Afrique," 154.

13. Bayart, *L'état en Afrique*. One must note (as Bayart acknowledges) that the subtitle "politics of the belly" is a Cameroonian expression fabricated by the instituting feminine imaginary, whose existence we signaled in an article published in 1987. See Jean Godefroy Bidima, "L'art négro-africain des 'sans-espoir,'" *Raison présente* 82 (1987).

14. See "Économie alimentaire," *Politique africaine* 37 (1990), 96 ff.

15. Jean Copans, "La Banalisation de l'état africain. À Propos de l'état en Afrique de J. F. Bayart." *Politique Africaine* 37 (1990).

16. Translator's note: *Arcana imperii* means "secrets of power" or of the state; *libido imperandi* means the "desire to control or command"; *libido manducandi* means the "desire to chew."

17. To be sure, economists employ the term "representation" in a very functionalist sense. Among managers, the term designates a professional distributor whose mission is to propose or to get contracts signed on behalf of businesses. And in a more narrow sense, it is a white collar worker charged with the interests of a business. On this subject, read *L'encyclopedie de la gestion*, vol. 1, ed. Yves Simon and Patrick Joffre (Paris: Economica, 1989), 45–46. In law, the notion of representation has many meanings depending on whether it is a matter of representing a thing, an institution, or a person. With respect to a thing, one speaks of representation when one presents something as evidence; this is the meaning one uses when one presents an original will to the court. The second sense of representation in law is defined as "action, by a person invested for this purpose, consisting of legal, judiciary or conventional power to carry out (representing), in the name and for the benefit of someone else incapable or prevented from doing so (the represented), a juridical act whose effects are directly felt by those so represented" (Gérard Cornu, *Vocabulaire juridique* [Paris: Presses Universitaires de France, 1987], 692). It is also in this sense that one speaks of mandate, procurement, administration, and management of affairs. This juridical sense of representation has at least one advantage and one inconvenience. The advantage would be that this notion of representation presupposes a transfer of power, a sort of alienation of power. Meanwhile, the inconvenience would be the very functionalist use of this notion: representation is first a function that one exercises and that one has exercised on one's behalf.

18. To be sure, "Summaries" are published on the representation of people in parliaments, and African economists speak of representation in the context of problems posed by multinational corporations in Africa, but neither of these bothers to rise to the level of the concept in order to think the concept of representation.

19. See Ludwig Wittgenstein, *Investigations philosophiques*, trans. Pierre Klossowski (Paris: Gallimard, 1961), 167.

20. Umberto Eco, *La guerre du faux*, trans. Myriam Tanant and Piero Caracciolo (Paris: Grasset, 1985), 225.

21. In Europe, the nation did not emerge from merchant capital in a mechanical fashion. Nation and state were constructed as two terms in a dialectical process in which multiple creativities converged. In Africa, the conditions of this same process did not exist: the state was imposed by a decision external to the social formation. It tried in turn to impose a nationality that was abstract and not selected by the hazards and determinations of a long common history. Despite constant criticism, we still suffer from the harmful effects of this artificial state, but what the state ought to do more often is practice a micropolitics that sets aside policy considerations and interacts with these microconsensuses that populate African "civil society."

22. A Gabonese university professor, Pambou [Tchivounda], writes tranquilly in a very general style: "The dimensions of the social body constitute the mold in which law congeals." Thus, law contributes to its formation. As M. Virally writes, "law is . . . a technique, a set of procedures put at people's disposition to arrive at certain ends. . . . Besides this role of transformation, law also assures

a function of mental acceleration. It could hardly be otherwise. . . . Observe and analyze the juridical rules applicable in a society, you will discover there the style of thinking characterizing those who compose it; as it evolves, this style brings with it the mutation of society itself." Guillaume Pambou Tchivounda, *Essai sur l'état africain postcolonial* (Paris: Librairie générale de droit et de Jurisprudence, 1982), 16.

This citation provokes at least two comments. First, law is a factor of progress and dynamism. Second, it is law that determines the pace and evolution of society, not the reverse. With respect to the first claim, it is not certain that law is necessarily a factor of advancement in a society, since to a certain extent, law cements, regulates, and conserves the *stare decisis* (the already-decided, the already-said, the already—instituted, in short the *already*). In no case does law occupy itself with the future, the *nondum*. Now, between the category of *stare decisis* and that of *nondum*, a society's progress is subordinated to the installation of an apparatus permitting, not the conservation of the *déjà*, but the anticipation and advent in reality of multiple ways in which the not-yet may be germinating.

In this very schematic analysis of law, we cannot touch on the dogmatic heritage of contemporary law through biblical and Roman-canonical survivals. The question of *unde* (where does it come from?) is never raised by African legal scholars. Why do these people neglect the symbolic and the unsayable as foundational references with which every normative system plays? How are the ordering and staging of the law woven together? How does the juridical text lead to the social capture of desire? We will not go so far as to say that "the foundation of law is imbecility, jurists having no pretense of thinking, but . . . merely holding symbols of the law." Pierre Legendre, *L'Empire de la vérité* (Paris: Fayard, 1983), 26. But it might be that legalistic techniques of control, of agreement, of contract, of evidence, appear to have a weight that is hard to distinguish from frivolity.

23. African juridical systems, like their French models, employ a language that is abstruse and ostentatiously old-fashioned. There are French archaisms one could easily avoid that render the text and discourse of law less explicit then they might be. In certain African civil codes, one can still find substantives like *serviteur, octroi, à la diligence de, faire diligence*, addresses like *Dame, Sieur*. These terms can very easily be replaced with *employé, autorisation, sous la responsabilité de, faire attention à*, or quite simply *Madame, Monsieur*. Certain prepositions, prepositional phrases and adverbs, *céans, attendu que*, can be very easily replaced with *ici* [here]. The same applies to certain adjectives and verbs: *Afférent*: replaceable with *qui se rapporte à* [related to]; *sis*: replaceable with *situé* [situated]; *diligenté par*: replaceable by *mené par* [led by].

24. Many thinkers have postulated that the French civil code, such as we know it, is only an overgrowth of a bourgeois tactic in which everything is orchestrated to create a pyramidal social structure. See André-Jean Arnaud, *Essai d'analyse structurale du code civil français* (Paris: Librairie générale de droit et de jurisprudence, 1973).

25. Maurice Bourjol et al., *Pour une critique du droit* (Grenoble: Presses Universitaires de Grenoble, 1978), 98.

26. Bourjol et al., *Pour une critique du droit*, 77.

27. Bourjol et al., *Pour une critique du droit*, 98–99.

28. The greatest violence being the *agrégation* in law (license of institutional power in a society where the majority are illiterate!). "On the plane of lived experience, the *agrégation* in law (strictly an internal competition, by contrast to the *agrégation* in humanities and human sciences and sciences) engenders in teachers a despotism and an atmosphere that is hardly conducive to scholarly work. . . . [B]etween the professors who have passed the *agrégation* and other teachers are woven personal bonds of dependency . . . linked to an elitist conception of recruitment, the *agrégation* allows jurists to be isolated and differentiated" (See Bourjol et al., *Pour une Critique du droit*, 100).

29. Karl Marx, *Grundrisse: Introduction to the Critique of Political Economy*, trans. Martin Nicolaus (New York: Vintage Books, 1973), 650.

30. Arnaud, *Essai d'analyse structurale*, 149–50.

31. Henceforth "in consciousness—in jurisprudence, politics, etc.—relations become concepts . . . the concepts of the relations also become fixed concepts in their mind. The judge, for example, applies the code, he therefore regards legislation as the real, active driving force. . . . Idea of Law. Idea of State. The matter is turned upside-down in *ordinary* consciousness." Karl Marx and Frederick Engels, *The German Ideology*, trans. W. Lough, ed. Roy Pascal, in *Karl Marx and Frederick Engels, Collected Works, Vol 5: 1845–1847* (New York: International Publishers, 1976), 92.

32. Patrick Charaudeau, *Langage et discours: Éléments de sémiolinguistique* (Paris: Hachette, 1985), 134.

33. Translator's note: A "delocutive" verb is linguistically derived from a performative, first-person expression, which it turns into a general behavior. The term was introduced by Émile Benveniste, *Problems in General Linguistics*, trans. Mary Elizabeth Meek (Coral Gables, FL: University of Miami Press), 1971, 239–46.

34. A. Grosser affirms, "Political leaders clearly do not believe everything they say, but it completely falsifies the analysis to suppose they are purely cynical, acting for the sake of a fully 'scientific' vision of reality. Hitler believed in international Judaism. Himmler believed in race. Leonid Brezhnev did not play at being a communist . . . the Pope does not evoke Christ for show when he considers political reality. Each 'decision-maker' has his mechanism for selecting, coloring, transforming; in short, of representing the world around him." Alfred Grosser, *L'Explication politique*, second ed. (Brussels: Éditions Complexe, 1984), 103, emphasis added.

35. Here we are thinking of the thesis of Christine Buhan and Étienne Kange Essiben, *La mystique du corps: Jalons pour une anthropologie du corps* (Paris: L'Harmattan, 1979).

36. Translator's note: The "implexe" is a concept used by the poet Paul Valéry, meaning a set of discontinuous impressions or sensibilities held together as much through human intention as through their own powers. Merleau-Ponty describes the interaction of multiple aspects of bodily experience, which are always anticipatory and desiring, in a similar way.

37. Maurice Merleau-Ponty, *The Visible and the Invisible*, trans. Alphonso Lingis (Evanston, IL: Northwestern University Press, 1968), 138.

38. Such a study has already been done by Jean-Thierry Maertens, *Ritanalyses*, vol. 1 (Paris: Jérôme Millon, 1987).

39. This approach will not be too occupied by body as "envelope" of tissues, a conception that comes from histology. Nor will it be viewed as a "volcano" in which enzymatic chains and cycles of synthesis, catabolisms, and anabolisms build on each other. This conception of the volcano-body is that of biochemistry. Another image of the body to avoid is that of the "machine" body, which treats the latter as an ensemble of detached parts, with thresholds of intensity, action and rest potentials, a cardiac pump, and renal filtration. Instead, we prefer the image of the body as mirror of society.

40. See Michel Foucault, *Histoire de la sexualité*, vol. 1, *La Volonté de savoir* (Paris: Gallimard, 1976), 79–80.

41. Michel Foucault, "The Eye of Power," in Jeremy Bentham, *Le Panoptique* (Paris: Pierre Belfond, 1977).

42. All the same, one must note with respect to makeup and Africa that the latter must deal with the commands of an ideal-ego imposed by fashion. The act of putting on makeup participates in the "ceaselessness" that permits the subject who uses cosmetics to have the illusion of renewal. Makeup only returns this person's body to herself in the form of a repressive identity. Put otherwise, the made-up body, designed to be looked at by others, is designated as desirable because as an already-desiring being, the African seeks an identity involving identification with "what someone will say."

43. Translator's note: For Lévinas, the face [*le visage*] is the invisible, expressive, and morally compelling aspect of a human person that appears in, but cannot be reduced to, the "front side" [*la face*] of his or her head; i.e., the physical eyes, nose, mouth, etc. See Emmanuel Lévinas, *Totality*

and Infinity: An Essay on Exteriority, trans. Alphonso Lingis (Pittsburgh: Duquesne University Press, 1969).

44. On the symbolic plane, it would be interesting to study the symbolism of the hole by means of the face [*visage*] that absorbs, integrates, and also eliminates!

45. One must begin by noting that in Africa, myth is torn between a foundational demand and the pressure of modernity. As archetypal model, it presents itself *ne varietur*, and at the same time it cannot remain aloof from the pressures of social tension and the competition from new myths (for example, eschatological myths coming from syncretism between Christianity, Islam, and traditional beliefs). This division at the heart of myth opens a gap, inside of which identitary logics become lodged.

46. See M. D'Hertefett, "Mythes et idéologies dans le Rwanda ancien et contemporain," in *The Historian in Tropical Africa,* ed. J. Mauny, R. Thomas and L. V. Vansina (London: Oxford University Press for the International African Institute, 1964).

47. If, to a certain extent, myth legitimates the order established by autocratic powers, the objection can also be raised that in some cases, by virtue of their spirit, myths have contributed to the reversal of the established order. The main thing to be grasped is the practical/active [*praxique*] function of myth.

48. Translator's note: *Soter* is Greek for "savior"; *fatum* is Latin for "fate" or "destiny."

49. This church claimed to be a veiled response to the situation of discrimination imposed by whites. Within Ethiopism, one must distinguish Ethiopism properly speaking and the churches called Zionist. Ethiopism was created in 1892 by a certain prophet Magena, who separated himself from the American Episcopalian church.

50. The first of these churches was created in the Natal region in 1911 by Isaiah Shembe (who proclaimed himself the black Christ), whose followers practiced vigorous political contestation. Our presentation of these movements is necessarily schematic.

51. The best known of these movements was the *Watu Wa ngu* (the people of God!) in which all adepts considered themselves as *arathi* (prophets!). Relying on biblical texts, the faithful claimed their divine origin as an "elect people," using the model of identification with the Jewish tradition. They proclaimed the liberation of Kenya, while also postulating the imminent arrival of God's kingdom. In this specific case, one is in the presence of a composite myth (myth of identification and of annihilation) in which the Bible and traditional belief are permanently intertwined.

52. Enrolled in the French army and baptized Catholic, this Congolese figure went to prison for having put together an African association with nationalist ideas. He died in prison. His companions, certain of whom had connections to the Kimbanguists (another messianic current in the Belgian Congo), founded Matsouanism.

53. On this point, read Martial Sinda, *Le messianisme congolais et ses incidences politiques* (Paris: Payot, 1972).

54. One notices this syncretism in their rituals: on the church altars, beside the flowers and candles, one finds a red cloth associated with a dagger and the photograph of Matsoua, while the whole background is dominated by the symbol V (for victory) formed of branches to which is fixed the cross of Lorraine.

55. These are the interiorized myths in which the stories are hardly emancipated from their reference to the first narrator. The latter becomes the absolute reference point for activity and temporality (everything is measured from the moment of before-Matsoua). It is Matsoua who is the depository of true language, the discourse that differs from and offers an alternative to the sinful world.

56. We find the same movements with the same hypostasis of interiority in Ivory Coast: the religion of Deima, celestial Christianity, and Harrisism.

57. This was an old principle of political legitimation used during the Middle Ages (fourteenth century) in France by Philip IV to constrain the clergy to give him subsidies. See Ernst Kantorowicz,

Mourir pour la patrie (Paris: Presses Universitaires de France, 1984), 119ff. But Kantorowicz indicates that the doctrine of *pro natalis patriae mori* was theological. It was used by St. Thomas Aquinas who also took up the *l'amor patriae* of Cicero and St. Augustine. Death *pro patria* was a kind of self-sacrifice, a *caritas*. See Kantorowicz, *Les deux corps du roi* (Paris: Gallimard, 1989), 172–99.

58. Curiously, and despite the fall of the *négus* (king), the Marxist Ethiopian revolution propped itself on this myth to justify/legitimate Amharic hegemony. The most typical case was the mythification/legitimation of Hailé Selassié. The latter was not only an autocrat, but around him were woven many myths destined to legitimate his power, and his person served as a guarantee of safety for the Rastafarian movement that gave birth to reggae music.

59. "By his fame outside the country, Hailé Selassié perpetuated the Solomonic myth in the middle of the twentieth century . . . to tell the truth, he was the only one who wanted to represent it."

60. All these ethnicities must be at the botton of the social ladder because they stem from the lineage of the cursed.

61. Having driven out the *négus*, those who govern in the military junta are Amharic and claim (with the support of Coptic Christian clergy) that, "in the name of their semitic filiation," they have the right to rule over other cursed peoples like the sons of Kush. Lately, Mengistu Haile Mariam has been driven out and many provinces have become autonomous, but the war is not finished.

62. François Fourquet, "L'Accumulation du pouvoir ou le désir d'état," *Revue Recherches* 46 (1982).

63. John L. Austin, *How to Do Things with Words*, 2nd ed., ed. J. O. Urmson and Marina Sbisà (Cambridge, MA: Harvard University Press, 1975), 109.

64. Oswald Ducrot and Tzvetan Todorov, *Dictionnaire encyclopédique des sciences du langage* (Paris: Seuil, 1972), 428.

65. Here we are ignoring extensive developments on the notion of verisimilitude in Gérard Genette as well as the pragmatic dimension suggested by the Jakobsonian functions of language.

66. The critics of jammed communication in the black African public space and the reservations that we have expressed vis-à-vis the state were concerned—at the moment of writing—with phenomena of the one-party state. Presently, African countries have adopted a form of political "pluralism" and a "democratization" that advance in the midst of multiple problems. Meanwhile, although out-of-date, these chapters allow us to see how the authoritarian state functioned on this continent, since phenomena of regression are not unknown to history.

67. For more information on this distinction, read Charaudeau, *Langage et discours*, 35ff.

68. The problem of enunciation is difficult to define in linguistics. Some recognize it and think that it is neither on the side of syntax nor the side of semantics, so perhaps it is on the side of pragmatics . . . but this is not sure, while what is sure, in any case, is "that one has a tendency to reject in the enunciation all the phenomena that have not yet found a satisfying place in linguistic theory." See Dominique Maingueneau, *Initiation aux méthodes d'analyse du discours* (Paris: Hachette, 1976), 99.

69. Eyadema, "Discours programme prononcé lors du congrès constitutif du Rassemblement du Peuple Togolais," in Claude Feuillet, *Le togo en général* (Paris: Éditions ABC, 1976), 147.

70. Joseph Désiré Mobutu, *Paroles du président* (Kinshasa: Éditions du Leopard, 1968), 29.

71. Mobutu, *Paroles du président*, 30.

72. Mobutu, *Paroles du président*, 31.

73. Roman Jakobson, *Essais de linguistique générale*, trans. Nicolas Ruwet (Paris: Éditions de Minuit, 1987), 177.

74. Pierre Legendre, *Le désir politique de Dieu* (Paris: Fayard, 1988), 47.

75. Legendre, *Jouir du pouvoir*, 159.

76. Roland Barthes, "The Old Rhetoric, an aide-mémoire," in *The Semiotic Challenge*, trans. Richard Howard (New York: Hill and Wang, 1988), 78ff.

77. Joseph Désiré Mobutu, *Le manifeste de la N'sélé, 20 Mai 1967* (Kinshasa: République de Zaire, Mouvement Populaire de la Révolution, 1982), 6.

78. Kant, "Perpetual Peace," 126.

79. Kantorowicz, *Mourir pour la patrie.*

80. Translator's note: The notions of "proximate power" and "sufficient grace" were central to the seventeenth-century dispute within the Catholic Church over the ideas of Cornelius Jansen, and over the extent to which similar doctrines by other philosophers could be declared heretical.

81. Blaise Pascal, *"Pensées" and "The Provincial Letters,"* trans. W. F. Trotter and Thomas M'Crie (New York: Random House/Modern Library, 1941), 330.

82. Maurice Merleau-Ponty, *Phenomenology of Perception,* trans. Colin Smith (London: Routledge & Kegan Paul Ltd., 1962), 184. In Wittgenstein there is also a strong relation between silence and language. This relation is circumscribed by the themes of the limit of language and of the unsayable. Silence is perceived here as that which, given the condition of saying, cannot be said.

83. This politics of silence is expressed by Baltasar Gracian, when he recommends holding oneself back more often than speaking. See Baltasar Gracian, *L'Homme de cour,* trad. Abraham Nicolas Amelot de la Houssaie (Paris: Éditions Lebovici, 1987), 108. As for relations between ruses, politics, opportunity, silence, and prudence, read Baltasar Gracian, *L'Homme universel,* trans. Joseph de Courbeville (Paris: Champ Libre, 1991), 145. This passage which addresses the "overall manner" was taken up and commented on by Vladimir Jankélévitch, *Le Je-ne-sais-quoi et le presque-rien,* vol. 1, *La Manière et l'occasion* (Paris: Seuil, 1980).

84. Joseph Dinouart, *L'art de se taire,* 2nd ed. 1771 (Paris: Jerome Millon, 1987), 57–58.

85. Dinouart, *L'art de se taire,* 63.

86. Soteriomania is a benign illness that seizes proud heads and brave hearts. Contagious affection (which affects politicians, intellectuals, and bankers) and whose manifestations convince the sick person that he is bearer of a great message, a great destiny, and a sublime historical action. State of a being who has renounced superfluousness and contingency.

87. Paul Veyne, *Le pain et le cirque* (Paris: Seuil, 1976), 665.

African Cultural Diversity in the Media

1. Kwame A. Appiah, *Cosmopolitanism: Ethics in a World of Strangers* (London: Allen Lane, 2006).

2. Claude Lefort, *Essais sur le politique, XIXe-XXe siècles* (Paris: Seuil, 1986), 25.

3. Vladimir Jankélévitch, *Le je-ne-sais-quoi et le presque-rien* (Paris: Seuil, 1981), 211.

4. Axel Honneth, *The Struggle for Recognition,* trans. J. Anderson. (Cambridge: Polity Press, 1995); Axel Honneth, *La société du mépris* (Paris: La Découverte, 2006).

5. Walter Benjamin, *Oeuvres,* vol. II. (Paris: Gallimard, 2000), 365.

6. The coup d'état should be understood here as a violent change in political regime by eliminating or sidelining the ruler and his government. Coups d'états in French-speaking Africa were started in 1963 in Togo, where soldiers assassinated the elected president Sylvanus Olympio. In 1964 it was Gabon's turn with the eviction of Léon Mba, who was reinstated by the French army. For a theoretical study of the coup d'état, see Gabriel Naudé, *Considérations politiques sur les coups d'états* (Paris: Gallimard, 2004).

7. *Subversive:* a term used by African political leaders who opted for the multiparty solution in their country after independence. The person opposed to that policy is a subversive. *Counter-revolutionary:* a term used several times by African Marxist regimes (Congo-Brazzaville from 1963 to the time of the Massamba regime) to indicate those opposed to central power. *Traitors to the nation, maquisards:* metaphors used during purges (the case of Sékou Toury in Guinea) to mark out those destined for state condemnation. *Mercenaries:* a catch-all term whose appearance and use go back to summer 1960, when Möise Tsombe proclaimed the Republic of Katanga, thus

effecting a secession from the young Democratic Republic of Congo, led at the time by President Kassavubu, Prime Minister Lumumba. and army Chief of Staff Joseph Désiré Mobutu. The word "mercenary" was used during the secession of Biafra in 1967–70 and in particular for the many coups d'états in the Comoros.

8. Marie-Hélène Gozzi, *Le terrorisme* (Paris: Ellipses, 2003).

9. Here the issue is to know whether old surveillance techniques for coups d'états are adequate for the prevention of terrorist acts.

10. Friedrich Nietzsche, *On the Genealogy of Morality and Other Writings*, trans. Carol Diethe, ed. Keith Ansell-Pearson (Cambridge: Cambridge University Press, 1994).

11. Sigmund Freud, "Instincts and Their Vicissitudes," in *The Standard Edition of the Complete Psychological Works of Sigmund Freud*, ed. James Strachey, vol. 14 (1914–16) (London: Hogarth Press, 1957), 139.

12. Max Scheler, *Ressentiment*, trans. William W. Holdheim, ed. Lewis A. Coser (New York: The Free Press of Glencoe, 1961), 45.

13. Scheler, *Ressentiment*, 46.

14. Scheler, *Ressentiment*, 46.

15. Scheler, *Ressentiment*, 46–47.

16. Béatrice Hibou, "Le 'Capital social' de l'état falsificateur, ou les ruses de l'intelligence économique," in *La criminalisation de l'état en Afrique*, ed. Jean-François Bayart, Stephen Ellis, Béatrice Hibou (Brussels: Complexe, 1997), 105–58; quoted in Xavier Raufer, *Dictionnaire technique et critique des nouvelles menaces* (Paris: Presses Universitaires de France, 1998), 10.

17. Raufer, *Dictionnaire technique*, 11.

18. Raufer, *Dictionnaire technique*.

19. George Simmel, *The Pauper*, trans. S. Draghici (Corvallis, OR: Plutarch Press, 2001).

20. Tatah Mentan, *Dilemmas of Weak States: Africa and Transnational Terrorism in the Twenty-First Century* (Aldershot, UK: Ashgate, 2004), 174ff.

Books between African Memory and Anticipation

I would like to dedicate this article to Élise Mbezele Mekoulou, Joséphine Ndzengue Bidima, Emmanuel Abina Mekoulou, and Roger Ebogo Bidoung.

1. Michel de Certeau observed that "ethnology occurs when the scene of the savage world acquires a homogeneity . . . as the space of 'objective' representation is detached from the observer's reason." *L'écriture de l'histoire*, (Paris: Seuil, 1975, 236); *The Writing of History*, trans. Tom Conley, European Perspectives Series (New York: Columbia University Press, 1988).

2. In the Beti language of Cameroon, *ayem kalara*, i.e., "he knows," is also used to designate "knowledge" and "book."

3. The book is a way for the subject to conjugate his or her historicity.

4. Cheikh Hamidou Kane, *L'aventure ambiguë* (Paris: Julliard, 1961). All quoted material translated by Lesley Kemp unless a specific English-language edition is cited.

5. Paraphrase from Mongo Beti, *Le pauvre Christ de Bomba* (Paris: Laffont, 1956); *The Poor Christ of Bomba*, trans. Gerald Moore (London: Heinemann, 1971), 30.

6. This is contrary to Philippe Laburthe-Tolra's thoughts on Cameroon, in *Vers la lumière ou le désir d'Ariel* (Paris: Karthala, 1999), 168.

7. F. Henneman, "Sieben Jahre Missionsarbeit in Kamerun," in *Zeitfragen aus der Weltmission 1*, (Aachen: Xavierius Verlag, 1918), 3. All quoted material translated by Lesley Kemp unless a specific English-language edition is cited.

8. N. Boeckheller, *Theodor Christaller, der erste deutsche Reichs-Schullehrer in Kamerun* (Leipzig: Emil Hermann Senior, 1897), 32.

9. Translator's note: This is a derogatory term in the French language to designate anything German.

10. See Laburthe-Tolra, *Vers la lumière*.

11. Laburthe-Tolra, *Vers la lumière*, 169.

12. H. Skolaster, *Die Pallotiner in Kamerun, 25 Jahre Missionsarbeit* (Limburg an der Lahn, 1924), 258.

13. Ian Linder, *Christianisme et pouvoir au Rwanda, 1900–1990* (Paris: Karthala, 1999), 65.

14. Cited in H. Froidevaux, *L'oeuvre scolaire de la France dans nos colonies* (Paris: Challamel, 1900), 20.

15. The philosopher Herbert Marcuse would describe as "repressive tolerance" this new form of censorship, which no longer keeps you from thinking, publishing, or reading, but which dictates how you should think, publish, and read.

16. This expression holds weighty implications, in that it relates to the subject who holds this memory and to the state of this memory. Can one speak of a "collective subject" who holds or produces this memory? The adventure of the "proletariat" as a "collective subject for-itself," messenger of humanity's emancipation, such as Marxist politicians and certain theorists have taught, is so eloquent that we tend to distrust the term "collective memory" with its corollary, "the productive collective subject" of this memory. The institution of the social is not a matter of an atomized individual either, since the creation of the instituting imaginary (Cornelius Castoriadis) cannot happen without the signifying community that, at the heart of a sociohistorical formation, prefigures the veracity and validity of the discourse each subject holds in regard to his or her history and its imbrications with other histories. As for the state of this memory, it remains a constantly gaping opening that further implies the state's end. The state is not static but a process of opening toward an elsewhere. One must always ask "state of what?" All this leads to considering the notion of collective memory not as a state, but as the provisional welding of dispositions, positions, and propositions, linking the subjects in a community of significations.

17. It is fitting to observe that the "past situation," once it has been captured by the historian's or the writer's discourse, becomes a construction. One reports an authentic event only by reconstructing it. See, in this regard, the epistemologists of history: Antoine Prost, *Douze Leçons sur l'histoire* (Paris: Seuil, 1996); Raymond Aron, *Dimensions de la conscience historique* (Paris: Plon, 1961); Marc Bloch, *Apologie pour l'histoire ou le métier d'historien* (Paris: A. Colin, 1960); Philippe Ariès, *Temps de l'histoire* (Paris: Seuil, 1986); Pierre Nora, "Passés recomposés: Champs et chantiers de l'histoire," in *Autrement* (Mutations series), (1985), No. 150–51.

18. Jacques Le Goff, *Histoire et mémoire* (Paris: Gallimard, 1988), 120. He quotes, but also comments on, Jack Goody's proposals in *La Raison graphique: La Domestication de la pensée sauvage*, trans. Alban Bensa (Paris: Éditions de Minuit, 1979), 192–93.

19. From an unpublished speech at UNESCO. It is the main point of his chapter, "La tradition vivante," in *General History of Africa*, vol. 1, *Methodology and African Prehistory*, ed. J. Ki-Zerbo (London: Heinemann Educational Books/Berkeley, CA: University of California Press, 1981), 166–203.

This proposition—which has been exploited—is naturally inaccurate. The library symbolizes knowledge; this sentence of Bâ's, in this sense, means that in Africa all elders are wise. This is false, because knowledge in traditional societies was a matter of elites. It was accessible only to those who passed the ordeals of initiation. There were indeed some old men who had failed these ordeals in their time. In addition, where does one find a society in which everyone is wise once they grow old? Knowledge is tension, conquest, trial and effort, and not a "state." Hampaté Bâ's sentence must be reviewed in the context of Africa's intergenerational struggle with its quarrels of legitimacy and hierarchy.

20. Paul Zumthor, *La lettre et la voix: De la littérature médiévale* (Paris: Seuil, 1987), 37: "By 'oral clues' I mean all that, inside of a text, informs us of the intervention of the human voice in its

publication: I mean in the mutation through which the text has passed . . . from a virtual state to an actual state. . . . Each text . . . demands a singular hearing: it contains its own oral clues."

21. See Hans Robert Jauss, *Pour une esthétique de la reception* (Paris: Gallimard, 1978); *Towards an Aesthetics of Reception,* trans. Timothy Bahti (Minneapolis: University of Minnesota Press, 1982).

22. See Didier Cahen, "Les Réponses du livre," in *Écrire le livre: Autour d'Edmond Jabès,* Actes du colloque de Cerisy (Seyssel: Champ Vallon, 1989), 57–70.

23. Brevié, *Bulletin de l'enseignement en AOF,* no. 74, 3. Cited in Abdou Moumouni, *L'education en Afrique* (Paris: Maspero, 1964), 54.

24. Brevié, *Bulletin de l'enseignement en AOF,* no. 83. Cited in Moumouni, *L'education en Afrique,* 54.

25. Ernest Nestor Roume, *Journal officiel de l'AOF,* no. 1024 (10 mai 1924). Cited in Moumouni, *L'education en Afrique,* 56.

26. Translator's note: This is a literary movement (approximately 1930–60) that began among French-speaking African and Caribbean writers living in Paris as a protest against French colonial rule and the policy of assimilation.

27. Paul Ricoeur, *Memory, History, Forgetting,* trans. Kathleen Blamey and David Pellauer (Chicago: University of Chicago Press, 2004), 81.

28. Jacques Lacan, *Encore: The Seminar of Jacques Lacan,* Book XX. *On Feminine Sexuality: The Limits of Love and Knowledge, 1972–1973,* ed. Jacques-Alain Miller, trans. Bruce Fink (New York: W. W. Norton, 1998), 120.

29. A. Marie Chartier, J. Hébrard, *Discours sur la lecture* (Paris: Fayard, 1989), 540.

The Internet and the African Academic World

1. Helen Fay Nissenbaum and Monroe E. Price, eds, *Academy and the Internet. Digital Formations, Vol. 12* (New York: Peter Lang: 2004).

2. Quoted in Georges Hardy, *L'enseignement au Sénégal de 1817 à 1854* (Paris: Larose, 1920), 57–58. All quoted material translated by Jean Burrell unless a specific English-language edition is cited.

3. Here readers are referred to the critique of this form of instrumental rationality by Max Horkheimer and Theodor W. Adorno, *The Dialectic of Enlightenment* (London: Verso, 1997).

4. Alioune Diop, "Le Sens de ce congrès." *Présence Africaine,* special issue (February–May 1959): 41.

5. Aimé Césaire, *Cahier d'un retour au pays natal* (Paris: Présence Africaine, 1956), 25.

6. Marcien Towa, *L'idée d'une philosophie négro-africaine* (Yaoundé, Cameroon: Editions Clé, 1979), 51–52.

7. Francis Jauréguiberry and Serge Proulx, eds, *Internet, nouvel espace citoyen?* (Paris: L'Harmattan, 2003), 9.

8. Jauréguiberry and Proulx, *Internet, nouvel espace citoyen?,* 9.

9. Nissenbaum and Monroe, *Academy and the Internet,* 43.

10. Nissenbaum and Monroe, *Academy and the Internet,* 40.

11. Paul Ricoeur, *Memory, History, Forgetting,* trans. Kathleen Blamey and David Pellauer (Chicago: University of Chicago Press, 2004), 413 (translation altered).

12. Ricoeur, *Memory, History, Forgetting.*

13. Valère Novarina, *Devant la parole* (Paris: P.O.L., 1999), 13.

14. Novarina, *Devant la parole,* 13.

15. Philippe Breton, *Éloge de la parole* (Paris: La Découverte, 2003), 19.

Works Cited

Abbele, A., et al. *Des prêtres noirs s'interrogent*. Paris: Cerf, 1956.

Abélès, Marc. "Aînesse et générations à Ochollo." In *Âge, pouvoir, et société en Afrique noire*. Edited by Marc Abélès and Chantal Collard. Paris: Karthala, 1985.

Adorno, Theodor W. *Critical Models: Interventions and Catchwords*, trans. Henry W. Pickford. New York: Columbia University Press, 2005.

Adotevi, Stanislas Spero. *Négritude et négrologues*. Paris: Union Générale d'Éditions, 1972.

Ageron, Charles-Robert. *L'Anticolonialisme en France de 1871 à 1914*. Paris: Presses Universitaires de France, 1973.

Ajala, Adekunle. *Pan-africanism*. London: A. Deutsch Ltd., 1973.

Al-Jabri, Mohammad 'Abed. *Arab-Islamic Philosophy: A Contemporary Critique*. Translated by Aziz Abbassi. Austin, TX: Center for Middle Eastern Studies: University of Texas, 1999.

Appiah, Kwame A. *Cosmopolitanism: Ethics in a World of Strangers*. London: Allen Lane, 2006.

Arendt, Hannah. *Between Past and Future: Eight Exercises in Political Thought*. New York: Penguin, 1993.

———. *Crises of the Republic*. New York: Harcourt, Brace and Co., 1972.

———. *Lectures on Kant's Political Philosophy*. Edited by Ron Beiner. Chicago: University of Chicago Press, 1982.

———. *Men in Dark Times*. New York: Harvest, 1970.

———. *On Revolution*. New York: Viking Press, 1963.

Ariès, Philippe. *Temps de l'histoire*. Paris: Seuil, 1986.

Aristotle, *Éthique à Nicomaque*. Translated by J. Tricot. Paris: Vrin, 1994.

———. *Rhetoric*. In *The Basic Works of Aristotle*. Edited by Richard McKeon. New York: Random House, 1941.

Arnaud, André-Jean. *Essai d'analyse structurale du code civil français*. Paris: Librairie Générale de Droit et de Jurisprudence, 1973.

Aron, Raymond. *Dimensions de la conscience historique*. Paris: Plon, 1961.

Atangana, B. "Actualité de la palabre?" *Études* 324 (1966).

Atienza, Manuel. "Juridicité." In *Dictionnaire encyclopédique de théorie et de sociologie du droit*. Edited by Andre J. Arnaud. Paris: Librairie générale de droit et de jurisprudence-Story Scientia, 1998.

Augé, Marc. *Théorie des pouvoirs et idéologie*. Paris: Hermann, 1974.

Austin, John L. *How to Do Things with Words*, 2nd ed. Edited by J. O. Urmson and Marina Sbisà. Cambridge, MA: Harvard University Press, 1975.

Bâ, Amadou Hampaté. "The Living Tradition." In *Methodology and African Prehistory*. Volume 1 of *General History of Africa*, 166–203. Edited by J. Ki-Zerbo. London: Heinemann Educational Books/Berkeley, CA: University of California Press, 1981.

Badiane, Aloiune, et al. *Pauvreté urbaine et accès à la justice en Afrique*. Paris: L'Harmattan, 1995.

Bakomba, Katik Diong. "La palabre africaine." In *Les imaginaires*. Paris: Union Générale d'Éditions, 1976.

Balanda, Gérard. "L'organisation judiciaire chez les Basakata, les Badja et les Boma." In *L'organisation judiciaire en Afrique*. Edited by John Gilissen. Brussels: Éditions de l'Institut de Sociologie, 1969.

Balandier, Georges. *Anthropo-logiques*. Paris: Le Livre de poche, 1985.

———. *Le pouvoir sur scènes*. Paris: Balland, 1980.

Bange, Pierre. *Analyse conversationnelle et théorie de l'action*. Paris: Hatier/Didier, 1992.

Barthes, Roland. "The Old Rhetoric, an Aide-Mémoire." In *The Semiotic Challenge*. Translated by Richard Howard. New York: Hill and Wang, 1988.

Bataille, Georges. *Inner Experience*. Translated by Leslie Anne Boldt. Albany: State University of New York Press, 1988.

———. *Écrits posthumes, Oeuvres complètes*, vol. 2. Paris: Gallimard, 1970.

Baudelaire, Charles. *Les fleurs du mal*. Translated by Richard Howard. Boston: David R. Godine, 1982.

Bayart, Jean-François. *L'état en Afrique: La politique du ventre*. Paris: Fayard, 1991.

Bayart, Jean-François, Achille Mbembe, and Comi Toulabor. *Le politique par le bas en Afrique noire*. Paris: Karthala, 1992.

Bazelaire, Jean-Paul and Thierry Cretin. *La justice pénale internationale*. Paris: Presses Universitaires de France, 2000.

Benjamin, Walter. *Oeuvres*, vol. II. Paris: Gallimard, 2000.

Bernault, Florence, ed. *A History of Prison and Confinement in Africa*. Translated by Janet Roitman. Portsmouth, NH: Heinemann, 2003.

Beti, Mongo. *The Poor Christ of Bomba*. Translated by Gerald Moore. London: Heinemann, 1971.

———. *Mission terminée*. Paris: Buchet-Chastel, 1957.

Bianchi, Hermann. *Justice as Sanctuary: Toward a New System of Crime Control*. Bloomington: Indiana University Press, 1994.

Bidima, Jean-Godefroy. *Théorie critique et modernité négro-africaine: De l'école de Francfort à la "Docta Spes Africana."* Paris: Publications de la Sorbonne, 1993.

———. *La Palabre: Une juridiction de la parole*. Paris: Éditions Michalon, 1997.

———. "Rationalities and Legal Processes in Africa." *Diogenes* 202 (2004): 69–72.

———. "African Cultural Diversity in the Media." *Diogenes* 55 (2006): 122–33.

———. "The Internet and the African Academic World." *Diogenes* 211 (2008): 93–100.

———. "Croire: Interrogations Philosophiques sur les Réligions en Afrique: Représentations, Institutions et Médiations." In *Philosophy of Religion*. Volume 10 of *Contemporary Philosophy*. Edited by G. Fløistad. Springer, 2010.

———. "L'art négro-africain des 'sans-espoir.'" *Raison Présente* 82 (1987).

Bloch, Ernst. *L'héritage de ce temps*. Paris: Payot, 1978.

———. *The Principle of Hope*, vol. 1. Translated by Neville Plaice, Stephen Plaice, and Paul Knight. Cambridge, MA: MIT Press, 1986.

Bloch, Marc. *Apologie pour l'histoire ou le metier d'historien*. Paris: A. Colin, 1960.

Boeckheller, N. *Theodor Christaller, der erste deutsche Reischs-Schullehrer in Kamerun*. Leipzig, Germany: Emil Hermann Senior, 1897.

Bonafé-Schmitt, Jean-Pierre. *La médiation: une justice douce*. Paris: Syros, 1992.

Botbol-Baum, Mylène, ed. *Bioéthique dans les pays du sud*. Paris: L'Harmattan, 2005.

Bourjol, Maurice, et al. *Pour une critique du droit*. Grenoble: Presses Universitaires de Grenoble, 1978.

Breton, Philippe. *Éloge de la parole*. Paris: La Découverte, 2003.

Breyer, Stephen. *Active Liberty*. Oxford: Oxford University Press, 2008.

Buhan, Christine, and Étienne Kange Essiben. *La mystique du corps: Jalons pour une anthropologie du corps*. Paris: L'Harmattan, 1979.

Bujo, Bénézet. *Foundations of an African Ethic: Beyond the Universal Claims of Western Morality*. Translated by Brian McNeil. New York: Crossroad Publishing, 2001.

Cahen, Didier. "Les reponses du livre." In *Écrire le livre: Autour d'Edmond Jabès*. Actes du colloque de Cerisy. Seyssel: Champ Vallon, 1989.

Campana, Robert. "De L'intervention punitive ou de l'extension du droit pénal aux relations internationales." *Studia philosophica* 64 (2005).

Carbonnier, Jean. *Flexible droit*. Paris: Librairie Générale de Droit et de Jurisprudence, 1975.

Cario, Robert. Preface. In Howard Zehr, *La justice restaurative. Pour sortir des impasses de la logique punitive*. Geneva: Éditions Labor et Fides, 2012.

Castoriadis, Cornelius. *The Imaginary Institution of Society*. Translated by Kathleen Blamey. Cambridge, MA: MIT Press, 1987.

Césaire, Aimé. *Cahier d'un retour au pays natal*. Paris: Présence Africaine, 1956.

———. *Discourse on Colonialism*. Translated by Joan Pinkham. New York: Monthly Review Press, 1972.

Charaudeau, Patrick. *Langage et discours: Éléments de sémiolinguistique*. Paris: Hachette, 1985.

Chartier, Anne-Marie, and Jean Hébrard. *Discours sur la lecture*. Paris: Fayard, 1989.

Cheza, Maurice, Henri Deroitte, and René Luneau. *Les évêques d'Afrique parlent, 1969–1991*. Documents Pour le Synode Africaine. Paris: Centurion, 1992.

Cioran, Emil. *Précis de décomposition*, in *Oeuvres*. Paris: Gallimard, 1995.

———. *Oeuvres*. Paris: Gallimard, 2003.

Clark, Philip. *The Gacaca Courts, Post-Genocide Justice and Reconciliation in Rwanda: Justice without Lawyers*. Cambridge: Cambridge University Press, 2010.

Comby, Jean. *Deux mille ans d'évangélisation*. Paris: Desclée de Brouwer, 1992.

Copans, Jean. "La banalisation de l'état africain. À propos de l'état en Afrique de J. F. Bayart." *Politique Africaine* 37 (1990).

———. "No Shortcuts to Democracy: The Long March towards Modernity." *Review of African Political Economy* 50 (1991).

Cornu, Gérard. *Vocabulaire juridique*. Paris: Presses Universitaires de France, 1987.

———. *Linguistique juridique*. Paris: Montchrestien, 1990.

Courtois, Gérard. "La vengeance, du désir aux institutions." In *La vengeance, Vol 4: La vengeance dans la pensée occidentale*. Paris: Éditions Cujas, 1985.

Crawford, Adam. "Justice de proximité—The Growth of Houses of Justice and Victim/ Offender Mediation in France: A Very UnFrench Legal Response?" *Social and Legal Studies* 9, no. 1 (2000).

Danblon, Emmanuelle. "Rhétorique, universalité et ritualité: Réflexions à propos de la palabre." In *Les cahiers de la MSHE Ledoux*. Transmission, identite, metissage, 2009.

Davidson, Basil, and Barry Munslow. "The Crisis of the Nation State in Africa." *Review of African Political Economy* 49 (1990).

Davis, Angela. *Are Prisons Obsolete?* New York: Seven Stories Press, 2003.

Decalo, Samuel. "The Process, Prospects and Constraints of Democratization in Africa." *African Affairs* 91 (1992).

De Certeau, Michel. *La culture au pluriel*. Paris: Union Générale d'Éditions, 1974.

———. *L'écriture de l'histoire*. Paris: Seuil, 1975.

———. *Histoire et psychanalyse entre science et fiction*. Paris: Gallimard, 1987.

Delsol, Chantal. *L'Âge du renoncement*. Paris: Éditions du Cerf, 2011.

Derrida, Jacques. *On Cosmopolitanism and Forgiveness*. Translated by Mark Dooley and Michael Hughes. Preface by Simon Critchley and Richard Kearney. London and New York: Routledge, 1997.

D'Hertefett, M. "Mythes et ideologies dans le Rwanda ancien et contemporain." In *The Historian in Tropical Africa*. Edited by J. Mauny, R. Thomas, and L. V. Vansina. London: Oxford University Press for the International African Institute, 1964.

Dia, Mamadou. *Nations africaines et solidarité mondiale*. Paris: Presses Universitaires de France, 1960.

Diagne, Pathé. "Accès à la justice dans les quartiers urbains pauvres: Dakar, Abidjan, Niamey, Ouagadougou." In *Pauvreté urbaine et accès à la justice en Afrique*, 27–116. Translated by Alioune Badiane et al. Paris, L'Harmattan, 1995.

Dinouart, Joseph. *L'art de se taire*, 2nd ed. [1771]. Paris: Jérôme Millon, 1987.

Diop, Alioune. "Le Sens de ce congrès." *Présence Africaine*, special issue (February–May 1959): 24–25.

Draï, Raphaël. *Le Pouvoir et la Parole*. Paris: Payot, 1981.

Dubouchet, Paul. *Le Modèle juridique, droit et herméneutique*. Paris: L'Harmattan, 2001.

Ducrot, Oswald, and Tzvetan Todorov. *Dictionnaire encyclopédique des sciences du langage*. Paris: Seuil, 1972.

Dufour, Dany-Robert. *L'individu qui vient . . . après le libéralisme*. Paris: Denoël, 2011.

Durand, Claude. *Les anciennes Coutumes pénales du Tchad*. Paris: L'Harmattan, 2002.

Duverger, Maurice. *Les partis politiques*. Paris: Armand Colin, 1952

Eco, Umberto. *La guerre du faux*. Translated by Myriam Tanant and Piero Caracciolo. Paris: Grasset, 1985.

Eboussi-Boulaga, Fabien. *Les conférences nationales en Afrique noire*. Paris: Karthala, 1993.

Edel, May Mandelbaum. "Property among the Ciga in Uganda." *Africa* 11, no. 3 (1938).

Elechi, O. Oko. 2006. *Doing Justice Without the State: The Afikpo (Ehugbo) Nigeria Model*. New York: Routledge.

Elungu, Pene Elungu A. *L'éveil philosophique africain*. Paris: L'Harmattan, 1985.

Epprecht, Marc. *Heterosexual Africa? The History of an Idea from the Age of Exploration to the Age of AIDS*. Columbus: Ohio University Press/University of KwaZulu-Natal Press, 2008.

Eyadema, "Discours programme prononcé lors du congrès constitutif du Rassemblement du Peuple Togolais." In Claude Feuillet, *Le Togo en général*. Paris: Éditions ABC, 1976.

Fanon, Frantz. *Black Skin, White Masks*. Translated by Charles Lam Markman. New York: Grove Press, 1967.

Farge, Arlette. *Subversive Words: Public Opinion in Eighteenth-Century France*. Translated by Rosemary Morris. University Park: Pennsylvania State University Press, 1995.

Ferry, Jules. *Discours sur la politique extérieure et colonial*. Paris: Armand Colin, 1897.

Flahault, François. "Le Fonctionnement de la parole." *Communication* 30 (1979).

Fleury, Cynthia. *Les pathologies de la democratie*. Paris: Fayard, 2005.

Foucault, Michel. *Histoire de la sexualite*, vol. 1, *La volonté de savoir*. Paris: Gallimard, 1976.

———. "The Eye of Power." In Jeremy Bentham, *Le panoptique*. Paris: Pierre Belfond, 1977.

———. *Discipline and Punish: Birth of the Prison*. Translated by Alan Sheridan. New York: Vintage Books, 1977.

———. *The Birth of Biopolitics, Lectures at the Collège de France 1978–1979*. Edited by Michel Senellart, translated by Graham Burchell. New York: Picador, 2008.

Fourquet, François. "L'accumulation du pouvoir ou le désir d'État." *Revue Recherches* 46 (1982).

François, G. and Marriol, H. *Législation coloniale*. Paris: Librairie Larose, 1929.

Frank, Andre Gunder. "No Escape From the Laws of World Economics." *Review of African Political Economy* 50 (1991).

Fraser, Nancy. "Rethinking the Public Sphere: A Contribution to the Critique of Actually Existing Democracy." In *Habermas and the Public Sphere*, 109–42. Edited by Craig Calhoun. Cambridge, MA: MIT Press, 1992.

Freedman, J. "Je suis Nyakagarura . . ." In *Âge, pouvoir, et société en Afrique noire*. Edited by Marc Abélès and Chantal Collard. Paris: Karthala, 1985.

Freud, Sigmund. "Instincts and Their Vicissitudes." In *The Standard Edition of the Complete Psychological Works of Sigmund Freud*, vol. 14, 1914–16. Edited by James Strachey. London: Hogarth Press, 1957.

Friedman, Lawrence M., Jean Guy Belley. "Juridicisation," in *Dictionnaire encyclopédique de théorie et de sociologie du droit*, ed. Ándre J. Arnaud. Paris: Librairie générale de droit et de jurisprudence-Story Scientia, 1998.

Froidevaux, H. *L'oeuvre scolaire de la France dans nos colonies*. Paris: Challamel, 1900.

Gadamer, Hans Georg. *Truth and Method*, 2nd rev. ed. Translated by Joel Weinsheimer and Donald G. Marshall. London: Continuum, 2004.

Garapon, Antoine. *Le gardien des promesses*. Paris: Odile Jacob, 1996.

———. *L'Âne portant des reliques: Essai sur le rituel judiciaire*. Paris: Le Centurion, 1985.

———. "Presentation." In *Pour une démocratie active*. Paris: Odile Jacob, 2007.

Gauchet, Marcel. "La dette de sens et les racines de l'Etat." *Libre, politique—anthropologie—philosophie* 77, no. 2 (1977).

———. "La dette de sens consubstantielle à la vie sociale." In *La condition politique*. Paris: TEL/Gallimard, 2005.

Genette, Gérard. *Seuils*. Paris: Seuil, 1987.

Gibbs, James L. "The Kpelle Moot: A Therapeutic Model for the Informal Settlement of Disputes." *Africa* 33, no. 1 (1963).

Glissen, John and Jacques Vanderlinden. "L'organisation judiciaire en Afrique noire." In *L'organisation judiciare en Afrique noire*. Brussels: Editions de l'Institut de Sociologie, ULB, 1969.

Godbout, Jacques T. *Ce qui circule entre nous, donner, recevoir, rendre*. Paris: Seuil, 2007.

Goffman, Erving. "The Interaction Order: American Sociological Association, 1982 Presidential Address." *American Sociological Review* 48, no. 1 (1983): 1–17.

Gonidec, Pierre F. *Les systèmes politiques africains*, 2nd ed. Paris: Librairie générale de droit et de jurisprudence, 1978.

———. and Alain Bockel, *L'état Africain*, 2nd ed. Paris: Librarie Générale de Droit et de Jurisprudence, 1985.

Goody, Jack. *La raison graphique: La domestication de la pensée sauvage*. Translated by Alban Bensa. Paris: Éditions de Minuit, 1979.

Gozzi, Marie-Hélène. *Le terrorisme*. Paris: Ellipses, 2003.

Gracian, Baltasar. *L'homme de Cour*. Translated by Abraham Nicolas Amelot de la Houssaie. Paris: Éditions Lebovici, 1987.

———. *L'homme universel*. Translated by Joseph de Courbeville. Paris: Champ Libre, 1991.

Grave, Jean. *La colonisation*. Paris: Publications des Temps Nouveaux, 1912.

Greimas, A. J. "Pour une sémiotique topologique" In *Sémiotique de l'espace*. Paris, Denoël-Gonthier, 1979.

Grosser, Alfred. *L'explication politique*, 2nd ed. Brussels: Éditions Complexe, 1984.

Guernais, M. E. "Aînés, aînées; cadets et cadettes." In *Âge, pouvoir et société en Afrique noire*. Edited by Marc Abélès and Chantal Collard. Paris: Karthala, 1985.

Habermas, Jürgen. *La pensée postmétaphysique. Essais philosophiques*. Paris: Armand Colin, 1993.

———. *Between Facts and Norms: Contributions to a Discourse Theory of Law and Democracy*. Translated by William Rehg. Cambridge: MIT Press, 1996.

———. *The Structural Transformation of the Public Sphere: An Inquiry into a Category of Bourgeois Society*. Translated by Thomas Burger with the assistance of Frederick Lawrence. Cambridge, MA: MIT Press, 1999.

Hardy, Georges. *L'enseignement au Sénégal de 1817 à 1854*. Paris: Larose, 1920.

Hartog, François. *Les régimes d'historicité*. Paris: Seuil, 2012.

Hebblethwaite, Peter. *Jean XXIII, Le pape du Concile*. Paris: Le Centurion, 1988.

Hegba, Meinrad. "Personnalité de l'Église particulière," *Telema*, January, 1979.

Heidegger, Martin. *Being and Time*. Translated by John MacQuarrie and Edward Robinson. New York: Harper & Brothers, 1962.

———. *On the Way to Language*. Translated by Peter D. Hertz. New York: HarperCollins, 1971.

Hengehold, Laura. *The Body Problematic: Political Imagination in Kant and Foucault*. University Park: Pennsylvania State University Press, 2007.

Henneman, F. "Sieben Jahre Missionsarbeit in Kamerun." In *Zeitfragen aus der Weltmission 1*. Aachen: Xaverius Verlag, 1918.

Hérault, George. "Modes informels de résolution des conflits dans les quartiers pauvres d'Ibadan." In *Pauvreté urbaine et accès à la justice en Afrique*, 401–19. Edited by Alioune Badiane et al. Paris, L'Harmattan, 1995.

Hibou, Béatrice. "Le 'capital social' de l'État falsificateur, ou les ruses de l'intelligence économique." In *La criminalisation de l'etat en Afrique*, 105–58. Edited by Jean-François Bayart, Stephen Ellis, and Béatrice Hibou. Brussels: Complexe, 1997.

Hofnung, Michèle Guillaume. "Que Sais-Je?" In *La médiation*. Paris: Presses Universitaires de France, 2000.

Honneth, Axel. *The Struggle for Recognition*. Translated by J. Anderson. Cambridge: Polity Press, 1995.

———. *La societé du mépris: Vers une nouvelle théorie critique*. Paris: La Découverte, 2006.

Horkheimer, Max. *Notes critiques (1949–1969)*. Paris: Petite Bibliotheque Payot, 2009.

Horkheimer, Max, and Theodor W. Adorno. *The Dialectic of Enlightenment*. London: Verso, 1997.

Hountondji, Paulin. *Sur la philosophie africaine*. Paris: Maspéro, 1977.

Hugo, Victor. "Discours sur l'Afrique, 18 mai 1879." In *La France colonisatrice*. Edited by Paul Arène et al. Paris: Liana Lévy, S. Messinger, 1983.

Irele, Francis Abiola. "Bidima Jean-Godefroy." In *Africana: The Encyclopedia of the African and African American Experience*. Edited by Kwame Anthony Appiah and Henry Louis Gates, Jr. New York: Oxford University Press, 2005.

Iwélé, Gode. *Mgr. Monsengwo, témoin et acteur de l'histoire*. Brussels: Duclot, 1995.

Jacques, Francis. *Espace logique d'interlocution*. Paris: PUF, 1985.

Jakobson, Roman. *Essais de linguistique générale*. Translated by Nicolas Ruwet. Paris: Éditions de Minuit, 1987.

Jankélévitch, Vladmir. *Le je-ne-sais-quoi et le presque rien*. Paris: Seuil, 1981.

Jauréguiberry, Francis, and Serge Proulx, eds. *Internet, nouvel espace citoyen?* Paris: L'Harmattan, 2003.

Jauss, Hans Robert. *Pour une esthétique de la reception*. Paris: Gallimard, 1978.

Jeol, Michel. *La réforme de la justice en Afrique noire*. Paris: Éditions A. Pedone, 1963.

Jouanjan, Olivier. "Nommer; Normer." In *99 Sciences et humanités, La dénomination*, no. 1 (1999).

Kabasele-Lumbala, François. *Le Christianisme et l'Afrique, une chance réciproque*. Paris: Karthala, 1993.

Kafureeka, Lawyer. "Multiparty Movement in Africa." In *Democracy and Democratization in Africa, Final Report*. The Hague: Institute of Social Studies and Global Coalition for Africa, 1993.

Kane, Cheikh Hamidou. *L'aventure ambiguë*. Paris: Julliard, 1961.

Kant, Immanuel. "Perpetual Peace: A Philosophical Sketch." In *Kant: Political Writings*, 2nd ed. Edited by Hans Reiss, translated by H. B. Nisbet. Cambridge: Cambridge University Press, 1970.

Kantorowicz, Ernst. *Les deux corps du roi*. Paris: Gallimard, 1989.

———. *Mourir pour la patrie*. Paris: Presses Universitaires de France, 1984.

Kaufmann, Pierre. *L'inconscient du politique*. Paris: Librarie Philosophique J. Vrin, 1988.

Kelsen, Hans. *Théorie pure du droit*. Paris: Dalloz, 1962.

Klute, Georg; Birgit Embaló, ldrissa Embaló, "Local Strategies of Conflict Resolution in Guinea-Bissau. A Project Proposal in Legal Anthropology." *Recht in Afrika* 2 (2006).

Kodjo-Grandvaux, Séverine. *Constructions et déconstructions de l'idée de "philosophie africaine": étude comparative des œuvres de Jean-Godefroy Bidima, Souleymane Bachir Diagne, Henry Odera Oruka et Kwasi Wiredu*. PhD diss., Université de Rouen, 2006.

Koselleck, Reinhart. *Futures Past: On the Semantics of Historical Time*. Translated by Keith Tribe. Cambridge, MA: MIT Press, 1985.

Laburthe-Tolra, Philippe. *Les seigneurs de la forêt*. Paris: Publications de la Sorbonne, 1981.

———. *Vers la lumière ou le désir d'Ariel*. Paris: Karthala, 1999.

Lacan, Jacques. *Encore: The Seminar of Jacques Lacan*, Book XX. *On Feminine Sexuality: The Limits of Love and Knowledge, 1972–1973*. Edited by Jacques-Alain Miller, translated by Bruce Fink. New York: Norton, 1998.

La justice dans les pays francophones. Paris: ACCT, 1995.

L'Afrique sous la domination coloniale 1880–1935. Volume 7 of *Histoire générale de l'Afrique*. Edited by Comité scientifique international pour la rédaction d'une histoire générale de l'Afrique (Unesco). Paris: Présence Africaine Édicef/UNESCO, 1989.

Lefort, Claude. *Democracy and Political Theory*. Translated by David Macey. Minneapolis: University of Minnesota Press, 1988.

———. *Les formes de l'histoire, Essais d'anthropologie politique*. Paris: Gallimard, 1978.

Le Goff, Jacques. *Histoire et mémoire*. Paris: Gallimard, 1988.

Legendre, Pierre. *Le Désir politique de Dieu*. Paris: Fayard, 1988.

———. *Dominium Mundi*. Paris: Mille et Une Nuits, 2007.

———. *L'empire de la verité*. Paris: Fayard, 1983.

———. *Jouir du pouvoir*. Paris: Éditions de Minuit, 1976.

———. *Leçons III: Dieu au miroir. Étude sur l'institution des images*. Paris: Fayard, 1994.

———. *Paroles poétiques échappées du texte*. Paris: Seuil, 1982.

Leroy, Étienne, *Le jeu des Lois, une anthropologie "dynamique" du droit*. Paris, LGDJ, 1999.

Lévinas, Emmanuel. *Le temps et l'autre.* Paris, Artaud, 1948.

Lévi-Strauss, Claude. *Race et histoire.* Paris: Denoël, 1967.

———. *Structural Anthropology,* vol. 2. Translated by Monique Layton. New York: Basic Books, 1976.

Linder, Ian. *Christianisme et pouvoir au Rwanda, 1900–1990.* Paris: Karthala, 1999.

Lopes, Daniel. "Médiations politiques africaines 'par le haut': Analyse empirique et essai de théorisation." In *Perspectives Internationales,* no. 3 (January–June 2013).

Loraux, Nicole. *The Divided City.* Translated by Corinne Pache with Jeff Fort. Cambridge, MA: Zone Books, 2002.

Luneau, René. *Laisse aller mon peuple! Églises africaines au-delà des modeles?* Paris: Karthala, 1987.

Lyotard, Jean-François. *The Différend: Phrases in Dispute.* Translated by Georges Van Den Abeele. Minneapolis: University of Minnesota Press, 1988.

Macaire, Pierre. *L'héritage makhuwa au Mozambique.* Paris: L'Harmattan, 1996.

MacIntyre, Alasdair. *Whose Justice? Which Rationality?* Notre Dame, IN.: University of Notre Dame Press, 1988.

Maertens, Jean-Thierry. *Ritanalyses,* vol. 1. Paris: Jérôme Millon, 1987.

Mahiou, Ahmed. *L'avènement du parti unique en Afrique noire.* Paris: Librarie générale de droit et de jurisprudence, 1969.

Main, D. "L'acte de juger." *Pouvoirs,* 55 (1990).

Manaï, D. in *Dictionnaire encyclopédique de théorie et de sociologie du droit.* Edited by A. J. Arnaud. Paris: Librairie générale de droit et de jurisprudence, 1988.

Maingueneau, Dominique. *Initiation aux méthodes d'analyse du discours.* Paris: Hachette, 1976.

Marcuse, Herbert, *Hegel's Ontology and the Theory of Historicity.* Translated by Seyla Benhabib. Cambridge, MA: MIT Press, 1987.

Martin, Denis-Constant. "La politique en Afrique noire: pouvoir, compétition, invention." *Études* 5 (1989).

Marx, Karl. *Le 18 Brumaire de Louis Bonaparte.* Paris: Éditions Sociales, 1969.

———. *Grundrisse: Introduction to the Critique of Political Economy.* Translated by Martin Nicolaus. New York: Vintage Books, 1973.

——— and Frederick Engels. *The German Ideology.* Translated by W. Lough, edited by Roy Pascal. In *Karl Marx and Frederick Engels, Collected Works, Vol 5: 1845–1847.* New York: International Publishers, 1976.

M'baye, Kéba. "Sacralité, croyances, pouvoir et droit en Afrique." In *Sacralité, pouvoir et droit en Afrique, Table ronde préparatoire du 4ème colloque du Centre d'Études Juridiques Comparatives organisée par le LAJP.* Edited by Mamadou Wane. Paris: Editions du CNRS, 1979.

Mbembe, Achille. *On the Postcolony.* Berkeley: University of California Press, 2002.

Mbonimpa, Melchior. *Idéologies de l'indépendance africaine.* Paris: L'Harmattan, 1986.

Meister, Albert. *L'Afrique peut-elle partir?* Paris: Seuil, 1966.

Meledje, Raymond Mel. "Emokr: Systèmes de gestion des conflits chez les Odjukru." PhD diss., École des Hautes Études en Sciences Sociales, 1994.

Melone, Thomas. *De la négritude dans la litterature négro-africaine.* Paris: Présence Africaine, 1962.

Menga, Guy. *La Palabre sterile.* Yaoundé, Cameroon: Éditions Clé, 1970.

Mentan, Tatah. *Dilemmas of Weak States: Africa and Transnational Terrorism in the Twenty-First Century.* Aldershot: Ashgate, 2004.

Merleau-Ponty, Maurice. *Phenomenology of Perception*. Translated by Colin Smith. London: Routledge & Kegan Paul Ltd., 1962.

———. *The Visible and the Invisible*. Translated by Alphonso Lingis. Evanston, IL: Northwestern University Press, 1968.

———. *The Prose of the World*. Translated by J. O'Neill. Evanston, IL: Northwestern University Press, 1973.

Middleton, John, and David Tait, eds. *Tribes without Rulers*. London: Routledge, 1958.

Mobutu, Joseph Désiré. *Le manifeste de la N'sélé, 20 Mai 1967*. Kinshasa: République de Zaïre, Mouvement Populaire de la Révolution, 1982.

———. *Paroles du président*. Kinshasa: Éditions du Leopard, 1968.

Moumouni, Abdou. *L'education en Afrique*. Paris: Maspero, 1964.

Montesquieu, *The Spirit of the Laws*. Translated and edited by Anne M. Cohler, Basia C. Miller, and Harold S. Stone. Cambridge: Cambridge University Press, 1989.

Moore, Gerald. *Seven African Writers*. London: Oxford University Press, 1962.

Morris, Ruth. *Penal Abolition: The Practical Choice*. Canadian Scholars Press, 1998.

Musso, Henri. *Critique des réseaux*. Paris: Presses Universitaires de France, 2003.

Nahoum-Grappe, Véronique. *Du rêve de vengeance à la haine politique*. Paris: Buchet-Chastel, 2003.

Naudé, Gabriel. *Considérations politiques sur les coups d'états*. Paris: Gallimard, 2004.

Negt, Oskar: *L'espace public oppositionnel*. Paris: Payot, 2007.

Nesbitt, Nick. *Universal Emancipation, the Haitian Revolution and the Radical Enlightenment*, Charlottesville: University of Virginia Press, 2008.

Nietzsche, Friedrich. *On the Genealogy of Morality and Other Writings*. Translated by Carol Diethe, edited by Keith Ansell-Pearson. Cambridge: Cambridge University Press, 1994.

Nissenbaum, Helen Fay, and Monroe E. Price, eds. *Academy and the Internet. Digital Formations*, vol. 12. New York: Peter Lang: 2004.

Ngal, Georges. *Aimé Césaire: Un homme à la recherche d'une patrie*. Paris: Présence Africaine, 1994.

Nkrumah, Kwame. *Africa Must Unite*. London: Heinemann, 1962.

———. *Consciencism: Philosophy and Ideology for De-colonization*. New York: Monthly Review Press, 1970.

Nora, Pierre. "Passés recomposés: Champs et chantiers de l'histoire." In *Autrement* (Mutations series) (1985): 150–51.

Novarina, Valère. *Devant la parole*. Paris: P.O.L., 1999.

Nyerere, Julius. *Freedom and Unity/Uhuru na Umoja: A Selection from Writings and Speeches, 1952–65*. London: Oxford University Press, 1967.

———. *Freedom and Socialism/Uhuru na Ujamaa: A Selection from Writings and Speeches, 1965–1967*. Oxford: Oxford University Press, 1968.

——— and Pierre Buis. *La Déclaration d'Arusha, dix ans après*. Paris: L'Harmattan, 1978.

Nzegwu, Nkiru Uwechia. *Family Matters: Feminist Concepts in African Philosophy of Culture*. Albany: SUNY Press, 2006.

Oppetit, Bruno. "Sur le concept d'arbitrage." In *Le droit des relations économiques internationales: Études offertes à Bertold Goldmann*. Edited by P. Fouchard, Ph. Kahn, and A. Lyon-Caen. Paris: Libraries techniques, 1982.

———. *Essai sur la codification*. Paris: Presses Universitaires de France, 1998.

Orecchioni, Catherine Kerbrat. *L'Implicite*. Paris: Armand Colin, 1986.

———. *Les interactions verbales*, vol. 1. Paris: Armand Colin, 1990.

Ost, François. *Du Sinaï au Champ de Mars. L'autre et le même au fondement du droit*. Brussels: Editions Lessius, 1999.

———. *Le temps du droit*. Paris: Odile Jacob, 1999.

———. *Dire le droit faire justice*. Brussels: Éditions Bruylant, 2007.

Owusu, Maxwell. "Democracy and Africa—A View from the Village." *The Journal of Modern Studies* 30, no. 3 (1992).

Oyono, Ferdinand. *Chemin d'Europe*. Paris: Union Générale d'Éditions, 1962.

Pageard, Robert. *Le droit privé des Mossi: Tradition et évolution*. Volume 1 of *Recherches voltaïques*. Paris: CNRS 1969.

Palmer, Vernon Valentine. *The Louisiana Civilian Experience: Critiques of Codification in a Mixed Jurisdiction*. Durham: Carolina Academic Press, 2005.

Pascal, Blaise. *Pensées* and *The Provincial Letters*. Translated by W. F. Trotter and Thomas M'Crie. The Modern Library. New York: Random House, 1941.

Pénoukou, Julien Efoué. *Églises d'Afrique: Propositions pour l'avenir*. Paris: Karthala, 1984.

Portalis, Jean-Étienne-Marie. *Discours préliminaire sur le projet de code civil*. Paris: Editions Confluences, 1999.

Prost, Antoine. *Douze leçons sur l'histoire*. Paris: Seuil, 1996.

Ramose, Mogobe B. "The Philosophy of *Ubuntu* and *Ubuntu* as a Philosophy." In *The African Philosophy Reader*, 2nd ed. Edited by Pieter H. Coetzee and Abraham P. J. Roux. London: Routledge, 2003.

Raufer, Xavier. *Dictionnaire technique et critique des nouvelles menaces*. Paris: Presses Universitaires de France, 1998.

Raynal, Maryse. *Justice traditionelle, justice moderne*. Paris: L'Harmattan, 1995.

Reich, Wilhelm. *Psychologie de masse du fascisme*. Paris: Payot, 1972.

Renan, Ernest. *La réforme intellectuelle et morale*. Paris: Lévy, 1871.

Ricoeur, Paul. "Entretien." In *Éthique et responsabilité*. Edited by Jean-Christophe Aeschlimann. Neuchâtel: À la Baconnière, 1994.

———. "Ethics and Politics." In *From Text to Action: Essays in Hermeneutics, II*. Translated by Kathleen Blamey and John B. Thompson. Evanston: Northwestern University Press, 1991.

———. *The Just*. Translated by David Pellauer. Chicago: University of Chicago Press, 2000.

———. *Oneself as Another*. Translated by Kathleen Blamey. Chicago: University of Chicago Press, 1992.

———. *Memory, History, Forgetting*. Translated by Kathleen Blamey and David Pellauer. Chicago: University of Chicago Press, 2004.

———. *Reflections on the Just*. Translated by David Pellauer. Chicago: University of Chicago Press, 2007.

Rivière, Madeleine. *Lettre de la psychiatrie française*, no. 90/99 (2000).

Rosanvallon, Pierre. *Democratic Legitimacy: Impartiality, Reflexivity, Proximity*. Translated by Arthur Goldhammer. Princeton: Princeton University Press, 2011.

Roux, Andre. *L'évangile dans la forêt*. Paris: Cerf, 1971.

Rubadiri, David. "Why African Literature?" *Transition* 4, no. 15 (1964).

Salas, Denis. *La volonté de punir. Essai sur le populisme penal*. Paris: Hachette, 2005.

Sarraut, Albert. *Grandeur et servitude coloniales*. Paris: Éditions du Sagittaire, 1931.

Sartre, Jean-Paul. *Orphée Noir. Black Orpheus*. Translated by S. W. Allen. Paris: Présence Africaine, 1976.

Schapp, Wilhelm. *Empêtrés dans des histoires: L'être de l'homme et de la chose*. Paris: Éditions de Cerf, 1992.

Scholem, Gershom. *Fidelité et utopie. Essai sur le judaïsme contemporain*. Paris: Calmann-Lévy, 1994.

Seneca. "De la colère," I, XVlll, 1. In *Entretiens. Lettres à Lucilius*. Paris: Robert Laffont, 1993.

Scheler, Max. *Ressentiment*. Translated by William W. Holdheim, edited by Lewis A. Coser. New York: The Free Press of Glencoe, 1961.

Senghor, Léopold Sédar. *Liberté I: Négritude et humanisme*. Paris: Seuil, 1964.

———. *Liberté II: Nation et voie africaine du socialisme*. Paris: Seuil, 1971.

Serequeberhan, Tsenay. *The Hermeneutics of African Philosophy: Horizon and Discourse*. New York: Routledge, 1994.

Silva Romero, Eduardo. *Wittgenstein et la philosophie du droit*. Paris: Presses Universitaires de France, 2002.

Simmel, George. *The Pauper*. Translated by S. Draghici. Corvallis, OR: Plutarch Press, 2001.

Simon, Yves, and Patrick Joffre, eds. *L'Encyclopedie de la gestion*, vol. 1. Paris: Economica, 1989.

Sinda, Martial. *Le messianisme Congolais et ses incidences politiques*. Paris: Payot, 1972.

Skolaster, H. *Die Pallotiner in Kamerun, 25 jahre Missionsarbeit*. Limburg an der Lahn, 1924.

Sloterdijk, Peter. *La compétition des bonnes nouvelles, Nietzsche évangeliste*. Paris: Mille et Une Nuits, 2002.

———. *Rage and Time: A Psychopolitical Investigation*. Translated by Mario Wenning. New York: Columbia University Press, 2010.

Soyinka, Wole. *The Burden of Memory, The Muse of Forgiveness*. Oxford: Oxford University Press, 1998.

Stiegler, Bernard. *Taking Care of Youth and the Generations*. Translated by Stephen Barker. Stanford: Stanford University Press, 2010.

Sylla, Lanciné. *Tribalisme et parti unique en Afrique noire*. Paris: Presses de la Fondation nationale des sciences politiques, 1977.

Táíwò, Olúfémi. *How Colonialism Preempted Modernity in Africa*. Bloomington: Indiana University Press, 2010.

Tchivounda, Guillaume Pambou. *Essai sur l'état Africaine postcolonial*. Paris: Librarie Générale de Droit et de Jurisprudence, 1982.

Thiénot, Champagne. *Rapport sur les études historiques*. Paris: Imprimerie impérial, 1868.

Timsit, Gérard. "Théorie des faces et analyse conversationnelle." In *Le Frais Parler d'Erwin Goffmann*. Paris: Minuit, 1989.

———. *Les noms de la loi*. Paris: Presses Universitaires de France, 1991.

Thomas, Louis-Vincent. *Le socialisme et l'Afrique*, 2 vols. Paris: Le Livre Africain, 1969.

Toe, J. Yado. "Les modes informels de regulation des délits et des conflits dans les quartiers pauvres de Ouagadougou." In *Pauvrété urbaine et accès à la justice en Afrique*, 317–52. Edited by Alioune Badiane, et al. Paris: L'Harmattan, 1995.

Touraine, Alain. *Pour la sociologie*. Paris: Éditions du Seuil, 1974.

Towa, Marcien. *Essai sur la problématique philosophique dans l'Afrique actuelle*. Yaoundé, Cameroon: Éditions Clé, 1971.

———. *L'idée d'une philosophie négro-africaine*. Yaoundé, Cameroon: Éditions Clé, 1979.

Van de Kerchove, Michel and François Ost. *Le Droit ou les paradoxes du jeu*. Paris: Presses Universitaires de France, 1992.

Van Hoof, D. C., D. Verbruggen, and C. H. Stoll, eds. *Elsevier's Legal Dictionary. In English, German, French, Dutch and Spanish.* Amsterdam: Elsevier, 2001.

Vernant, Jean-Pierre. *The Origins of Greek Thought.* Ithaca, NY: Cornell University Press, 1982.

Veyne, Paul. *Le Pain et le cirque.* Paris: Seuil, 1976.

Wagret, Jean Michel. *Histoire et sociologie politiques de la République du Congo (Brazzaville).* Paris: Librairie générale de droit et de jurisprudence, 1963.

Wilson, Richard A. *The Politics of Truth and Reconciliation in South Africa: Legitimizing the Post-Apartheid State.* Cambridge: Cambridge University Press, 2001.

Wittgenstein, Ludwig. *Investigations philosophiques.* Translated by Pierre Klossowski. Paris: Gallimard, 1961.

Wondji, Christophe. "De la bouche de l'ancien." *Courrier de l'UNESCO* (April 1996).

Zehr, Howard. *The Little Book of Restorative Justice.* Intercourse, PA: Good Books, 2002.

Žižek, Slavoj. *Did Somebody Say Totalitarianism? Five Interventions in the (Mis)use of a Notion.* London: Verso, 2001.

Zumthor, Paul. *La lettre et la voix. De la littérature médiévale.* Paris: Seuil, 1987.

Index

About the Author and the Translator

Jᴇᴀɴ Gᴏᴅᴇғʀᴏʏ Bɪᴅɪᴍᴀ is Professor and Yvonne Arnoult Chair of French Studies at Tulane University. He is author of *Théorie critique et modernité négro-africaine: De l'école de Francfort à la "Docta Spes Africana"* (1993) and the titles *La philosophie négro-africaine* (1995) and *L'art négro-africain* (1997) in the PUF Que Sais-Je? series. *La Palabre* (1997) is his first full-length book translated into English.

Lᴀᴜʀᴀ Hᴇɴɢᴇʜᴏʟᴅ is Associate Professor of Philosophy at Case Western Reserve University. She is the author of *The Body Problematic: Political Imagination in Kant and Foucault* (2007).

www.ingramcontent.com/pod-product-compliance
Lightning Source LLC
Chambersburg PA
CBHW020751300326
41914CB00050B/123